At Home with God

DICKEY

At Home with God

FAMILY DEVOTIONS FOR THE SCHOOL YEAR

ANNE BROYLES

SUE DOWNING

PAUL AND ELIZABETH LYND ESCAMILLA

MARILYN BROWN ODEN

UPPER
ROOM BOOKS®
NASHVILLE

At Home with God: Family Devotions for the School Year
© 2002 by Upper Room Books®. All rights reserved.

The Upper Room Web site: http://www.upperroom.org

Cover and interior design: Steve Laughbaum
*Cover Photos: Children in Swing © George Shelley / Corbis Stock Market; Woman and Boy
© Steve Weinrebe / Photonica; Man and Girl © Peter Beck / Corbis Stock Market*

First Printing: 2002

Library of Congress Cataloging-in-Publication

At home with God / Anne Broyles…[et al.].
        p. cm.
    Includes bibliographical references.
    Contents: Family devotions for the school year.
    ISBN 0-8358-0933-1
    1. Family—Prayer-books and devotions—English. 2. Devotional calendars.
    I. Broyles, Anne, 1953–

BV255 .A88 2002
249—dc21   2002017377

Contents

Introduction

Dear Parent,

We hope that you will find this family devotional user-friendly. It requires no preparation beforehand, except for the occasional gathering of simple supplies that are noted at the end of the devotion on the day before they are needed. For each day's devotion you will need only this book and your Bible. We suggest that you also keep paper and pencils with your Bible.

You can complete each devotional in ten to fifteen minutes. If family devotions are a new practice for you, you may want to experiment with different times until you find the one most convenient for your family. Although this book contains daily devotions, each stands alone so that if you miss a day, the next day's devotion is not affected. It is written specifically for families with children in grades one through five, but most of the activities could include younger or older children as well.

Each day's devotion contains several elements, but if you find that your family is really enjoying exploring one particular element in depth, feel free to stay with that. Completing all elements in a day's devotion is less important than allowing family members to engage fully in one that seems significant.

Though you could simply turn to today's date and begin, we suggest you read the next section entitled Getting Started. It contains helpful information on such topics as preparing a space, reading the Bible with children, prayer, storytelling, etc. An appendix at the back includes optional activities with content related to specific daily devotions. These can be used anytime when you want to extend the time of your devotions. You will also find a list of books for adults and for children.

We pray that your family will be blessed in these times of prayer and conversation and that you will experience God's presence with you on this journey together.

The Writers

Getting Started

Like many parents, you may feel confident to lead young children in bedtime or mealtime prayers, but you are unsure about leading them to an intimate knowledge of God as they enter school and become more independent thinkers. It can be overwhelming to learn that the family is the first and most natural place for spiritual development and that you, as a parent, are the major influence on your child's faith.

How does a parent engage a school-age child in faith-centered conversation and a sharing of Christian faith? Where do today's busy adults find time and energy to prepare for such encounters, no matter how eager they are to start?

At Home with God offers great help to parents with these concerns. Designed for daily use during the school year (September–May), its Bible selections, prayers, storytelling, shared questions, and activities have been developed to build a family's foundation of faith. You will find that drawing the family together consistently to focus on the Bible and questions of faith can develop spiritual growth in and of itself. As the days go by, use of this resource will establish a family's regular pattern of praying together and talking comfortably about the Christian life. Coincidentally, it will also open doors of understanding and communication about other matters a family often faces during a child's elementary school years.

Some ideas for getting started with your family devotions are presented here in the following order:

1. Preparing the Place
2. Reading the Bible Together
3. Praying Together
4. Sharing Together
5. Dramatizing a Bible Story
6. Storytelling

PREPARING THE PLACE

Creating sacred space in the home can help children (and adults!) make the transition from the ordinary, sometimes hectic, pace of the day to a special, sacred time. Using the same place and routine every time you gather for devotions can also help. But of course, as in most of family life, some flexibility is also important. Here are some simple suggestions:

- Choose a place—perhaps the kitchen table, a coffee table in the living room, or the family room floor in front of the fireplace.
- Clear the area and provide a sense of order

and beauty. If you're at the kitchen table, clear away the dishes; if you're in the family room, put away the mail, the remote control, etc.

- Turn off the radio, TV, telephone, computers, and any other electronic gadgets that may interrupt the time.

- Place a candle in the setting that you can light as you begin your time together. When you light the candle, you may want to add a simple prayer such as "Come, O Lord. We are open to your spirit." Or use words such as these: "As we light this candle, God, we open our hearts to you."

- Since children respond to concrete symbols, you may want to add a cross or religious picture or items from nature such as some beautiful leaves or flowers, a bowl of nuts or pinecones, a few stalks of wheat, an interesting rock, a few gourds, or some shells. Or there may be an object that has a special meaning for your family. Keep the item simple so that it can either remain in place or be set up easily.

- Make sure the children are settled and ready to listen. Before you begin, encourage them to put their toys or homework away, to find a seat, and to relay any urgent message that won't wait until later.

Remember that although the physical setting can enhance your time together, the important thing is that family members allow themselves to be present to one another and to God's spirit in the moment and the place.

READING THE BIBLE TOGETHER

One of the most significant parts of this special time is reading together from the Bible. Give all members of the family opportunities to hold the Bible; look up the scriptures (with help if needed); and, if they are able, read the selected verses to the family. Being chosen to read the Bible for the day is an honor, and most children delight in having a turn. Be sure that the skills of the reader fit the difficulty of the passage so that the experience will be a positive one. A child who is too young to read the Bible can bring the Bible to its special place in your worship center and find the appropriate chapter and verse, previously marked with a ribbon or piece of paper.

Although the *New Revised Standard Version* of the Bible is quoted most often in this book, your family may use whatever Bible translation you prefer. It is a good idea, however, to choose a translation that uses simple language. The language of the King James Version, while quite beautiful, is difficult for most children to understand or read. You will find several translations available with more contemporary, simpler language.

But what if you, as a parent, are not as familiar with the scriptures as you wish you were? How can you help your children find scripture passages when you don't have a clue yourself where to find, for example, the Book of Jeremiah? Fortunately, Bibles, just like other books, have tables of contents. There are separate tables of contents for the Old Testament and the New Testament. If you place a bookmark at the page containing these tables of contents, you can find them easily. Simply locate the particular book of the Bible you want, and you will see the page number where it begins. You can then easily help your children find the chapter and verse for the reading. As children continue in their practice of daily devotions, their familiarity with the Bible will increase. Most Bibles also contain other reference materials such as maps and chronological charts of biblical events. If possible, take the time to review these and see which ones are of interest to the family.

You can involve your children in many ways in the selected scripture reading. If the scripture passage relates a story and if you know the story well, telling the story instead of reading it can make the story more memorable for children. Children love repetition. Repeating a phrase or verse over and over again like a chant is an excellent way to involve children in a scripture passage. This method works particularly well with psalms. A variation of this method is to read five or six words and then have listeners repeat them after you. Jesus' parables and the creation story lend themselves well to this way of reading scripture.

Another way to help children relate to a scripture passage is to encourage them to use their imaginations to become part of the scene. We can help them do this by asking questions. For example, these questions relate to some of the better-known scripture passages:

- How would you feel if the disciples asked you for your lunch? Can you see all the people on the hillside? What colors do you see around you?
- How would I feel if God told me to pack my things and move to a strange land? I wonder; how many days will it take to get there? What should I take with me, and what should I leave behind?
- How would it feel to be one of the women who went to Jesus' tomb on that first Easter? What does the garden look like in the early morning? How do the plants and flowers smell? What do you see when you get to the tomb?

Though directions for reading the scriptures are generally given in these family devotions, feel free to read the Bible in ways that are most meaningful for your family. The method of entering into the scripture is not nearly so important as our commitment to do so.

PRAYING TOGETHER

Praying is one of the most important things we can do with our children. Prayer helps children know that God is always present to them, that God always has time to listen to them, and that God can be trusted to do what is best for them. Prayer helps children know that God loves them unconditionally, forgives them, and values them for the unique individuals they are.

It's never too early or too late to begin praying with children. The practice of praying aloud a one-sentence prayer over the infant in the crib, calling the child's name aloud, can lay the foundation for a family life in which praying together is the norm.

Some guidelines for praying with young school-age children are:

- Stay simple. One-sentence prayers of thanksgiving are a good way to start.
- Pray anytime and anywhere. It's not necessary to wait for a particular time and place. Nonetheless, establishing regular times of prayer is an important way to incorporate prayer into your family's busy schedule.
- Help children understand that prayer is listening to God as well as talking with God and to be comfortable with short periods of silence.
- Help children know God as a friend or as a tender shepherd. A child's image of God affects the way he or she prays. Children may come to think of God either as a Santa or as a police officer in the sky. As parents, we need to be gently proactive in helping our children grow into another concept of God.
- Help children know that they can say anything to God. In *Children and Prayer*, Betty Cloyd writes, "Tell children that God is big enough to handle whatever they want to say to God....To be secure enough to bring to God all of our needs and desires is one of the main goals in prayer."

- Last, but very important, let children see you and other significant adults in their lives praying.

As with the Bible readings, directions for praying and prayers are generally provided in the daily sessions but feel free to pray your own prayers and to do so in the most meaningful ways for your family.

SHARING TOGETHER

Time for family members to talk about faith is a vital part of these sessions together. When questions are included during the Sharing Together section, be sure to take one question at a time and deal with it fully so that everyone has a chance to speak (but is not pressured to do so). It is not necessary to cover all the questions. More important is that family members feel that this is a special and safe time to speak openly about their faith, about their doubts and fears as well as their certainties.

At times, a parent may be tempted to focus on giving advice rather than on listening—that would be a good time to remember that God gave us (even us parents) two ears and only one mouth!

DRAMATIZING A BIBLE STORY

Dramatizing a Bible story can be great fun and a great learning experience. Asking children a lot of questions may push them into a more adult-oriented, intellectual way of thinking, but drama and play open up other learning possibilities. Through drama, children can experience the story on a level that they can relate to immediately and directly.

If you find that more structured sharing times are a challenge in your family, you may want to try some acting. Also, if a particular story really speaks to one or more of your fam-

ily members in a special way, drama allows an opportunity for that meaning to unfold further. We cannot predict when a child (or an adult, for that matter!) will latch on to a Bible story in a heartfelt way, but we can certainly be open to such discovery when it happens. Drama is one way to encourage discovery. Here are some suggestions:

• Act it out

This is most easily done with an adult being the narrator who tells the story. Other family members take parts (sometimes several parts each) and act them out. A simple cloth or a chair turned a certain way or some other prop can add to the scene but isn't necessary. Most of the parables can be dramatized using only our bodies and voices.

• Mime

In mime, the story is acted out with no words, only actions. (Tremendous lessons are often learned with the mouth in a closed position!) Try mime with the story of the Good Samaritan (Luke 10:25-37), the Parable of the Sower (Mark 4:1-9), or Jesus' blessing of the children (Mark 10:13-16).

• Use toys, dolls, or puppets

If your household has a variety of toys, consider building tabernacles with blocks (Exodus 35–36, Nov. 28), or acting out the Mary and Martha story (Luke 10:38–42, Nov. 7–9) with small dolls. Ruth, Naomi, and Boaz could be simple puppets (Book of Ruth, Nov. 23–25). If such things are not available, they can be drawn on paper, cut out, and taped onto a block or stick.

Use whatever you can find among your toys and dolls to assemble the scene, the props, and the characters. Allow children to move the characters around as the story unfolds.

Enacting drama with dolls or other toys may take some preparation time. It could be an extended part of the devotional time or carried over to another evening. For example, one person could gather characters and props and set the scene before other family members gather.

Remember that what matters most is having Bible stories become part of our thinking, feeling, imagining, and actions. Drama is simply one more way to weave scripture into our daily lives.

STORYTELLING

Stories are basic to the way we experience life and learn our Christian faith. The fact that Jesus told many stories as a part of his teaching and healing ministry suggests their importance—even centrality—to our faith.

In an age of technology, oral storytelling can give a child dimensions of life and experience not accessible in other media. As a child listens to a story being told, his or her imagination creates its own pictures. Further, storytelling has the capacity to meet children at their own level and inner need and to nurture them deeply in ways that are difficult to measure.

While many of us feel that only experts can spin a yarn or retell a story or even read one aloud from a book, it is simply not so! All day long we tell stories of all kinds—short, long, funny, sad. Sometimes we report only facts; other times we embellish a bit to add humor or interest. Storytelling is not merely a hobby for some—it is a way of life for all of us. With practice, any of us can tell stories for devotional purposes too.

Good storytelling requires only two things: a good story and someone who feels the need to tell it. In other words, telling a story has less to do with the teller's skill and talent than with his or her belief in the story's importance. Here are some suggestions for telling stories as part of your family's devotional time:

- Begin simply. Choose simple, straight-forward Bible stories to read or tell. Read the stories aloud as a basic storytelling method. Without being overly dramatic, express the story's emotions and emphases. What the story means to you should come through in the way you read the story to others.
- After you grow comfortable reading stories aloud, try moving off the page. That is, try telling a Bible story in your own words. Make note beforehand of key characters, phrases, and story development.
- Finally, you may want to make up your own stories. These can come from your own life experience, or you may create imaginary characters and situations. They should reflect the same tensions, dilemmas, emotions, virtues/ vices, and resolutions that would be found in a Bible story. The younger the listener, the more basic these stories should be.

Children in grades one through three tend to relate well to stories of nature and animals, while children in grades three through six usually appreciate stories of adventure and hero figures.

Below are two story starters for the younger age level. Notice how basic their structures are.

The little squirrel scampered up the pecan tree and down again. She was working hard to gather nuts for winter....

The red oak tree had held its leaves green and supple through spring and summer, and then held them through autumn winds while they rustled and stirred. But now the tree let them go, one by one, until....

One last word—you can begin this book on any day of the school year. Your family may want to repeat the daily readings and activities again in future years. You'll be surprised at the difference a year makes! Welcome to *At Home with God*.

SEPTEMBER

September 1

READING THE BIBLE TOGETHER

Let one family member read Ecclesiastes 3:1, and then the whole family can repeat it together.

A STORY

On a sunny day in September, a young woman named Julie packed to leave home and start a new job. As Julie's parents helped her, they thought about the many beginnings in Julie's life up to this point. They remembered the day she was born, the day they brought her home from the hospital, and the moment she took her first step. They remembered each birthday and the day she entered first grade. They had special memories of the family's move to a new city and joining a new church. They remembered when Julie began piano lessons and what a wonderful beginning that was for her. And now Julie was experiencing another beginning with her new work.

Our lives are filled with beginnings. Some are big. Some are small. There are happy beginnings and sad ones. But each new beginning is important. Each helps to shape us and make us who we are.

SHARING TOGETHER

In Ecclesiastes 3:1, God tells us there is a time for everything. Give each person a chance to share memories of beginnings in his or her life. What feelings do you associate with these beginnings? How were they important in your life?

Perhaps this daily devotional time is a new beginning for your family. If so, talk about the hopes and goals you have for this time. Write down the hopes and goals each person has shared, and keep them in a special place. Review your list from time to time to help you remember them. You may also want to make changes in your list from time to time.

FAMILY LITANY

Ask one person to read the litany and signal to the family to join in with the words, *Be with our family as we begin.*

Reader: Dear God,
All: **Be with our family as we begin.**
Reader: Help us to feel your loving presence with us.
All: **Be with our family as we begin.**
Reader: Give us the desire to spend time with you every day.
All: **Be with our family as we begin.**
Reader: Fill us with love and thankfulness for you and one another.
All: **Be with our family as we begin.**
Reader: Be with our family throughout all the times of our lives. Amen.

OPTIONAL ACTIVITY
See page 264.

September 2

READING THE BIBLE TOGETHER

The Bible is filled with stories about new beginnings. One of the greatest of these stories is found in Genesis 1:1–2:3. It is God's story of the beginning of our world and of all living things.

A STORY

Family members can take turns reading from this story based on Genesis 1–2:3. One way would be to take turns reading what happened on each day. Be sure that the whole family repeats the last line of the story together.

In the beginning, God thought, *I have a great idea! Why not create a world, a world that is good?* In the beginning, God decided, This is what my plan will be. In the beginning, that is how all of creation began.

Day 1 – God said, "Let there be light and darkness. Let there be day and also night."

Day 2 – God said, "Let there be the firmament," and the earth's atmosphere was created!

Day 3 – God said, "Let there be the seas and the land. Let there be the plants and the trees."

Day 4 – God said, "Let the sun, moon, and stars shine. Let the seasons, days, and years be here."

Day 5 – God said, "Let there be birds soaring above, and let there be every creature of the sea."

Day 6 – God said, "Let animals roam the land." God also created man and woman, both in God's own image.

Day 7 – God smiled and said, "Creation is complete. I am going to rest!"

All: (One person reads the line below and then the family repeats it together.)

Now we say, "Praise and thanks to God for our beginning! "

SHARING TOGETHER

God had a definite plan when our world was created, and we can be thankful for our beautiful world. Often we begin something new without making a plan and without asking for God's blessing. What do you want to create with your life? Perhaps you have an idea or some dreams. Do you have a plan? Have you prayed about your ideas and dreams for your life?

PRAYING TOGETHER

Repeat together the words of Psalm 104:24 (NIV):

How many are your works, O Lord!
In wisdom you made them all;
the earth is full of your creatures.

OPTIONAL ACTIVITY

See page 264.

September 3

READING THE BIBLE TOGETHER

Say this scripture verse together several times: "I can do all things through him who strengthens me" (Phil. 4:13).

A STORY

Once there was a special grandmother. Her family called her Gram. Gram never drove a car. When she was not riding with someone, she walked. Gram loved to walk!

But one day, Gram fell and broke her hip. Doctors repaired her broken hip, and it healed well; but Gram had to learn to walk again.

One of the physical therapists explained to Gram how he would help her, but that she must do her part too. She would have to exercise her legs each day in order to walk again. The therapist said, "It won't be easy. I can't exercise for you; I can only help. You must be determined to do this!"

The therapists soon found out that Gram was very determined! Even though she did not always feel like it, she continued to exercise her legs daily. She told her family that she knew she was not alone. God was with her.

Gram was like the engine in *The Little Engine That Could*, the classic children's story by Watty Piper. As the little engine chugged and pulled to get over the mountain, it kept saying over and over, "I think I can! I think I can!" Only Gram was also saying, "With God I know I can!" What a wonderful example Gram became to all who knew her!

SHARING TOGETHER

Sometimes life presents us with difficult new beginnings. Here is a way to help us remember to begin when it seems too hard. Think about each letter in the word beginning the sentence.

B – Believe you can do it!
E – Expect good results!
G – Give it your all!
I – Imagine God's loving presence with you.
N – Now is the time to begin—not later!

PRAYING TOGETHER

Repeat together the scripture verse above as a closing prayer.

September 4

READING THE BIBLE TOGETHER

Read Genesis 9:11-17.

A STORY

Let different family members read each paragraph. Discuss the questions.

God said to Noah, "You must build a huge boat because a great flood is coming, and your family will need something that floats! Gather your material and begin right now. Very soon, lots of water will cover all the land." (Imagine you are Noah. How would you feel?)

"Next, I want you to do something else," God said. "Find every animal and bring them on board two by two."

Noah answered, "Yes, God, I will obey." He worked on the ark day and night. Finally the ark was complete with enough room for Noah's family and all the animals. (What would you take on the ark with you?)

Other people laughed and made fun of Noah. They said, "No flood will ever come!" But soon, dark clouds filled the sky. Lightning could be seen and thunder heard not far away. Then the rains poured down. For forty days and forty nights, it rained and rained. All during this time, the ark kept Noah's family and the animals safe. (Have you ever been laughed at? How did it feel?)

When the rains finally ended, Noah sent a dove to search for evidence of dry land. What joy, what celebration, what shouts of glee could be heard when the dove returned with an olive branch! Then a beautiful rainbow appeared in the sky. God spoke to Noah's family, "This rainbow is my sign to you of eternal hope. It is also my promise of a new beginning and of my everlasting love for you." (What does God's promise mean to you today?)

PRAYING TOGETHER

The following is an echo prayer. One family member will read a line of the prayer, and the rest of the family will repeat the same words.

Reader:	For the promise of a rainbow,
All:	**For the promise of a rainbow,**
Reader:	For the promise of hope,
All:	**For the promise of hope,**
Reader:	For the promise of your love,
All:	**For the promise of your love,**
Reader:	We give you thanks, Lord.
All:	**We give you thanks, Lord. Amen.**

Read the section in Getting Started entitled Reading the Bible Together, pages 10–11.

LOOKING AHEAD

Parents will need to have mementos of each child's birth for tomorrow's devotion. You might bring baby albums, birth certificates, or baptismal certificates.

September 5

READING THE BIBLE TOGETHER

Read Genesis 17:1-7, 15-22.

A STORY

Abraham and his wife Sarah were both very old when God appeared to Abraham. God said, "I will bless Sarah. She shall give birth to a son. Your son's name is to be Isaac and from him shall come many nations and kings. I will establish my covenant between Isaac and me. Through Isaac, I will establish an everlasting covenant for all of Isaac's children."

When Abraham heard this, he laughed and

laughed! He thought to himself, *This is really absurd! At the ages of ninety and one hundred, Sarah and I are too old. The chances for us to bear a child are gone!*

But the words of God are true forever. With God we can always begin anew. So in spite of her age, Sarah gave birth to Isaac. What a celebration! What joy there was! As promised, Isaac was the beginning of many nations and kings.

SHARING TOGETHER

Look at mementos of your children's births. Let the family talk about the birth of each child in the family. Remember that every person is a blessing from God, just as Isaac was. Be sure to share the feelings and expectations surrounding each child's birth and how each birth marked a new beginning for the family. For example, what changes and new challenges did each birth bring to your family?

PRAYING TOGETHER

God, you are an AWESOME GOD! With you all things are possible. With you we can dream big! With you there are no limits to what we can achieve. We are created in your image. WOW! That makes us AWE-SOME too! Amen.

OPTIONAL ACTIVITY

See page 265.

September 6

PRAYING TOGETHER

Dear God, some in our family attend school. Others hold jobs, and we all need time to play. There are meetings, errands, chores, sports to play, lessons to take. There are special outings, meals to prepare, groceries to buy, rooms to clean. There are video games to play, television shows to watch, e-mails to send; and sometimes there seems no end to the homework we have. We visit with our friends and sometimes take vacations. We seem so busy with places to go and things to do.

Dear God, we know the most important activity our family can share is to spend daily time with you. Please guide us and show us how to love you more and more each day. Help us to place you first! Amen.

SHARING TOGETHER

Imagine that you have been given the gift of a day to do whatever you choose. What are the top five activities you would select? List them in order of their importance. Talk together about your choices. Is spending time with God on your list? How do we make sure that we have time to pray and talk to God each day?

READING THE BIBLE TOGETHER

Read Exodus 20:3.

FAMILY LITANY

Let one person read a verse and make the appropriate motion, and then the rest of the family can repeat it.

Verse 1
God is so good. (Lift arms up.) (Repeat twice.)
So good to me. (Point to self.)

Verse 2
God's love is here. (Cross hands over heart.)
(Repeat twice.)
God's love is in me. (Point to self.)

Verse 3
God, help me see (Point to eyes.) (Repeat twice.)
The good in others. The good in me. (Point to self.)

Verse 4
God, help me to…(Praying hands.) (Repeat twice.)
make time for you. (Lift arms up.)
Praise God. Amen! (Repeat twice.)
We love you, God!

September 7

A STORY

Rick's family has a small cabin on a beautiful lake not too far from his home. His mother and father have been taking him there since Rick was a baby. At the cabin, Rick is reminded of all of nature and the wonderful world God created for us. He loves to walk along the lake and listen to the sounds of the water and the birds in the trees. When he is there, Rick feels very close to God. It is as if he could almost reach out and touch God! Rick thinks of the cabin as a sacred place because he is always reminded of God's presence when he is there.

SHARING TOGETHER

Think and talk about how your family can create a sacred place in your home where you can gather together and pray to God. Let each family member make a suggestion or two.

- Decide on an area in your home for this special place and choose a central focal point, such as a table to arrange things on.
- Plan together the things you can bring there to remind you of God (family Bible, candle, cross, treasures from nature such as flowers, a seashell, a robin's egg, leaves, a colorful rock, an evergreen branch, etc.). Consider also whether to include a family picture or a religious picture, a special prayer, or work of art a family member has created.
- Each person can take responsibility for changing the items in your sacred place periodically.

PRAYING TOGETHER

All: **Come into our home, Lord.**
Reader: May it be a place that welcomes you. May it be a place where our family feels your loving presence surrounding us. May it be a place where others find comfort, peace, and your love.

All: Come into our home, Lord.

Reader: May it be a place that says, "God is here."

All: Come into our hearts, Lord.

Reader: May we always remember we are created in your image. May we know that you are forever with us and that we are never alone. May we spread your love wherever we go.

All: Come into our hearts, Lord.

Reader: May we be a family that says, "God is here." Come into our home.

All: Come into our hearts. Come be with us, Lord. Amen.

READING THE BIBLE TOGETHER

Read Psalm 96:7-9a.

Parents can find suggestions for Preparing the Place on page 9.

September 8

READING THE BIBLE TOGETHER

Begin today's devotion by having one person read Matthew 18:20 and then the rest of the family repeating it together.

SHARING TOGETHER

Think about this devotional time and imagine God being a special guest in your home. Decide on a spot where you could offer God a place to sit. Focus on this place and picture God there. Take time for each family member to greet and welcome God into your home. What do you want to tell God? What are the good things in your life that you want to point out to God? What concerns do you want to share? What persons or circumstances need your prayers? What areas of your life need forgiveness? Give each person the opportunity to share with other family members what their conversations might be.

PRAYING TOGETHER

Dear God, we always have a place for you. We welcome you into our home. Help us to feel your loving presence and to know that you never leave us. Guide and direct our family throughout each day. Thank you for being with us, God. Thank you for being our constant companion. Amen.

September 9

IMAGINE THIS

One person reads the following meditation pausing after each question to give the family time to respond.

Close your eyes. Picture in your mind the outside of your home. Imagine the front door. Someone's standing at the door. Listen, someone is knocking at your door. Knock, knock, knock, knock. Slowly you walk to the door and open it. Imagine that Jesus is standing there waiting. What does Jesus look like? What expression is on his face? What does Jesus say to you? How do you feel about Jesus being there? Does Jesus seem more like a friend or a stranger to you? What would you say to Jesus?

What would you want to show Jesus and do with him?

READING THE BIBLE TOGETHER

Read Revelation 3:20.

A FAMILY LITANY

One family member will read the lines marked for the reader. The rest of the family can respond with the words *Knock, knock, knock,* or make a knocking sound on the table.

All: **Knock, knock, knock.**
Reader: Someone's waiting patiently. Someone's knocking. Who is there?
All: **Knock, knock, knock.**
Reader: Someone's knocking. Someone's close. Can you hear? Listen.
All: **Knock, knock, knock.**
Reader: Jesus wants to come in today. Jesus wants to remain in our hearts.
All: **Knock, knock, knock.**
Reader: Jesus would like us to be his disciples. Let's answer Jesus and say,
All: **Come in!**

PRAYING TOGETHER

Pray this prayer as an echo prayer.

Come in, Lord Jesus.
Come in, Lord Jesus.
Come into my heart today.

Come in, Lord Jesus.
Come in, Lord Jesus.
Come into my heart and be with me always.
Amen.

CONSIDER THIS

Jesus does not force himself into our hearts, our home, or our lives. We each choose whether to open the door and let Jesus in, or simply leave Jesus on the outside. Think about what we can do as a family to be sure that we are opening the door of our lives to Jesus.

September 10

SHARING TOGETHER

Let several family members take turns reading the following.

We have choices to make every day, and we wonder, What should I say? What should I do? Shall I give something or take something? Should I help others or ignore them? Should I be quiet or speak, frown or smile? Shall I work or play, be mean or kind? Should I give up or try again, lie or be truthful, say yes or no? Will I decide to make fun of others or encourage them? Will I be honest or cheat, get angry or forgive? Will I be able to love others or keep on hurting people?

We have choices to make every day, and we wonder, What should I say? What should I do? The answer is to look at and listen to Jesus. He's there for each of us. When we ask, "What would Jesus do?" we receive help in what to do. Talk together about what decisions your family is facing now.

READING THE BIBLE TOGETHER

Read John 14:5-6.

FAMILY LITANY

The family will repeat the phrase, *For each choice we have to make*.

One family member will read the reader's part of the litany.

Reader: Dear God,
All: **For each choice we have to make,**
Reader: help us to know we are not alone.
All: **For each choice we have to make,**
Reader: help us to follow the example of Jesus.
All: **For each choice we have to make,**
Reader: help us to show your love.
All: **For each choice we have to make,**
Reader: help us to be thankful.
All: **For each choice before us now,**
Reader: help us to do your will, God. Amen.

September 11

READING THE BIBLE TOGETHER

Read Psalm 34:1, 8.

A STORY

Jeff and his family decided to plant a tomato garden one spring. They wanted to have juicy, red tomatoes to eat and to share with their friends. Jeff's family knew that this

whole process would involve several important steps. First they located an area in their yard that would receive plenty of sunshine. Then they cleared the area of grass and loosened the soil. Next, holes needed to be dug. Jeff wanted to do this. He got a small hoe and made a little hole for each plant.

His dad placed a plant in each hole and pushed the dirt up around the plant. Jeff's mother spread fertilizer around the plants, and, at last, Jeff gently watered each plant. Jeff was tired, but he was pleased that they would have tomatoes in their garden.

Then Jeff's dad reminded him that they had to tend the garden every day if they wanted healthy tomatoes. So they all agreed to set aside a specific time of day to weed and water the tomatoes.

After all their effort, tiny green tomatoes gradually appeared, and before long they grew into beautiful red, ripe tomatoes, ready to be picked.

What joy and satisfaction Jeff's family found in growing tomatoes together and sharing them with others!

IMAGINE THIS

Imagine your family as a garden. You want to plant seeds of faith so your family will grow in Christian faith and become the family God wants you to be. What steps do you take? What tools do you need? What activities are essential for spiritual growth? Who needs to be involved? How often do you work at it?

FAMILY LITANY

Let one family member teach the family the response line and motions and then read the lines marked for the Reader.

All: **We are family.**
(Clasp one another's hands.)
We grow together!
(Raise clasped hands.)

Reader: We have a place for God in our home and with our family.

All: **We are family. We grow together!**

Reader: We know that God loves us and is with us. We read the Bible and we pray.

All: **We are family. We grow together!**

Reader: We help one another, and we share God's love. We celebrate our times together.

All: **We are family. We grow together!**

Reader: Praise God. Amen.

LOOKING AHEAD

For your devotion time tomorrow, gather photos or videos taken at special family times, such as birthdays, Christmas, vacations, and family reunions.

READING THE BIBLE TOGETHER

The Bible is a memory book of the family of God. We are a part of that family. Each time we read and study the Bible, we learn more of our family history as followers of Jesus Christ.

Read 1 John 3:2.

SHARING TOGETHER

Begin by looking at family pictures together and talking about some of the occasions represented. Share together the feelings and memories you associate with them. Remember when they occurred and the reason for these special times.

Take turns sharing a special memory of something your family has done together. Parents may also want to share a childhood memory that the children may not have heard or one worth sharing again.

Think together about your hopes for your family devotions. What kinds of memories do you hope will result from these family times?

PRAYING TOGETHER

God, help our family to make loving and happy memories. Help us to see how our memories teach us more about you and your love for us. Through our times of sharing and prayer, help us to grow into the people you want us to be. Amen.

over us every moment of every day. We can return God's love by giving God this precious gift. What does this mean? It simply means that we need to take time for God. In all we do, God is present with us. God is with us when we walk and run, work and play, laugh and cry. God comes and goes with us, listens and talks with us, celebrates and hurts with us. We have the opportunity to take time for God. In all we do, God is forever by our side. Let's begin today to think of how we take time for God.

September 16

SHARING TOGETHER

Talk about the many ways your family can give God the gift of time. (Getting together for daily family devotional times is one very special way!) Use these other suggestions as a guide for your discussion.

- Belong to and be active in a church. Ask the question, "What gifts do I have to contribute to my church?"
- Pray and read the Bible to continue to grow in your Christian faith.
- Choose to share God's love with others, wherever and whenever you can. Remember that our actions speak the loudest.

READING THE BIBLE TOGETHER

Read Psalm 36:5-10.

PRAYING TOGETHER

Dear God, thank you for your love and for always taking time for each of us. Give us willing hearts and guide us to take time for you too. Amen.

READING THE BIBLE TOGETHER

Read Psalm 32:6-7.

SHARING TOGETHER

Make a list together of all the things you are reminded of when you think about prayer. What is prayer? Why do we pray? When do we pray? How do we pray? Where do we pray? Take turns sharing how you would complete the phrase, "Prayer is…." For example, maybe it is just one word to describe prayer, the name of a place, something or someone you have prayed about, or where you were or what you were doing when you prayed. Think about times you and your family have prayed. Maybe there's a familiar prayer that comes to mind.

CONSIDER THIS

- Prayer is talking, listening, whispering, shouting, thinking, singing, laughing, crying. Prayer is all this, and even more.
- Prayer is bowing heads, folding hands, kneeling, sitting, standing, walking, dancing, running, holding, touching. Prayer is all this, and even more.
- Prayer is thanking, praising, giving, receiving, questioning, believing, caring, hoping, growing, and even being sorry. Prayer is all this and even more.

- Prayer is praying anyplace, anytime, anywhere, alone or with others. Prayer is spending precious time with God. Prayer is all this and even more.

SINGING TOGETHER

Sing to the tune of "Jesus Loves Me" or say the words.

Take the time for daily prayer.
Let God hear what's on your heart.
Know that God is there for you.
Waiting, listening for each prayer.
Say, "God, I thank you!" (sing three times)
You fill my heart with joy.

PRAYING TOGETHER

Pray together silently. Encourage family members to tell God about anything that is in their hearts and to listen for what God may be saying to them. A parent can close the time of silence with these words:

We give praise and thanks to you, God, for listening to us, for loving us, and for never leaving us. Amen.

PRAYING TOGETHER

Let one family member read the lines of the prayer with special voice and motions, and the rest of the family can repeat them. Then the family may want to add other responses as well.

We can shout our prayers! (Shout) Alleluia, Amen.
We can whisper our prayers. (Whisper) Forgive me, God.
We can sing our prayers. (Sing) Praise God from whom all blessings flow!
We can act out our prayers. (Raise hands upward.) I love you, God!
We can show love for others as our prayers. (Hug someone.)
We can dance our prayers. (Hold hands. Raise arms upward. Move in a circle.)
We can think our prayers and listen for our prayers. (Close eyes and leave a brief time of silence.)
We can write, draw, or paint our prayers. (Pretend to write, draw, or paint.)
We can pray in many ways, anytime, anywhere. (Join hands, heads bowed.)
God, we can pray because you care for us and are always there for us. We can pray because we are your children. Amen.

READING THE BIBLE TOGETHER

Read 1 Thessalonians 5:16-18.

SHARING TOGETHER

Let each family member share a special way that he or she would like to express a prayer. Use these prayers as part of your family devotion time together.

September 18

READING THE BIBLE TOGETHER

Read Luke 11:1.

CONSIDER THIS

In answer to the disciples' request, Jesus gave them the Lord's Prayer. The Lord's Prayer is Jesus' loving gift to show us how to pray and what to pray about. It is a prayer to be said over and over again. It is a prayer from which we can learn each time we say it.

READING THE BIBLE TOGETHER

Family members can take turns reading one line of Matthew 6:7-13 at a time.

TELL US MORE

Families may notice that the Bible does not include one phrase that we say when we pray the Lord's Prayer at church, "For thine is the kingdom, and the power, and the glory, forever. Amen." The church added the phrase as a closing to the prayer.

SHARING TOGETHER

Now read the Lord's Prayer one phrase at a time and talk together about what the words mean. Encourage all family members to express their feelings and the understanding they have about the Lord's Prayer. As each person does this, encourage everyone to put the Lord's Prayer into words that are a part of your family's vocabulary. Here's one way of doing that, but your family will have other ideas too.

Dear God,
Praise and thanks to you, for you are the source of all we are, have, and hope to become. Praise and thanks to you for your abundant, everlasting love. Give us the desire to follow you. Help all the people in our world to show love to one another and to know of your great love for them. Forgive us when we ignore your commandments and do hurtful things that make you unhappy. Give us forgiving hearts when others wrong us. Lead us to make the right choices and to serve you in all we do. Amen.

PRAYING TOGETHER

Close by praying the Lord's Prayer together. Stand in a circle and hold hands as you pray. You may use the prayer as it is printed in Matthew 6:9b-13.

LOOKING AHEAD

Tomorrow you will need a basket and paper and pencils.

September 19

READING THE BIBLE TOGETHER

Let someone read Psalm 92:1 and then lead the family in repeating it.

CONSIDER THIS

A very special part of prayer is offering our thanks to God for the many, many blessings God gives to us each day. Just as we appreciate it when other people thank us for something we have done or said, it pleases God when we give thanks for all our blessings.

Close your eyes. Think about today and what you have to be thankful for. Think about your family, friends, church, home, school, job, the world God created, the ways people have reached out to you.

Take time for everyone to name at least five blessings. Record each blessing on a slip of paper and place the slips in the Basket of Thanks.

PRAYING TOGETHER

Lord, we offer thanks for our many blessings. We know that you are the Giver of these blessings. Thank you for our family, each one of our friends, and your never-ending love.

Thank you for our food and clothes and for those who take the time to care. Thank you for the stars, the moon, and the sun; for rainbows, clouds, and the air we breathe. Thank you for the earth, sky, and sea. Thank you for green grass, flowers, trees, and leaves, for our pets and all other animals. Thank you for our home.

Thank you for people who willingly give and share; thank you for hugs and the smiles of others. Thank you for the Bible, especially the stories that your son Jesus told. Thank you for creating each one of us as special, unique. Thank you for the wondrous beginning of each new day. Thank you for showing us the way and for your abundant love.

Lord, we offer thanks for our many blessings. Help us never to forget that you are the Giver of all these blessings. Amen.

September 20

SINGING TOGETHER

Sing the words below to the tune "If You're Happy and You Know It" or say the words. The family can echo the words after one person reads it aloud and indicates the motions.

If you love God and you know it, pray to God.
(Praying hands.) (Repeat.)
If you love God and you know it,
Then your prayers will surely show it.
If you love God and you know it, pray to God.

If you love God and you know it, read God's
    word. (Palms together and open.) (Repeat.)

If you love God and you know it,
What you read will surely show it.
If you love God and you know it, read God's word.

If you love God and you know it, show God's love. (Outstretched arms.) (Repeat.)
If you love God and you know it, then your acts will surely show it.
If you love God and you know it, show God's love.

If you love God and you know it, do all these. (Repeat all motions.) (Repeat.)
If you love God and you know it, then your life will surely show it.
Yes, I love God and I know it.
Yes, I do! (Hands crossed over heart.)

PRACTICING WHAT JESUS TAUGHT

What could your family do to show your love and praise for God this week? Maybe your family could…

- Invite another family to attend church with you.
- Visit a shut-in or elderly person.
- Take a meal to a family in need.
- Send a special thank you to someone who's been kind to your family.
- Surprise a neighbor with a home-baked gift!

Talk, decide, and then carry out your plan!

September 21

SINGING TOGETHER

Say or sing the words to "Kum Ba Yah" (Come by Here).

Come by here, my Lord. Come by here.
(Sing three times)
O Lord, come by here.

Someone needs you, Lord. Come by here.
(Sing three times)
O Lord, come by here.

CONSIDER THIS

Do you make lists in your family? Most families have all kinds of lists to help them remember things. We make shopping lists, gift lists, Christmas card lists, guest lists, to-do lists. What other lists do you make? Lists are reminders to us. They say, "Don't forget. This is important!"

Some families keep another special list, a *Prayer List*. They place on this list the names of people whom they know need prayers. It may be the name of a family member, neighbor, friend, schoolmate, someone in the news, a fellow church member, or someone they have been asked to pray for. They keep this list in a special place as a reminder to pray. When family members see the list, they also remember that prayer is one of the most loving gifts they can give to someone else. Sometimes they might be the only people praying for a particular person.

SHARING TOGETHER

Create a family prayer list. Think and talk together about persons whom you feel need to be on your list. Encourage each family member to contribute. Write down each person's name and the reason you are praying for him or her.

PRAYING TOGETHER

Let a family member pray for those you have included on your prayer list. Hold hands as you pray. Conclude the prayer by saying or singing together again these words from "Kum Ba Yah."

Someone needs you, Lord. Come by here.
(Sing three times.)
O Lord, come by here.

READING THE BIBLE TOGETHER

Repeat Matthew 21:22 together.

September 22

READING THE BIBLE TOGETHER

Read Psalm 46:10 and then all whisper it together.

TELL US MORE

We often think of prayer only as talking to God. But listening is a part of prayer we may forget about or ignore. Maybe this happens because we are busy asking for something or telling God something. It is important to remember that when we pray, we also listen to hear God's voice.

Be still. Listen. We can hear God's voice in the rustling of the leaves, the whisper of the wind, the pitter patter of the rain, the sound of a cricket, the singing of birds, softly falling snow, ocean waves lapping against the shore, and the stillness of the night. Listen. God speaks to us through all of creation.

Be still. Listen. We can hear God's voice in our desire to pray, to hug, and to smile. God's voice can be heard in our being thankful for our blessings, forgiving one another, helping those in need. We can hear God's voice when we treat others as we want to be treated, follow Jesus, read the Bible, attend church, and show love. God speaks to us through our hearts.

Be still. Listen. God is speaking to us in the kind words and actions of friends, the encouragement of a teacher, the loving guidance and support of family, and the help we receive when we feel alone. God speaks to us through others.

Be still. Listen. What is God saying to you?

SHARING TOGETHER

Beginning with a parent, take turns talking about times you have felt God was speaking to you. Think about all the ways God speaks to us. Did God speak to you in some way during the past few days?

PRAYING TOGETHER

Pray the following prayer as an echo prayer.

Help me to be still and listen.
Help me to hear and do.
Help me to love and love again.
Help me to know you, God. Amen.

September 23

READING THE BIBLE TOGETHER

Read Colossians 4:2.

CONSIDER THIS

Windows are different sizes, shapes, and even colors. They are like big eyes that help us to see. Windows are a part of homes, churches, and other buildings. We see windows in cars, buses, and airplanes.

Have you ever thought of a window as a reminder to pray? What could you see through a window that might remind you to pray?

SHARING TOGETHER

What might you see from the windows of your home that reminds you to thank and praise God? Do you see the beauty of God's creation? Do you see friends or people who help you in special ways such as a mail carrier, garbage collector, or repair person? Do you see children playing or a family pet? a school or church?

What needs do you see from your windows that you can pray for? Do you see the home of a sick neighbor? an ambulance, fire truck, or police car? a stray or hurt animal? Do you see people passing by?

Go now to the different windows of your home, together or separately. Take several minutes to think silently about what you see from each. Then gather and share with one another the observations you have made. Have a family member record on paper what is said.

PRAYING TOGETHER

Sit or stand together in a circle. One person can lead the prayer and leave pauses so that family members can mention things they saw.

Dear God, we looked out our windows and saw the many ways you have blessed our family. Praise and thanks to you for….(Family members name what they saw.)
Dear God, we looked out our windows and before our eyes we saw so many needs for your loving presence and care. Please help and guide….(Family members name the concerns they felt.)
Dear God, as we look out our windows, wherever we are, help us to imagine them as opportunities for prayer. Then help us not to hesitate to pray. Amen.

September 24

CONSIDER THIS

Have you ever given much thought to pockets? Sometimes it is not the complicated inventions that help us the most but the simple things! Aren't pockets like that? They are simple things, but think of how useful they are. Pockets give us a spot to warm our hands and a place for treasures we find. Pockets can hold things we forgot we had or thought we had lost. Lists of every kind, a note from a friend, pens, pencils, and pictures can all be found in pockets. In a pocket we might keep a tissue to dry our tears, a snack, a key that unlocks a door or starts a car, gloves for a winter day, or a small flashlight to help us find our way in the dark.

Pockets help free our hands to do other things. There are pocketbooks, pocket Bibles, and wallets full of pockets. What we carry in our pockets tells a great deal about us. (For example, who we are or what we like, or maybe what we do or where we live.) Did you know that pockets can also carry gentle reminders for us of God's love? Why not put a prayer in your pocket today?

A STORY

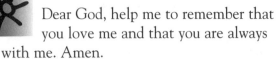

Granddad always kept a tiny metal cross in his billfold pocket. Printed on the cross were the words, *God loves you.* This was a constant reminder to Granddad that he was a child of God and that nothing could separate him from God's steadfast love. If he was sad or afraid, he would reach into his pocket and take out the cross. This always helped him to remember that God was near to him. He also liked to give these crosses away so others could keep this message in their pockets too. Granddad found a wonderful way to spread the message of God's love.

PRAYING TOGETHER

Dear God, help me to remember that you love me and that you are always with me. Amen.

READING THE BIBLE TOGETHER

Read Psalm 136:1-9.

SHARING TOGETHER

Family members can create their own sentence prayers. Write the prayers on slips of paper, and let each person keep his or her own prayer to carry in his or her pocket. Use today's scripture if you wish. Consider trading prayers occasionally or putting a prayer in someone else's pocket for that person to find.

OPTIONAL ACTIVITY

See page 265.

September 25

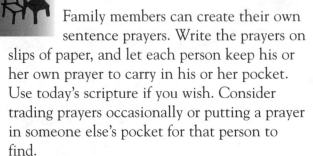

READING THE BIBLE TOGETHER

Let different family members look up and read these well-known passages:
Matthew 19:13-15 (Jesus and the children),
Luke 6:31 (The Golden Rule),
Matthew 28:18-20 (The Great Commission),
Mark 12:28-31 (The Great Commandment).

CONSIDER THIS

Do you have a favorite pair of jeans? Jeans come in different sizes, colors, and styles and are available at many stores.

But we often find that when we buy a new pair of jeans, they feel stiff and new. It is only after we begin to wear them and we wash them a number of times that our jeans begin to soften and become more comfortable. In fact, the longer we wear them, the better they feel.

But we do have to wear our jeans. If we select a pair and simply allow them to hang in a closet or remain in a drawer, our jeans will continue to be stiff, new, and unfamiliar to us.

Just like those unworn jeans, many Bibles are never opened or read. People buy them but then leave them unopened on tables or bookshelves or tucked away in drawers where they are rarely noticed. Sometimes Bibles just gather dust and are forgotten about!

We have to use our Bibles—open them, look through them, study them, read the stories again and again—before we can begin to know what the Bible is all about and what it has to say to us.

When we use our Bibles, we learn more about what it means to be a follower of Jesus Christ. We continue to grow in our understanding of Jesus and of God's love for us. And our Bibles become more and more important to us.

PRAYING TOGETHER

Dear God,
thank you for the gift of the Bible.
Help our family to read and listen to your word.
Help our family to study and learn your word.
Help our family to live your word. Amen.

LOOKING AHEAD

Gather one or several candles before your devotion time tomorrow. Put them into holders in a central place on your worship area. Place an open Bible close to them, and have a match ready to light them.

September

CONSIDER THIS

This candle represents light, all kinds of light. Close your eyes and picture in your mind as many different kinds of lights as you can. Think about all the different uses for lights. Why do we have lights? What do they do for us? What if there were no lights?

READING THE BIBLE TOGETHER

Repeat several times the words found in Psalm 119:105.

SHARING TOGETHER

Opening the Bible can be like turning on the light. Consider the letters in the word *light*.

L– Lets us see more clearly.
I – Illuminates our path.
G – Gives us direction.
H– Helps us to live better.
T – Takes us out of darkness.

When you open the Bible, what light does it give you?

FAMILY LITANY

All: Let there be light.

Reader: Let there be...fireflies to chase on a summer's evening, stars shining in the sky, the dawning of a new day, candles flickering on a birthday cake, light appearing at the end of a tunnel, headlights beaming through rain and fog, twinkling lights on a Christmas tree, the glare of a floodlight, a flashlight penetrating the darkness, a full moon illuminating the sky, stoplights flashing on and off, a night-light softly glowing, daylight streaming through a window.

All: Let there be light.

Reader: Let there be...light to guide and direct, light to help us see the way and give us hope. Let there be light as we read and study the Bible which is a lamp to our feet and a light to our path so that we might come to know the teachings of Jesus, who is the light of the world.

All: Praise and thanks to God for giving us the light.

PRAYING TOGETHER

Dear God, help us to open our Bible and let its light brightly shine to direct and guide us as a family and show us what is right. Help us to open our Bible and let us learn of the great love you have for us. Help us to open our Bible so that it can be a lamp to our feet and we can spread your love to those we meet wherever we go. Help us to open our Bible so that our faith can grow and grow. Amen.

September 27

IMAGINE THIS

Did you know that you have a special friend who is always with you? This friend loves you no matter what you do or say, wherever you might be.

You have a special friend with you whether you are crying, acting silly, playing, going to school, or just gazing at a cloud. Did you know you have a friend wherever you are?

Who is this friend who stays by your side? the friend who comforts, guides, listens, loves, and helps you grow?

Did you know your friend's name is God? Take time to thank and praise God for being such a friend.

SHARING TOGETHER

Parents, share with your children an experience you had where God's loving presence was real to you. Even though we cannot see God, God is always with us. We are never alone. God lives in our hearts. Discuss as a family how it feels to know you have such a special companion.

READING THE BIBLE TOGETHER

Read Psalm 139:7-10.

SINGING TOGETHER

One family member sings a phrase of this song and the others echo the words to the tune of the hymn, "What a Friend We Have in Jesus," or say the words.

God is always walking with me.
God's forever by my side.
No need to feel alone or fearful.
God's there to listen, guide, and love.
Alleluia, God, I love you!
Help me never to forget.
God, you're always walking with me.
You're forever by my side.

September 28

A STORY

The Golden Egg Book by Margaret Wise Brown is a wonderful children's book for people of all ages. The story begins with a duck that is inside an egg. He feels all alone in a small dark world. When he breaks through the egg's shell and discovers a bunny, they become good friends. The story ends by saying, "And no one was ever alone again."*

CONSIDER THIS

Sometimes, like the duck in *The Golden Egg Book*, we feel all alone in the world. We think we do not have any friends, and the world seems like a dark place.

God is our special friend who always wants to be in communication with us and spend time with us. When we choose to love and spend time with God, our friendship with God will continue to grow and grow! When we choose to ignore God and forget to pray, we may feel lonely inside. And it makes it difficult for our relationship for God to grow.

SHARING TOGETHER

Take time for each family member to tell his or her own story about a special friendship. Let each person share a response to the following questions: What does the friendship means to you? How did you meet and become friends?

READING THE BIBLE TOGETHER

Say the words of Proverbs 17:17*a* together several times: A friend loves at all times.

PRAYING TOGETHER

Invite each family member to contribute to a prayer about friendship. Then someone can close the prayer with these words:

For the gift of friendship, for the gift of your loving presence with us, we thank and praise you, Lord! Amen.

*Margaret Wise Brown, *The Golden Egg Book*, Racine, Wis.: Western Publishing Company, 1947.

September 29

READING THE BIBLE TOGETHER

Read Mark 6:46.

SHARING TOGETHER

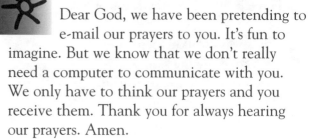

How do you feel when you receive a special note or letter from someone? What does it tell you about the person who sent it? Do you ever send mail to friends and family? How do you feel when you do this?

Sending e-mail has become very popular. Before you can blink, the computer sends a message!

Everyone loves to receive mail. We feel good knowing that someone cares enough about us to send us a personal message. We can send messages to those we love on all kinds of occasions. Maybe it's a birthday greeting, a thank you, congratulations, a note saying "I'm sorry," a special announcement, or just a letter to let someone know we are thinking about him or her.

Prayer is like sending mail to God. God loves us and wants to hear from us anytime or anywhere. It pleases God when we take the time to pray. When we pray, we are saying, "God, we know that you are present with us, and we want to tell you what we are thinking and feeling just now."

Imagine that your family is sending God an e-mail. If a computer is available, gather around it to write your message. If not, use paper and pencil to pretend to create an e-mail for God. Let each family member help to write it. When the e-mail is complete, pray the entire message together.

PRAYING TOGETHER

Dear God, we have been pretending to e-mail our prayers to you. It's fun to imagine. But we know that we don't really need a computer to communicate with you. We only have to think our prayers and you receive them. Thank you for always hearing our prayers. Amen.

READING THE BIBLE TOGETHER

The LORD has heard my supplication;
the LORD accepts my prayer (Ps. 6:9).

September 30

READING THE BIBLE TOGETHER

Read Matthew 18:12-14.

TELL US MORE

In this parable, Jesus tells us that God is like the shepherd in the story. When we have gone astray and find ourselves lost, God will patiently seek us out. God never gives up until we are safe and cared for again. God loves us that much! We are all God's precious children.

A STORY-POEM

Take turns reading a verse at a time. Create your own motions if you wish.

Verse 1
A hundred sheep in the wilderness one day.
All are there to play and graze.
One leaves the flock. A sheep is gone!
Only ninety-nine sheep together this day.

Verse 2
A shepherd in the wilderness one day,
To keep his sheep from wandering afar.
He counts his sheep and what does he find?
One has left. A sheep is gone this day.
He looks and searches until he can find,
His little lost sheep that wandered afar.
All one hundred sheep together again this day.

Verse 3
A shepherd tells neighbors
and friends one day,
"Oh, what a joyful time it is!
I've got my sheep that wandered afar.
This sheep was lost but it's back in the fold
Rejoice with me. Let's celebrate this day!"

A STORY

When Julie was four years old, her dad took her Christmas shopping. While they were shopping, Julie wandered away from her dad while he was paying for the gift they had chosen.

When Julie's dad realized that she was gone, he forgot about the gift and began shouting her name. He asked others to help in the search too. Nothing mattered but finding Julie!

Julie was soon found playing in a big clothes rack nearby. Immediately, Julie's dad scooped her into his arms, held her tight, and said, "Julie, I love you! I don't want you to be lost from me ever again! I'm so happy that I found you and we're together!"

SHARING TOGETHER

How do you think Julie's dad felt? How do you think Julie felt? How do you feel when you think that God will always seek us, even when we are lost in some way?

READING THE BIBLE TOGETHER

Read Psalm 23.

OCTOBER

October 1

READING THE BIBLE TOGETHER

Read the story in Luke 18:35-43, and then see who can answer these questions:

- What did the blind man want and need?
- Whom did he think could give him what he needed?
- How did he ask for what he wanted?
- What did Jesus say to the blind man?
- What was the blind man's response when he could see?

CONSIDER THIS

 When the blind man received his sight, the first thing he did was to follow Jesus and praise God. He had just experienced Jesus' power; his life had been changed; he would no longer have to sit by the side of the road and beg for money. Instead, he would follow Jesus!

When any of us knows Jesus, when we let ourselves feel his power as the blind man did, don't we too want to follow Jesus? Aren't we ready to praise God and give thanks for the wonderful things Jesus has done?

SHARING TOGETHER

People who follow Jesus are called Christians. Those who follow Jesus come in all shapes, sizes, colors, and ages. They live in every country of the world and speak any of thousands of languages. But they have one thing in common—they believe in Jesus Christ and his power to make a difference in their lives.

Why do you believe in Jesus? How have you seen his power?

PRACTICING WHAT JESUS TAUGHT

Following Jesus means more than going to church and saying, "I am a Christian." To follow Jesus means to live as he taught us to live and to ask in every situation, "What would Jesus do?"

How can you live in a way that is more like Jesus? What small steps can you take today to be a faithful follower of Jesus?

SINGING TOGETHER

 While you sing these words (or say them if you don't know the tune), think of what it means to follow Jesus:

I have decided to follow Jesus (Sing 3 times.)
No turnin' back, no turnin' back.

Though none go with me, still I will follow (Sing 3 times.)
No turnin' back, no turnin' back!

My family with me, we'll follow Jesus!
(Sing 3 times.)
No turnin' back, no turnin' back!

The world around me, the Lord before me
(Sing 3 times.)
I'm movin' on, I'm movin' on!

PRAYING TOGETHER

Jesus, we know you love us and you want to change our lives. Thank you for the opportunity to follow you. Help us to always look to you as our leader and friend. Amen.

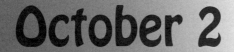

October 2

CONSIDER THIS

Followers of Jesus listen carefully to God's voice.

A STORY

Joan of Arc, a Christian who lived a long time ago (1412–31 C.E.), is still famous today for her courage. When she was only twelve, Joan began hearing voices that she believed came from God. The voices told her she had been chosen to save her country, France, from the English invaders. Despite the fact that she was young, female, and untrained as a soldier, Joan convinced French leaders that God wanted her to lead the soldiers. She led French forces to victory again and again, and she became a hero in her country.

Unfortunately, Joan was captured, sold to the English, and put on trial for not following official church beliefs such as women not wearing men's clothing. She was burned at the stake when she was only nineteen years old—but later, people realized she had been faithful to what she heard God saying.

No one else heard God speak to Joan. Many didn't believe that God would really communicate with a young girl, let alone give her the power to lead troops to battle. Some people thought Joan was crazy, but her actions proved she was indeed listening to God's voice.

TELL US MORE

The Bible is full of stories of how God spoke to a variety of people. As a young boy, Samuel heard God's voice calling him, but he needed Eli's help to understand who was speaking (1 Sam. 3:1-19). Mary heard God speaking through an angelic messenger (Luke 1:26-38). Joseph heard God in a dream (Matt. 1:18-25). Throughout the ages, God has spoken to people, sometimes in words, sometimes in thoughts or dreams, sometimes in the words of other people.

SHARING TOGETHER

Think about the ways God communicates with each of us:

- In what ways do you talk to God?
- Have you ever felt God was speaking to you?
- Is it easy or hard to listen for God's voice?
- What can we do to be good listeners?

PRAYING TOGETHER

Close with this prayer or your own:

Loving God, we are so glad that you want to communicate with us. You are always there when we need to talk to you. Thank you for the many ways you speak to us. Help us to be good listeners. In the name of Jesus Christ, who came that we might know you better. Amen.

OPTIONAL ACTIVITY

See page 266.

October 3

CONSIDER THIS

Followers of Jesus have a vision of the world as God intends it to be and are not afraid of taking action to make things better for all.

A STORY

Martin Luther King Jr. grew up as the son of a minister. Every Sunday he sat in church and heard Bible verses about how God wants peace, harmony, and wholeness for our world. Yet Martin could see that God's vision was not happening—everywhere around him were signs saying, For Whites Only or No Colored Allowed. People were mistreated because of the color of their skin or the fact that they were poor or uneducated.

Martin grew up as a strong Christian and became a Baptist minister. Then, he was the one preaching from the Bible about a new heaven and a new earth. He became an important force not only in his local church but also in the civil rights movement in the United States. He spoke not only to people in the church, but he also shared his vision of what God desired with all people—black and white, Christian and non-Christian, the powerful and the powerless. He urged people to work for change in ways that wouldn't hurt anyone. Because of his leadership, laws were changed. Little by little, the world became a bit more like God intended it to be because Martin Luther King Jr. kept lifting up God's vision of wholeness.

In one of his most famous speeches Martin spoke these words: "I have a dream that my four little children will one day live in a nation where they will not be judged by the color of their skin but by the content of their character. I have a dream today."*

Unfortunately, Martin was killed by someone who did not share his dream. Thirty-five years after his death, though, the influence of Martin Luther King Jr. is still felt as people today hold up his example of peaceful ways to work for change.

READING THE BIBLE TOGETHER

Read Isaiah 65:17-25.

- What images stand out for you?
- How is this "new earth" different from the earth on which we live?
- With this vision of how God intends our world to be, what work needs to be done to bring about such a new earth?

Close by reading Galatians 6:9-10 in memory of Martin Luther King Jr., a faithful follower of Jesus.

*The Words of Martin Luther King, Jr., selected and compiled by Coretta Scott King (New York: Newmarket Press, 1983), 95.

October 4

CONSIDER THIS

Followers of Jesus notice and care for suffering people.

READING THE BIBLE TOGETHER

Read Paul's words in Ephesians 2:8-10.

How is each of us created in Christ Jesus for good works? How can we help meet the needs of suffering people?

A STORY

Born in Yugoslavia, Mother Teresa was originally named Agnes. By the time she was twelve, Agnes knew that she wanted to help the poor. She trained to be a Christian missionary and, at eighteen, took vows as a nun. For nineteen years, Sister Teresa taught in a convent in Calcutta, India, but she still felt called by God to work with the poor. In 1946, she left the convent school and began to work among the poor in the slums of Calcutta.

Teresa started an open-air school for homeless children and then founded the Missionaries of Charity whose goal was to care for poor and outcast persons who had no other help. Mother Teresa and her Missionaries of Charity founded children's homes, clinics, a leper colony, and homes for the dying. When she won the Nobel Peace Prize, Mother Teresa said, "With this prize…I am going to try to make the home for many people that have no home. Because I believe that love begins at home, and if we can create a home for the poor—I think that more and more love will spread."

Mother Teresa helped other people not because she was trying to be famous but because she wanted to follow Jesus. Everything this humble woman did, she did because she believed what Paul wrote to the church in Ephesus long ago.

PRAYING TOGETHER

Jesus, our example and our friend, please show each of us ways to help those who suffer. Let us never forget that we were made to do good works in your precious name. Amen.

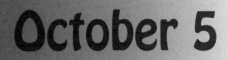

October 5

CONSIDER THIS

Followers of Jesus speak the truth about justice even when it may be dangerous to do so.

A STORY

Oscar Romero was a Catholic archbishop in a tiny Central American country. El Salvador was ruled by a few wealthy citizens who seemed to care little for the many extremely poor Salvadorans. The government's national guard even murdered innocent farm workers without cause. Numerous church workers were killed for their actions on behalf of the poor. El Salvador was in turmoil.

Archbishop Romero spoke out against the violence. He pleaded with the soldiers to stop the killing. Having seen several friends who were priests murdered by the National Guard, he knew the risks he was taking. "I have often been threatened with death. Nevertheless, as a Christian, I do not believe in death without resurrection....If the threats come to be fulfilled, from this moment I offer my blood to God for the redemption and resurrection of El Salvador."*

In 1980, as Romero preached, a shot rang out and the archbishop fell dead at the front of the sanctuary. His death rocked the country, moving more and more people to action. Romero's brave witness inspired others to work for justice. He followed Jesus who said, "Just as I have loved you, you also should love one another" (John 13:34).

PRACTICING WHAT JESUS TAUGHT

Most of us won't live in such dramatic circumstances, but all of us have times when we must choose to speak for justice or to remain silent. Take turns answering what you might say in the following situations:

- A classmate tells a joke that makes fun of people in a certain ethnic group.
- You see some children mistreating a dog.
- When you go to a toy store, a group of people is protesting the sale of war toys.
- You overhear another person making racist or sexist remarks.
- Someone who is very popular is making fun of someone you know who doesn't have many friends.
- You've promised to help your Sunday school class with a service project, but then you get invited to a party that sounds as if it would be a lot of fun.

Can you think of times in your life when you have chosen to stand up for what was right even when it was the hard thing to do? Tell how you made your decision and what the consequences were.

READING THE BIBLE TOGETHER

Reading Philippians 4:1, 4-9 in honor of Oscar Romero, a faithful follower of Jesus.

*Mary Craig, *Candles in the Dark: Six Modern Martyrs* (London: Hodder and Stoughton, 1984), 201.

October 6

CONSIDER THIS

The past few days, we've looked at some people who have brought others closer to God by living a faithful Christian life. See what your family can remember about following Jesus before looking at the list below.

- Followers of Jesus listen carefully to God's voice.
- Followers of Jesus have a vision of the world the way God wants it to be and are not afraid of taking action to change the way things are.
- Followers of Jesus notice and care for suffering people.
- Followers of Jesus speak the truth about injustice even when it may be dangerous to do so.
- Followers of Jesus live in a way that brings other people closer to God.

What other things would you add to the list of what a faithful follower of Jesus does? Joan of Arc, Martin Luther King Jr., Mother Teresa, and Oscar Romero are now with God, but they lived and loved in the same world in which we live and love. Some people in their everyday lives did not understand the work they did. None of these four was perfect, but they all tried to live as followers of Jesus and sought to put God first in their lives.

 ## SHARING TOGETHER

Think of someone you know who puts God first, tries to follow Jesus, and inspires you to be a faithful Christian. This could be someone in your family, church, or neighborhood. You can also look at newspapers and magazines to see who in other parts of the world is doing God's work. Talk about those persons and what they do.

 ## READING THE BIBLE TOGETHER

Read John 10:27-28.

What is the reward Jesus gives those who follow him?

 ## PRAYING TOGETHER

Stand in a circle, holding hands, and name some of those people who have shown the world the way Jesus wants us to live. After each name is called out, everyone can say together, "Thank you, God, for your faithful people." Be sure to remember the people in your family's life as well as famous people.

 ## OPTIONAL ACTIVITY

See page 266.

 ## LOOKING AHEAD

You will need a timer for tomorrow's devotion.

October 7

 ## SHARING TOGETHER

God made so many creatures! Set a timer for two minutes, and then see how many different kinds of animals you can name in that time. Let family members take turns calling out the name of an animal, fish, bird, or reptile. Be specific and let your mind wander among forests, jungles, deserts, and mountain homes to think what might live there. Ready, set, go!

 ## CONSIDER THIS

Isn't God creative? From the tiniest fish to the tallest giraffe, each creature is God's handiwork. When we see a ruby-throated hummingbird or an intricately striped zebra, we get a hint of how great God's imagination is.

MORE SHARING TOGETHER

What animals are your favorites? Name those special creatures, then give everyone a moment to think about the question: If I could be another living thing, what would I be? Starting with the youngest person, share your choice and why you would like to be that particular creature.

READING THE BIBLE TOGETHER

Ask a family member to read Genesis 1:20-25.

Keep your place marked in the Bible as you talk about this passage. How do you think God felt God after creating "swarms of living creatures of…every kind"? (We read that God saw that it was good, so we can assume that the Creator felt happy about creating anteaters, sharks, frogs, grizzly bears, and all the other wonderful animals that live on our earth.)

Next, read Genesis 1:26-31. Here's the big question: If God was so happy with everything that had been created, why did God go one step further and create human beings? See if each person in your family can come up with at least one possible reason why, after spending so much energy creating all the different living creatures, the Almighty also made people like you and me.

PRAYING TOGETHER

Stand in a circle and close with an echo prayer. One person reads a line and the others repeat it.

God, you are a wonderful Creator.
Thank you for all the incredible creatures you made.
Thank you for making us, too.
Help us to appreciate other living beings.
Help us to care for everything that lives.
We are your creation, your helpers, your children.
In your good name, we say, Amen.

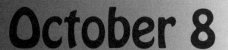

October 8

READING THE BIBLE TOGETHER

Read Genesis 1:27.

SHARING TOGETHER

Look at members of your family. Each of them was made in God's image. Is everyone identical? No, human beings are each uniquely made.

Make a list of all the ways people can look different from each other (hair, skin, eye color, shape of nose, height, etc.). Think about other ways people are not all the same. Some like brussels sprouts, and some don't. One person is afraid of dogs, and the next person loves them. A human being can live anywhere on earth,

have any kind of job, and wear a variety of clothes. Someone may travel around the world while another never leaves home. In what other ways are people different from one another? Share your ideas.

CONSIDER THIS

Given all of these differences, how can every person be made in the image of God? How is that possible? What does it mean to be made in God's image? How does each one of us show what God is like?

TELL US MORE

When we see how unique each person is, we once again realize God's imagination and creativity. So many colors of eyes! So many body shapes and hair textures! No two voices sound quite the same, and every personality is one of a kind. Yet we know that each person was made to be like God.

Although we may all look original on the outside, each of us has the light of God inside of us. Think of who you know God to be—how can human beings be like God? How do our lives show the God-part inside us?

MORE SHARING TOGETHER

Share with one another times someone in your family showed their God-likeness.

Say, "I saw how you were like God when you (name what the person did)." You may want to thank the other persons for how they showed God to you. When we are loving, kind, helpful, and understanding, we show that we are made in God's image.

Go to a room where there is a mirror big enough for you to see all members of your family. Stand together in front of the mirror and say together, "So that's what God looks like!"

October 9

IMAGINE THIS

Have one person read this guided meditation while the others close their eyes, relax, and use their imaginations to see themselves in the story.

You are lost. The others all ran ahead and now you are alone, wondering if anyone will even notice that you're not with the rest. Everything around you is strange. You have never seen this place before. It's getting dark, and you begin to feel afraid. You want to call out for help, but there is no one near enough to hear your voice.

It is cold, and the ground is hard. You settle close to the earth, sure it is going to be a long and lonely night. You feel sad, wondering if anyone even misses you. Does anyone care?

Just when you are feeling lower than low, you hear a sound in the distance. Is it a voice? You listen carefully, trying not to get your hopes up, but far away, faintly, you hear someone call your name. "Here I am!" you try to say, but no sound comes out of your mouth. Will you ever be found?

Closer and closer comes the voice. You are standing now, shivering; still, no sound leaves your mouth. You hear someone calling your name, over and over. Suddenly, a form bends over you. "There you are, my precious little one!" You feel yourself scooped up into strong arms, hugged close so that the chill begins to leave your cold body. "I'm so glad I found you! You were lost, but now you're found."

(Reader: give a few moments of silence before asking others to open their eyes.)

SHARING TOGETHER

Talk about how you felt during the guided meditation. Have you ever felt lost and alone in real life?

READING THE BIBLE TOGETHER

Read Luke 15:3-7.

Jesus is saying that we can count on God. We may sometimes get lost, but God will always look for us. "Rejoice with me, for I have found my sheep that was lost."

PRAISING GOD TOGETHER

Stand up to do a family cheer with these words:

Praise God who finds us when we're lost!
Praise God who loves us without cost!
Hip, hip, hooray!
God's here today.
P—r—a—i—s—e God!

October 10

SHARING TOGETHER

Take turns playing *Find the Coin*. While the others hide their eyes, one person takes a quarter and hides it in one room. The person hiding the coin then calls out, "Find the coin!" Whoever successfully finds the quarter is the next to hide the coin. After a few minutes of play, gather together with your Bibles.

READING THE BIBLE TOGETHER

Let a young reader turn to Luke 15:8-10 and read aloud.

- Why did the woman search for the coin?
- What difference might one silver coin make?
- Why is she so happy to find the coin?
- What does she do and say when she finds it?
- Does any part of this story sound familiar?

The shepherd who found the lost sheep also said, "Rejoice with me," for he had just found what was lost.

CONSIDER THIS

Why do you think Jesus told these stories? What do we know about God from hearing about the shepherd and the woman who lost her silver coin? How do you feel about a God who wants to find you?

Jesus is talking about more than being lost in an unknown place. Yes, God does care for you if you get separated from your loved ones and can't find your way home. God also cares for you if you are lost in other ways. Maybe you do something that does not show the spirit of God inside you. That is being lost. Or you decide it's not so important to obey family rules. That is being lost. In what other ways do people sometimes get lost? (Some examples: hurting other people, saying mean things, telling lies, not keeping promises.)

Even when we are lost, God knows where we are. God wants us to be found. Sometimes, for instance, when we do something that hurts another person, we feel lost. But if we say we're sorry to that person and then ask God for forgiveness, God is ready to find us. Are we ready to be found?

SINGING TOGETHER

Sing the first verse of "Amazing Grace" together. It reminds us that God wants us to be found.

Amazing grace! How sweet the sound
that saved a wretch like me!
I once was lost, but now am found;
was blind, but now I see.

October 11

READING THE BIBLE TOGETHER

Look up the story of the Prodigal Son in Luke 15:11-32.

Choose how your family wants to experience this Bible passage (also known as the story of the Loving Father). You could read the story, then take turns telling its plot from memory with one person continuing where another leaves off. Or your family might read the story aloud, each taking a different part to speak: the father, younger brother, older brother, servants, and the narrator who will say everything that is not spoken by a character in the story.

You could also act out the story using simple props (a baseball cap for the younger brother, a suit coat or briefcase for the older brother, a hat for the father, a broom and rake for the servants, a robe and pair of slippers to be given to the lost son). Designate where home and a foreign country are with the road connecting them. Encourage all actors to be as dramatic as possible.

SHARING TOGETHER

However you experience the story of the Prodigal Son/Loving Father, take time afterward to share your answers to these questions together:

- Which character are you most like?
- What does this story tell us about God?
- What does this story tell us about human beings?

PRAYING TOGETHER

God, you are the parent who always welcomes us home. When we run away, when we make bad choices that hurt others or ourselves, you are still there with open arms, ready to hold us close to you. Thank you for your faithful love that is greater than any mistakes we can make. We praise you in the name of Jesus Christ. Amen.

October 12

READING THE BIBLE TOGETHER

Ask one family member to read again the story of the Prodigal Son in Luke 15:11-32.

SHARING TOGETHER

Tell which character each of you identifies with and why ("I am like the older brother because…"). Pass around a ring to symbolize the ring the father wanted to give his younger son when he returned home. The person whose turn it is to hold the ring answers one of the following questions:

- Why do you think the younger son wanted to go out on his own?
- Why do you think the older son was angry that his younger brother got a party?
- Do you think the father was right to celebrate that his lost son was found?
- Why did Jesus include this story with the stories of the shepherd searching for a lost sheep and the woman searching for a lost coin?
- Why does each of these stories talk about rejoicing?
- What is your favorite part of the story?

IMAGINE THIS

Ask everyone to close his or her eyes while one person reads:

Imagine a hot, dusty road along which a young and weary traveler sadly trudges. An older man stands far down the roadside, his hands cupped over his eyes as he tries to see into the distance. When the young traveler is still a long way off, the old man begins to run as fast as his arthritic knees will allow. He runs until he is close enough to wrap his arms around the young man. Tears run down his cheeks. "My son is alive! He who was lost is found." The young man forgets his years of hard living; he feels only his father's strong embrace.

And we, when we feel lost, can just as surely run to God who will welcome us with open arms and words of joy. Thanks be to God!

A FAMILY LITANY

One person reads each of the following lines, pausing for the others' response: "God is always ready to find us!"

Reader: No matter where in the world we go . . .
All:　　**God is always ready to find us!**
Reader: Even if we forget who we are . . .
All:　　**God is always ready to find us!**
Reader: No matter what we do . . .
All:　　**God is always ready to find us!**
Reader: Whether or not we are looking for God…
All:　　**God is always ready to find us!**

October 13

CONSIDER THIS

Most of us wouldn't describe God as a bird, but the Bible tells us some ways God is like two very different birds: a strong, powerful eagle and an ordinary, humble chicken.

READING THE BIBLE TOGETHER

Read Deuteronomy 32:11-13.

Can you imagine God as that mighty eagle that cares for its young high on the mountaintop? The eagle's strength and swiftness show its ability to protect its young, so when we read in Exodus 19:4 the words, *You have seen what I did to the Egyptians, and how I bore you on eagles' wings and brought you to myself*, we realize that God could be like an eagle.

But how is God like a chicken? Jesus uses this image when he is feeling sad about the way the people in Jerusalem are acting. Read Matthew 23:37. Here Jesus is that clucking hen who shelters her young under her wings.

So we could think of God as an eagle strong enough to carry us on its wings or as a hen caring enough to give us refuge close to its feathered breast. Images like these do not mean we think God is a big bird up in the sky; they simply give us one more way we can glimpse the greatness that is God.

God is so great that our Creator cannot be neatly wrapped up and put in a box so we can open the box and say, "Oh, so this is God." God is the loving father, the powerful eagle,

the brooding mother hen, the comforting presence, the imaginative creator of the universe.

PRAYING TOGETHER

If you know the song "On Eagle's Wings," you can sing it as your closing prayer. If not, close with this prayer:

Strong and loving God, you are beyond any image we can think of for you. Thank you for upholding us like a strong eagle and for caring for us like a mother hen cares for her chicks. Thank you for all the ways you love us! Amen.

October 14

CONSIDER THIS

There is so much for us to learn about our Creator. God knows us much better than we can ever know the One who created us! God has known and loved us even longer than our parents have! Because we feel so loved, we continue to search for clues that help us know God better.

SHARING TOGETHER

God is more than any human words can pin down. Yet we need words so we can begin to understand our experience of knowing the God who loves us. The Bible uses many different images to describe God. Take turns reading from the list on the next page. If some of the words are new to you, you can always use a dictionary to see what they mean and how they might apply to God. Pick which of these words fits who you think God is.

Love   Breath   Dove   Hope

Rock   Fortress   Comfort

Lamb   Counselor   Cloud   Presence

Mercy   Life   the Way

Judge   Defender   Fountain   Wisdom

Shelter   Comfort   Giver

Savior   Shepherd   Stillness   Spirit

Help   Guide   Almighty

Power   Blessing   Creator   Redeemer

October 15

CONSIDER THIS

John the Baptist was well-known for preaching to people about their need to repent or change the way they were living. "Come be baptized, and start your life over in God," he told the many people who journeyed to the Jordan River to be baptized. John was clear that he himself was not the Messiah.

READING THE BIBLE TOGETHER

Read Psalm 62:5-8.

How does the person who wrote this psalm feel about God?

PRAYING TOGETHER

Give family members a chance to say a sentence prayer, using whatever words express God for them. When everyone has had a chance to pray, a parent can close with these words:

Great and gracious God, you are much more than our words can express. Help us to patiently learn about you. Remind us that you are more than our minds may ever understand, but your love is with us every moment of our lives. In the name of Jesus, who came that we might know you better, we pray. Amen.

LOOKING AHEAD

You'll need paper, scissors, markers or pens, and tape for tomorrow's devotional time.

READING THE BIBLE TOGETHER

Read Mark 1:9-11 that tells what happened when Jesus came to be baptized.

Then answer the following questions:

- Why did Jesus come to John to be baptized?
- What unusual thing happened when Jesus was baptized?
- What do you think the heavenly voice meant (verse 11)?

IMAGINE THIS

When we read Bible stories, we can picture in our minds how we think the action unfolded. We have no video footage, no still photographs to mark those moments; but in our own mind's eye, we can make the Bible come alive. Close your eyes as one family member reads the verses from Mark 1:9-11 again.

Imagine the faces of John and Jesus during the baptism. How does each of them react when the heavenly voice delivers its message?

Whose voice speaks?

SHARING TOGETHER

Using the pattern on this page, make paper doves for each person in your family. On each dove, write these words: *You are my beloved child. I am pleased with you.* Each person can place his or her dove where it will be regularly seen (on a mirror, bedroom door, the front of a notebook).

PRAYING TOGETHER

God, we know that you love us. As you were pleased with your son, Jesus, you are pleased with us and offer us new life too. Thank you for that gift. Amen.

OPTIONAL ACTIVITY

See page 266.

October 16

SOMETHING TO CONSIDER

Baptism welcomes us into the family of God. Some people are baptized as babies or young children. Their parents as Christians make baptismal promises for them. Others are baptized as youth. For them, baptism may be one of their first adult decisions. Many people are baptized as adults when they decide to make Jesus part of their lives.

SHARING TOGETHER

Yesterday we read about Jesus' baptism. Ask someone to tell again how and where he was baptized (Mark 1:9-11). Say together the words that you printed on the doves: *You are my beloved child. I am pleased with you.* Share stories about baptisms in your family. (This is a good time for a parent to share memories of those special times in the children's lives. Also, if they can remember the details, the adults can tell about their own baptisms as well.)

If no one in your family has been baptized, you may have witnessed someone else's baptism. What was that experience like? If someone in your family has not yet been baptized but desires baptism, you may want to make an appointment with your pastor to discuss baptism.

READING THE BIBLE TOGETHER

Read Acts 2:38-39.

MORE SHARING

Take turns kneeling in the center of the circle of family members while they place their hands on each person's head. Say in unison, "You are God's beloved child. God is well pleased with you." When each person has had a chance to be in the center, close with a family hug.

OPTIONAL ACTIVITY

See page 266.

LOOKING AHEAD

You will need a pitcher, large bowl, and water for tomorrow.

October 17

SHARING TOGETHER

Fill a pitcher with water and place a large bowl on a table around which your family can gather. As one person slowly pours water from the pitcher into the bowl, the others close their eyes and listen to the sound the water makes as it enters the bowl. When the bowl is filled, everyone can open his or her eyes.

Let each person take turns swishing her or his hands in the bowl. Family members may take turns placing their hands on other family members' heads and saying, "Remember your baptism and be thankful." (Anyone who is not yet baptized could say, "I am thankful God offers me the water of life.")

Stay by the bowl as you talk about the following:

- What did you think while the water was being poured into the pitcher?
- What are other times you notice the sound of water?
- Why is water important?
- Baptism has been called the "water of life."

Do you think this is a good way to talk about joining the family of God?

READING THE BIBLE TOGETHER

Read Deuteronomy 33:12.

CONSIDER THIS

These words were said about Benjamin, the youngest brother of Joseph, but they are words that apply to all of God's children. How often we forget that each of us is God's beloved child! Our families should be the place we best remember God's love. Yet sometimes, in the midst of busyness, family conflicts, and trying to meet our individual needs, we forget to remind each other, "You are God's beloved child. God is pleased with you."

MORE SHARING

Set a timer for three minutes. Close your eyes, hold hands with one another, and sit quietly together while each person thinks of the other family members and silently says, "(Name of the person), you are God's beloved child. God is pleased with you." When the timer goes off, squeeze hands, open your eyes, and smile!

LOOKING AHEAD

Tomorrow you'll need several colors of construction paper or tagboard, scissors, a hole punch, markers or pens, and string or yarn. If you don't have access to these supplies, you can use paper and pencil.

October 18

SHARING TOGETHER

Work together on a list of precious jewels. See how many different jewels you can list, then ask the following questions about each one:

- Why is this stone considered so beautiful?
- Would it cost a lot to buy one of these?
- Why would someone want to own jewelry made with this stone?

READING THE BIBLE TOGETHER

Read Revelation 21:11.

How might these words apply to a family?

CONSIDER THIS

Having a family who loves you is worth even more than the rarest diamond. Each person is an important part of a family. Just as a skilled jeweler knows how to create a spectacular necklace out of rubies and diamonds, God has created family members to fit together perfectly. Families come together in different ways: by blending two families, by adoption, by a mother and father having children together. No matter how a family is formed, each person is a precious jewel who contributes his or her own part to the beauty that is the family.

MORE SHARING

Each family member can cut colored paper into different shapes of jewels and then make necklaces for the other family members. On a paper jewel, write a word or two that tells something about a family member (loving, plays baseball with me, good listener). Try to think of as many positive things for each family member as you can so that everyone has a large number of jewels. Finish your time together with each person giving the others their jewels and reading aloud the words they picked for them. Use a hole punch with string or yarn to make the necklaces.

PRAYING TOGETHER

O God, we thank you for the way you have made us each a precious jewel in your sight and in the warmth of this family. Help us to value one another. Together, we are more precious than diamonds! In the name of Jesus, who brings us closer to one another, we pray. Amen.

October 19

CONSIDER THIS

Some people are easy to love. Jackson's sweet toddler face easily lights up in a smile; he is hardly ever grumpy. Lucy is almost eighty, and her hip hurts her most of the time. Maybe the pain makes her so crotchety—and the fact that she lives alone and feels abandoned by her children. To be with Jackson is to remember how good life is and how even the simplest things can bring joy. A few minutes with Lucy make many people want to run from her bitterness. Which of these two do you think most needs to feel loved? The sweet, happy toddler or the lonely old woman? Both!

READING THE BIBLE TOGETHER

Read Paul's words about how to live in Philippians 2:3-4.

How might Paul's words apply to young Jackson and old Lucy?

PRACTICING WHAT JESUS TAUGHT

Even though we might want to avoid someone like Lucy, if we put her interests first, we can take a few minutes to talk to her, listening even when she irritates us. Following Jesus is not about doing what we think is most fun or best for us. Instead, as Paul wrote, we are to look to the interests of others.

Who are the people you know who are hardest to love? Be honest. Name those people you find challenging. Whom do you try to avoid? Someone who makes you mad or sad or just doesn't seem worth your time? Let each person choose one difficult person to focus on. Begin by sitting, eyes closed. Imagine that person in your mind's eye. Try to see beyond the things the person does that irritate you. What might be going on inside that makes the person difficult?

IMAGINE THIS

Now, with your eyes still closed, imagine saying to that person, "You are God's beloved child." Try to see that person as you think God might see him or her. Say again, "You are God's beloved child." When ready, open your eyes.

SHARING TOGETHER

Share with one another what it was like to imagine saying that. Was it easy or hard to bless the other person? Could you see the person through God's eyes?

PRAYING TOGETHER

Close with each family member saying a one-sentence prayer for his or her difficult person.

October 20

CONSIDER THIS

We reach out to others because, as beloved children of God, we try to recognize that every person God created is worthy of love. It may be easier to recognize the belovedness of a friend with whom we have much in common or a teacher we like than that of a stranger on the street. However, Christian love reaches far beyond just those we know and like.

A STORY

Do you remember the October 4 devotion about Mother Teresa? She was known for her compassionate work among the poor and homeless of Calcutta, India. When someone asked her how she could stand to touch a leper who was dying, she replied, "I see in him the face of Jesus." Mother Teresa's words echo Jesus' words when he said, "Truly I tell you, just as you did it to one of the least of these who are members of my family, you did it to me."

READING THE BIBLE TOGETHER

Read Matthew 25:31-40.
In these verses Jesus tells a story about reaching out to strangers in love.

PRACTICING WHAT JESUS TAUGHT

Ask yourselves the following: When has our family given the hungry food? The thirsty drink? Welcomed the stranger? Clothed the naked? Cared for the sick? Visited the prisoner? As we did those things, were we able to see the face of Jesus in those we helped?

It may be hard to think of exact moments in the past when you have met the needs of others. So how about looking to the future? Brainstorm how any of you might be able to see the face of Jesus in these people:

- a homeless street person
- the playground bully
- a grouchy teacher
- a disaster victim you read about in the newspaper
- someone new to your neighborhood
- a church visitor
- a frustrated parent dealing with children in a grocery store

PRAYING TOGETHER

Close with a time of prayer. See if one of the children in your family will offer a spontaneous prayer. Or stand in a circle and individually pray as you think of ways to see Jesus' face (belovedness) in each and every person who crosses your path.

OPTIONAL ACTIVITY

See page 266.

October 21

CONSIDER THIS

It's not always easy to follow Jesus. Sometimes it's really hard to do the right thing, say the kind word, reach out to the needy. That's one reason why we need to read the Bible. We learn from the example of Jesus, and we find practical advice about how to live in love.

READING THE BIBLE TOGETHER

Look at Romans 12:9-13 to see the marks of a true Christian.

Read each of these lines separately, pausing after each one to let a family member say what he or she thinks it means:

Let love be genuine;

hate what is evil, hold fast to what is good;

love one another with mutual affection;

outdo one another in showing honor.

Do not lag in zeal,

be ardent in spirit,

serve the Lord.

Rejoice in hope,

be patient in suffering,

persevere in prayer.

Contribute to the needs of the saints;

extend hospitality to strangers.

Then have one reader repeat the entire Bible passage. Let each person tell which of these actions is easiest for him or her to do and which is the hardest to do. Is it easy to pray but hard to be patient in suffering? Each of us can help the others to grow in suggested areas.

We want to be like Jesus because we know that each of us is God's beloved child. We know that, as God said to Abraham, God also says to us, "I will bless you...so that you will be a blessing" (Gen. 12:2).

SHARING TOGETHER

Write out the letters *BLESSING* vertically so that you can make a word puzzle about living in such a way as to be a blessing to others. (You can do individual word puzzles or one as a family, depending on family members' ages.) So B might be *Bless others with your love* or *Be like Jesus.* Close by sharing your word puzzle(s) as a reminder of how to live as a blessing.

October 22

SHARING TOGETHER

Take turns telling who is your best friend. Then ask yourself this question: Who knows me most completely in all the world. (This may or may not be the best friend.) How does it feel to be able to tell that person all about yourself? Does a best friend help you feel special?

All of us need people who love and understand us. Good friends and loving family help us feel safe and at home in the world. But no matter how much we are loved by friends, parents, and siblings, there is One who loves us even more.

READING THE BIBLE TOGETHER

Read Psalm 139:13-18, and then answer together the questions below:

- How long has God known each of us?
- How well does God know us?
- Where can we hide from God?
- When is God with us?

MORE SHARING

Work together to write a poem that tells how you feel when you think about God's love (or, if everyone is old enough, write individual poems). You could create your own form of poem or use the format below and just complete the sentences. Remember that poems can be rhymed or unrhymed.

Before I was born, God . . .
As I have grown, God . . .
God knows me better than . . .
All of my days, God . . .
When I think about God's love, I . . .
So every day, I give thanks because . . .

READING THE BIBLE TOGETHER

Read or say Psalm 23 in unison.

This psalm tells how God is with us at all times, even the hard times when we are sick or with people who frighten us. Repeat verse 6 three times, letting your voices get quieter and quieter until the last time when you are speaking in a whisper.

LOOKING AHEAD

For tomorrow you will need to pull together the supplies listed under the section Reading the Bible Together, page 10.

October 23

A STORY

"You're lucky you're older," Jake said with a scowl.

Laurie shook her head. "Are you kidding? I have more responsibilities. And I always have to be good in case you follow my example."

"But Mom lets you do all the fun stuff. It's not fair!"

"Hey, when I was your age, she never let me have a Disneyland birthday party. It's so obvious that she loves you more than me."

"She does not! She's always saying you're just like her," Jake pointed out. "She likes you best."

In the next room, Laurie and Jake's mother sighed. Would they ever understand that she loved each of them the same amount? True, she didn't treat them exactly the same way, but the two children were different ages with different personalities. Wasn't it clear that she loved them both according to their needs?

READING THE BIBLE TOGETHER

Read Matthew 20:1-16.

Jesus told this story that illustrates our human need to compare. We often wonder if someone got more than we did. Use a handful of beans or clothespins to stand for the landowner and workers in the story. Decide where the vineyard is. (You might even use a few plastic plants to decorate it.) As one person reads the Bible passage, children can move the beans or clothespins to act out the story.

SHARING TOGETHER

When you have acted out the story, share your ideas about these questions:

- Why did the landowner pay everyone the same wage?
- How would you have felt if you had worked the longest hours?
- How might you have felt if you only worked a short time?
- What does this story say to us as families?

SINGING TOGETHER

Reread Matthew 20:14-16 and sing or say these verses:

God is so good. (Sing 3 times.) God is so good to us.
God loves us so. (Sing 3 times.) God is so good to us.

Trust there's enough/ blessings for all. Trust there's enough. God is so good to us.

October 24

Remember when we read the story of the Prodigal Son on October 12. Read again the portion in Luke 15:25-32.

A STORY

Have you ever wanted something someone else had? Felt jealous when a friend got to do something you didn't get to do? Resented it when someone else got all the attention? These are all very human feelings, and that's how the prodigal son's older brother felt when his younger brother came home. Pretend that you are listening to the older brother as he shares his feelings. Have someone in the family read these words that the older brother might have thought.

Just who does he think he is? First, he demanded what Dad wasn't even ready to give him, then rushed away from us to live the big life far away. Who knows how he spent all that money—but I bet he wasted it in the worst ways possible.

Meanwhile, as he was living it up, who stayed here doing all the work? Me, of course. Mr. Responsible. He partied, and I worked the fields. I was Dad's right-hand man, never taking time off to have fun. Doing the work of two sons.

He was gone so long, I practically forgot his name. Dad, on the other hand, made a fool out of himself, moping around, wondering aloud where my brother was. I remember how he went down to the road every day, looking up and down the highway as if the skunk would be home any day. Did we hear one word? Did we even know if he was dead or alive? Did I care?

Then suddenly he was home—the prodigal returned. And how my dad celebrated! It made me sick. The fatted calf, new clothes, a ring for his finger, shoes for his feet, and a party like I've never had. That burned me up!

SHARING TOGETHER

What could you say to this brother? What advice do you have that might help him deal with his resentment?

60

READING THE BIBLE TOGETHER

Read Romans 12:15.

What might these words say to someone in the older brother's situation? Do these words apply to any situation in your family's life?

PRAYING TOGETHER

God, sometimes we can't seem to help feeling jealous or wanting what others have. Help us instead to be happy when others are happy. Let us live in your love. Amen.

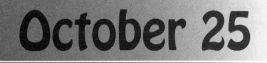

Octobr 25

CONSIDER THIS

Since God made us, God understands everything about us. So God knows that sometimes we have feelings of anger, jealousy, or resentment. In the story of the Prodigal Son, many of us can identify more with the older brother than the younger prodigal (Luke 15:25-32). However, we also know that God wants us to move past our anger, jealousy, or resentment. We can begin to do that by acknowledging our feelings, talking to others about our feelings, and asking God to help us so we can be more like Jesus.

READING THE BIBLE TOGETHER

Read Ephesians 4:26, 31-32.

If the older brother could have heard and understood words like these, would he have stayed outside the party, letting his anger get in the way of celebrating his brother's return?

The story of the Prodigal Son ends with the father and older son standing outside the party. When his father comes to invite him in to the celebration, the older son spills out all his anger and resentment. The father responds, "Son, you are always with me, and all that is mine is yours. But we had to celebrate and rejoice, because this brother of yours was dead and has come to life; he was lost and has been found."

IMAGINE THIS

Put your heads together and imagine how the conversation might have gone at this point if the older brother could have taken the words from Ephesians to heart. Did the older brother respond to his father in a positive way? Was he able to put aside his resentment, go inside, and greet his brother? What might have happened then? How would he have felt? Take turns being the father and older brother and act out possible scenes that might have occurred. See how many endings you can come up with, and then take a vote to see how your family wants to resolve the story.

A FAMILY LITANY

Close with the following cheer. One person yells out a line, then the others yell it back:

Give up anger!
   Give up anger!
Don't be mad.
   Don't be mad.
Let love flow through you,
   Let love flow through you,

And you won't be sad.
And you won't be sad.
Forgive each other.
Forgive each other.
Accept God's grace.
Accept God's grace.
Let kindness guide you
Let kindness guide you
In every place.
In every place.
Amen.
Amen.

October 26

 ## CONSIDER THIS

One of the reasons the Bible still speaks to us in a fresh way even though it was written long ago is that humans have not changed much over the centuries. The people for whom the Bible was first written were much like us. They had good days and bad days, times when they acted as their best selves and times they did mean-spirited things they later regretted. They needed encouraging words to help keep them on the right path, just as we today need encouragement.

 # READING THE BIBLE TOGETHER

Ask someone to read these words from Paul: Ephesians 4:1-3, 29–5:2 and Galatians 6:2.

Paul's was writing to people who were trying to live in a Christ-like community. Isn't that what we're trying to do in our family lives? Go back and read the Bible verses again, slowly. Put into your own words what they mean for your family. For instance, Ephesians 4:3 might be translated as *try to get along*. One family member can write down the family's understandingof Paul's words.

PRACTICING WHAT JESUS TAUGHT

After you have a list of what Paul's advice might be for your family, take time to reflect on:

- How do these words apply to your family?
- What is the easiest positive behavior for you to do?
- What is the hardest positive behavior for you to do?

A FAMILY LITANY

Close your time together by saying these excerpts from Ephesians 4 and 5. Give each person one or more lines to speak. Stand in order of speaking so everyone knows when his or her turn comes.

Be kind to one another,
tenderhearted, forgiving one another,
as God in Christ has forgiven you....
Be imitators of God,
as beloved children,
and live in love,
as Christ loved us.

October 27

CONSIDER THIS

When a baby is born, its family members offer love and immediate welcome to the world. Families are based on love. But, as much as we talk about love, love can be hard to pin down and understand. Work together to see if you can answer these questions:

- What is love?
- How do we show love?
- Why do we love?
- Can you love God and hate your sister or brother at the same time?

READING THE BIBLE TOGETHER

Take turns reading the verses in 1 John 4:7-12, letting each person read one verse at a time, pausing between verses. Then ask someone to read slowly through the entire passage but every time the word *love* is written, the reader will point to the other family members who will chime in with that important word.

Look back at the above questions. Did these words from 1 John 4 give you any new insights or answers?

Have an adult read the following phrases, making sure to pause after the comma in the second phrase:

> **No-matter-what love.**
> **No matter what, love**.

The first phrase describes the kind of love strong families need: *no-matter-what love* means I love you—no matter what. There will be times when it is hard to love. It's not long before that sweet infant who was unconditionally welcomed into the family is a growing child with wants and needs of its own—wants and needs that may conflict with the wants and needs of others in the family. When a brother and sister fight over a toy, there needs to be *no-matter-what love* between them. When a parent is disappointed with a child (or vice versa), what is needed? *No-matter-what love*. Almost every day that we live together in families, we need to say, *I love you—no matter what*.

The second phrase summarizes much of the Bible's message: *No matter what (happens), love!* So when we're tempted to blame or yell or feel resentful, maybe we can remember the little voice in the back of our minds that whispers, *No matter what, love!*

PRAYING TOGETHER

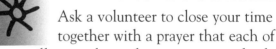

Ask a volunteer to close your time together with a prayer that each of you will remember to have *no-matter-what love* for one another and *no matter what, love!*

October 28

READING THE BIBLE TOGETHER

Have someone read 1 John 3:11, 23, and 2 John 6.

Doesn't the message about love sound clear? Yet, for most of us, there are moments when it is not so easy to walk in love. We may feel angry, disappointed, hurt, left out, rejected, ignored by our parents or siblings. And we're still expected to love!

SHARING TOGETHER

Role-play the following situations that might occur in a family, using the ideas on love from 1 John 4:7-12 (from yesterday) and 1 John 3:11, 23 and 2 John 6. There may be more than one person who wants to try to act out a given situation.

- A younger brother breaks his sister's favorite toy. How could the sister work this out with her brother?
- A father finds out his child has lied to him. How might he discuss this with the child?
- A mother promises to be present at an important event but doesn't arrive until the event is finished. How might the child share the feelings of disappointment?
- An older brother is rude to a younger brother and his friends. What can the younger brother say or do to express his feelings?
- A child has to choose between hanging out with friends and visiting his or her grandparents. How might the child make this decision?

A FAMILY LITANY

Close by, asking two readers to take parts and read aloud:

1. And this is love, that we walk according to his commandments;
2. this is the commandment just as you have heard it from the beginning—you must walk in it.
1. Beloved, let us love one another, because love is from God.
2. God is love, and those who abide in love abide in God, and God abides in them.
1. We love because he first loved us.
2. Those who say, "I love God," and hate their brothers or sisters, are liars;
1. for those who do not love a brother or sister whom they have seen, cannot love God
2. whom they have not seen.

Both: The commandment we have from him is this: Those who love God must love their brothers and sisters also.

LOOKING AHEAD

You will need a timer or clock for tomorrow's devotion.

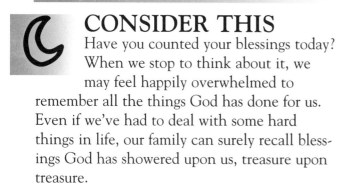

October 29

CONSIDER THIS

Have you counted your blessings today? When we stop to think about it, we may feel happily overwhelmed to remember all the things God has done for us. Even if we've had to deal with some hard things in life, our family can surely recall blessings God has showered upon us, treasure upon treasure.

SHARING TOGETHER

It's time for a treasure hunt! Each of you can go to any part of your home to search for treasures: things that remind you of God's good gifts. Set a timer for three to five minutes and look for your own idea of treasures. Come back together and take turns talking about the items you found. Why is each thing meaningful? Why do we need reminders of God's good gifts?

After everyone has had a chance to share, see if you can think of ways God has given your family good things. Let one or two family members take turns writing down the blessings.

READING THE BIBLE TOGETHER

Read Psalm 136:1-9, 23-26 together.

One reader can lead these verses while everyone else joins in with the refrain that repeats every other line: *for his steadfast love endures forever.* (If you are reading a translation other than the NRSV, use whatever refrain is at the end of each verse.) Practice that phrase a few times before the reader begins to read.

LOOKING AHEAD

Have paper available to make a mural. This could be butcher paper or newsprint, posterboard, or brown paper grocery bags cut open and turned inside out—any paper to make a surface at least three feet long. You will also need markers or paints to make your mural, along with smaller paper and scissors.

OPTIONAL ACTIVITY

See page 267.

October 30

READING THE BIBLE TOGETHER

God has promised to be with us at all times, through thick and thin. Read Isaiah 43:1-4a.

SHARING TOGETHER

Work together to make a mural that illustrates this passage. How might you show the waters and fire? As you draw or paint, talk about how this passage does not only mean that God saves us from fire and flood but also is there with us for all the hard parts of our lives. What might be some difficult times when we need God with us? What experiences has your family undergone when you leaned on God for strength? This could include natural catastrophes, loss of employment, the death of a loved one, or a move to a new city.

When you have finished your family's mural or pictures, write these words on it: Do not fear, for I have redeemed you; / I have called you by name (Isa. 43:1b).

Cut paper in the shape of a heart for each person and write, *You are precious in my sight, / and honored, and I love you* on the hearts. After decorating your hearts, form a parade and walk to each person's bed and hang that person's heart as a reminder of how much God loves each of us and will be with us at all times.

PRAYING TOGETHER

Read Isaiah 43:1-4a again and close with this prayer:
God, we know you love us and will be with us in all our tough times. Help us always to feel your loving arms around us. In the spirit of Jesus we pray. Amen.

October 31

CONSIDER THIS

Today is Halloween, a day when many children enjoy dressing up in costumes. Originally, for Christians, this was a day of preparation for All Saints' Day (November 1). Think about how we could dress up if we were focusing on All Saints' Day. Never mind princesses, goblins, witches, and cartoon characters. What about wearing a costume that shows how all of us are supposed to be dressed in the whole armor of God?

READING THE BIBLE TOGETHER

Read Ephesians 6:10-18.

SHARING TOGETHER

Work together to fashion a costume out of odds and ends you have around the house. See if you can you find items to represent:

- the belt of truth
- the breastplate of righteousness
- the shoes ready to proclaim the gospel of peace
- the shield of faith
- the helmet of salvation
- the sword of the Spirit (Word of God)

When the costume is ready, family members can take turns modeling the outfit. Have someone read the Ephesians passage again as the model points to the various costume parts. Remember that in this biblical passage, Paul is not describing a typical warrior going into battle, but rather, he wants us to understand that if we are to live as faithful followers of Jesus, we must consciously prepare ourselves just as a soldier going into battle prepares. In reality, it's not the clothes but our attitude that matters. Be strong in the Lord and in the strength of his power, Paul writes. Pray in the Spirit at all times. Reread Ephesians 6:10-18.

PRAYING TOGETHER

God, please clothe us in your love that we may always stand strong as your faithful people. Remind us that our strength is in you, our Rock and our Redeemer. For the gift of that strength and all your good gifts, we give you thanks and praise. Amen.

NOVEMBER

November 1

READING THE BIBLE TOGETHER

Read Philippians 1:3-5.

TELL US MORE

In the Bible, the word *saints* is sometimes used to describe all people who love God and are a part of the church. In our reading, taken from a letter in the New Testament, Paul is remembering saints who have been special in his life and in his faith.

Each year, the church observes All Saints' Day on the first day or first Sunday of November. It is a time to remember those people who have died and who were good teachers, good friends, and good examples.

SHARING TOGETHER

Give each family member a chance to answer these questions:

- Can you think of someone special to you who is no longer living?
- What do you remember about that person?
- How did the person you named help you or teach you?

Have someone read the scripture verses again. This time, keep in mind the people you have talked about.

PRAYING TOGETHER

Let two family members read the following prayer, either in unison or alternating lines:

Thank you, God, for teachers who were kind
  to us, and wise,
for grandparents who loved us well,
for family or friends who have died, but still
  mean a lot to us.
Thank you for their examples, their attention
  to us, their love for us.
Thank you for the ways they showed us what
  you are like.
Thank you, God, for these and all the saints.
Amen.

November 2

READING THE BIBLE TOGETHER

Read Philippians 4:9.

CONSIDER THIS

Somebody once said that a saint is a person who is like a window to God. When you look at the saint's life, you see such goodness that you understand something more

68

about God's goodness too. And you understand a little better how to live and show that goodness yourself.

A STORY

When Robert was growing up, his family often attended church in the small town where his grandparents lived. The church was so small that often Robert and his brothers and sisters were in the same Sunday school class. After Sunday school, the children would sit together in the worship service. Mrs. Nooner was the children's Sunday school teacher, and somehow she always wound up on the same pew with them during the service. She would help them find the right pages in the hymnal and point out the words as they sang. Mrs. Nooner taught the children about the Bible and prayer, and she taught them about worship. But mostly, because Mrs. Nooner loved the children, she taught them about God's love. Mrs. Nooner was a living saint for Robert and his family.

SHARING TOGETHER

Some saints or holy people have already died. But other saints are living. We may see them on the news, in our churches, schools, neighborhoods, or even our own home. They are ordinary people like us, but they are special people because they try hard to live the way they believe God wants them to live.

Who are the living saints in your life right now? In other words, who shows you God's love by teaching, caring, encouraging, or simply by being interested in you?

_____

_____

_____

Have someone read the scripture verse again. This time think about the living saint in your life that you named earlier. Write a letter, card, or e-mail, or make a phone call to those you have named and let them know what they mean to you.

PRAYING TOGETHER

Let two family members read the same prayer you prayed yesterday, either in unison or alternating lines:

Thank you, God, for teachers who are kind to us and wise,
for grandparents who love us well,
for family or friends who mean a lot to us.
Thank you for their examples, their attention to us, their love for us.
Thank you for the ways they show us what you are like.
Thank you, God, for these and all the saints.
Amen.

November 3

READING THE BIBLE TOGETHER

Read Luke 2:41-45.

TELL US MORE

When Jesus was twelve years old, he went with his family from their home in Nazareth to the capital city of Jerusalem for the Passover festival. Passover is a very important holiday when the Jewish people remember how God freed them from being slaves in Egypt. Like most Jewish families, Jesus' family probably went to Jerusalem to celebrate Passover every year. Extended families and friends traveled together, and the children mixed and mingled with aunts, uncles, cousins, and grandparents throughout the trip. Jerusalem was very crowded during the Passover, with people coming and going throughout the Temple and the city.

SHARING TOGETHER

Can you remember a time when you were lost from your family or when one family member became separated from the rest of the family? What feelings do you remember? How do you think Jesus' father and mother felt when they realized that he wasn't with them?

SINGING TOGETHER

If you know the tune, sing together this song, called "His Banner over Me Is Love." Otherwise, you can say the words to each other:

The Lord is mine and I am His, His banner
    over me is love,
The Lord is mine and I am His, His banner
    over me is love,
The Lord is mine and I am His, His banner
    over me is love,
His banner over me is love.

PRAYING TOGETHER

God, even when we are lost, you are still near us. When we are alone, you are still beside us. When we feel empty with fear, you are still inside us. Amen.

OPTIONAL ACTIVITY

See page 267.

November 4

READING THE BIBLE TOGETHER

Read Luke 2:46-49.

TELL US MORE

When Mary and Joseph finally found Jesus after three days of searching, he didn't seem worried at all. In fact, he seemed surprised this his parents were worried. There he was, learning from the teachers and leaders in the temple. "Didn't you know I would be here?" he asked Mary and Joseph.

SHARING TOGETHER

How do you think Jesus felt sitting there with the teachers? What might he have been asking and learning as he sat with them? Who would have taken care of Jesus for three days while he was there without his parents?

Is there someone in your church whom you could ask certain questions about God? What questions would you like to ask that person?

PRAYING TOGETHER

Let two family members read the following prayer, either in unison or alternating lines:

Thank you, God, for teachers who are kind to us and wise,
for grandparents who love us well,
for family or friends who mean a lot to us.
Thank you for their examples, their attention to us, their love for us.
Thank you for the ways they show us what you are like.
Thank you, God, for these and all the saints. Amen.

November 5

READING THE BIBLE TOGETHER

Read 2 Timothy 1:5. It is a short verse; try repeating it together in unison.

TELL US MORE

In this letter, Paul is writing to a young Christian named Timothy. Paul must have known Timothy's grandmother and his mother and known of their strong faith in God. He believes that this same faith lives inside Timothy as well.

A STORY

When Hector was a child, his grandfather always said the same prayer at mealtimes. Perhaps it was a prayer that Hector's grandfather had learned in his childhood. It went this way: *Bless this food to our use, and us to thy service. We ask for Christ's sake. Amen.* Sometimes Hector's mother would also say that prayer at mealtimes when they were at home. Now that Hector is a father himself, he sometimes says that same prayer at his family's mealtimes. Now his children are growing up with the prayer. What began with Hector's grandfather continued with his mother, then with him, and now with his children. Perhaps someday Hector's children will say the prayer with their children.

SHARING TOGETHER

Can you think of a prayer or Bible verse, a song, a wise saying, or a certain activity or practice that one of your parents or grandparents has taught you? Share some of these together. What faith practices does your family have now that the children in the family might pass on when they are adults?

PRAYING TOGETHER

Let each family member offer a prayer of thanksgiving for the gifts that have been handed down from parents or grandparents.

Thank you, God, for (name each gift). Amen.

LOOKING AHEAD

If tomorrow night is a good time to build a fire or have a cookout, start planning now. Be sure to have some extra pieces of wood.

November 6

READING THE BIBLE TOGETHER

Read 2 Timothy 1:6.

CONSIDER THIS

Timothy was a young Christian who had learned about the faith through his mother and grandmother. They both handed down what they believed and practiced, and here Timothy is being encouraged to *rekindle* that gift.

Rekindle is a word we use to describe what we do to a fire that is about to go out. We add more kindling or wood to make it burn bright again. If you have ever been around a campfire or a lighted fireplace, maybe you have seen the fire rekindled in such a way. A fire that is not rekindled will eventually go out.

SHARING TOGETHER

What would it be like to have something inside of us become strong again after it was weak or forgotten? Maybe we have gotten away from a good practice or habit and picked up a bad one. Then something happens, and we return to the good practice again. Maybe we have known God in a special way or spent time praying or reading the Bible or going to worship or Sunday school. Then maybe something changes, and we begin to forget or ignore those practices. Or maybe we have used a gift in God's service in the past but have ignored it lately. Talk about things that you, individually or as a family, would like to rekindle. If you are gathered around a fire, add a piece of kindling to the fire as you share something you would like to have rekindled. Ask God to warm and deepen your faith.

SINGING TOGETHER

If you know the tune, sing this song, called "Give Me Oil in My Lamp." If you don't know the song, let someone read the words aloud, or say the words echo style.

Give me oil in my lamp, keep me burning—
    Give me oil in my lamp, I pray.
Give me oil in my lamp, keep me burning—
    Keep me burning 'til the break of day.
    Sing hosanna, sing hosanna,
        sing hosanna to the King of Kings.
    Sing hosanna, sing hosanna,
        sing hosanna to the King.

PRAYING TOGETHER

Dear God, the way you made us is awesome—with gifts inside us that can be enjoyed and shared. Rekindle these gifts in us, so that our hearts will be like a warm fire. Amen.

November 7

READING THE BIBLE TOGETHER

Read Luke 10:38.

TELL US MORE

Once he began his ministry, Jesus traveled a lot. He moved from place to place, receiving whatever hospitality was offered to him. In today's story, Jesus is headed toward Jerusalem, the place where he will experience trouble with the authorities and finally be killed. Maybe he has these things on his mind; maybe he is weary from traveling long miles on foot; maybe he has gone a long time without a home-cooked meal. Whatever the case, he has been invited into the home of a woman named Martha. Martha and her sister, Mary, and their brother, Lazarus, were friends of Jesus.

SHARING TOGETHER

How do you suppose Jesus felt being welcomed into someone's home? What do you think Martha would have done to welcome him? What would it be like to welcome Jesus into your home? How would you prepare for such a visit? How would you make Jesus feel welcome? Give everyone a chance to share ideas.

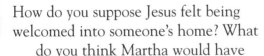

Even when we are not at our house, we can help someone *feel at home*. Think of a time when you have helped someone feel welcome at school or work, in your church or in your neighborhood. Take turns sharing a time when you've felt welcomed by others.

A STORY

Linda had moved to a new neighborhood and a new school. Just before moving, she had cut her hair really short. On the first day at her new school, people teased Linda all morning, calling her a boy and making up new names for her. Linda tried to laugh with her new classmates, but their teasing did not seem funny at all. By lunchtime, she felt a hurt deep inside. She sat alone at the lunch table, trying hard not to cry.

"Hi, my name's Rosa. You're Linda, right?" Linda looked up to see a girl from her class who had sat down next to her! The two girls talked while they ate lunch. Linda's hurt feelings began to go away.

The rest of the day, Rosa showed Linda around, and at the end of the day they traded phone numbers.

"Call me if I can help with anything," Rosa offered. As Linda walked home, she knew that, thanks to Rosa, her new school would be a good place after all.

PRAYING TOGETHER

Thank you, God, for putting people in the world to welcome us. Help us to see when we can welcome someone else. Amen.

LOOKING AHEAD

You will need a candle and matches for tomorrow.

November 8

READING THE BIBLE TOGETHER

Read Luke 10:38-39. Have one person read verse 38, and someone else read verse 39.

TELL US MORE

Jesus had been invited to visit a friend named Martha in her home. Mary, Martha's sister, was there too. While Martha worked hard to prepare things for Jesus' visit (she was probably cooking a meal), Mary was quietly listening to Jesus talk.

SHARING TOGETHER

If Martha was welcoming Jesus by her work, do you suppose being quiet and listening was Mary's way of welcoming him? How do you think Jesus felt being listened to?

Does someone listen to you sometimes the way Mary listened to Jesus? How does this make you feel?

PRAYING TOGETHER

One way we can listen to Jesus today in our lives is to be silent together as a family. Try this: Light a candle, and sing a simple song, such as "Jesus Loves Me," or "Oh, How I Love Jesus." Agree beforehand that after you finish the song, you will all remain silent and pray for one or two minutes until a designated person says, "Amen."

Try leaving the gathering place in silence afterward. Encourage each person to think about Jesus during the silence.

OPTIONAL ACTIVITY

See page 267.

LOOKING AHEAD

You'll need a bowl or basket tomorrow, in addition to paper and pencils or crayons.

November 9

READING THE BIBLE TOGETHER

Read Luke 10:40-42. You may want to read the entire story of Mary and Martha (Luke 10:38-42) from your Bible, or tell the story in your own words.

SHARING TOGETHER

How do you think Martha was feeling toward her sister when she asked Jesus to "tell her to help me"? How do you think Martha felt when Jesus told her that she was worried by many things and that Mary had "chosen the better part"? What do you think Jesus meant by that? How do you think Mary felt when Jesus said that?

When Jesus said to Martha, "There is need of only one thing," he might have been referring to a meal she was preparing—meaning she needed to cook only one thing rather than many dishes. Or he could have meant that the one important thing was to be with Jesus and listen to him, rather than be busy in other ways. What do you think Jesus meant when he said that to Martha?

Share worries or concerns that might distract you or your family from listening to God. Write or draw these on paper, then tear the paper into small pieces and place them in a bowl or basket to be burned or thrown away.

SINGING TOGETHER

Sing "He's Got the Whole World" together:

He's got the whole world in his hands. (Sing 4 times.)
He's got the wind and the rain . . .
He's got you and me, brother . . .
He's got you and me, sister . . .

PRAYING TOGETHER

If you have written down and torn up your worries, place them in the middle of your circle during this time of prayer. Have two readers share this prayer, using alternating lines, and everyone reading the responses.

Reader 1: God, in our lives there are worries and problems.
All: **We surrender them to you.**
Reader 2: God, in our lives there is busyness and hurry.
All: **We want to listen to you.**
Reader 1: God, in our lives there are many paths that can distract us.
All: **We choose to follow you. Amen.**

November 10

READING THE BIBLE TOGETHER

Read Matthew 25:31-40.

CONSIDER THIS

When Jesus told stories, he used examples that were familiar to people in his time. Although we may find a story of sheep and goats strange, many people in Jesus' day knew about taking care of sheep or goats. Jesus told this story as a way of saying that whenever we show kindness to a stranger or someone in trouble, it is like showing kindness to Jesus himself. And whenever we ignore someone who needs our help, it is like ignoring Jesus.

SHARING TOGETHER

Whom do you know who might need kindness shown to them like the people in Jesus' story?

Do you know someone who is hungry or sick or in prison?

In what other ways can people be in trouble and need our help?

What about people who are lonely or who have had something sad happen, like a death in the family?

Use crayons or colored pencils to draw a picture of a person or group in need. Draw them with the face of Jesus as you think he looked.

PRAYING TOGETHER

As a family, pray for those persons or groups you know who are in special need right now, beginning with these words: *Jesus, please help us to care for* (name the person or group) *as we would care for you.*

Repeat the phrase for each person or group you think of.

November 11

READING THE BIBLE TOGETHER

Read Matthew 25:31-40.

A STORY

Today we remember Saint Martin, who lived out the lesson of this Bible story long ago.

It was a November day. Heavy gray clouds covered the sky, and a strong wind was pulling the last leaves off the trees. Martin and a group of other knights were riding along a country road in France. They were under orders from the emperor to go to a new area, and they were

in a hurry to arrive before dark. It started to rain hard. The ground was beginning to freeze. The riders had to slow down so their horses wouldn't slip.

Once darkness had fallen, one of the men called, "I can see the city. We must hurry to arrive before the city's gates close."

"He is right," another answered. "We must ride faster now, and our horses can rest during the night." They began to gallop faster.

But Martin, concerned for the safety of his horse, gradually fell behind the others. The wind picked up, and the rain turned into snow. Martin tucked his chin into his wide, warm cloak.

It was late when Martin reached the city, but the enormous gates were still open. As he began to ride through the gates, he noticed a poor man sitting by the roadside, trying to stay out of the cold wind and snow. The man shivered from the cold.

Martin stopped. He had already given away almost everything he owned; he had nothing except his knight's uniform and his cloak. But without hesitating, he drew his sword and cut his cloak in two, giving half to the poor man.

Late that night, Martin reached his destination, found his bed, and fell asleep. Legend tells us that in the night he was awakened by a great light. Christ appeared before him, wrapped in half a cloak—he looked just like the poor man by the road! He spoke to the angels around him, saying, "Martin has given this cloak to me."

The experience stirred Martin's heart deeply. He decided that from then on he wanted to serve Christ with his whole life. He was baptized and spent the rest of his life working among the poor. Others followed his example as well. Martin died many years later, on November 8, 397.

PRAYING TOGETHER

Dear God, we cannot see you, but we can see people who are in need. We cannot offer you a place to stay or a cup of water or warm clothes, but we can give these things to others who are in trouble. Help us to remember that when we do this, we are really loving you. Amen.

LOOKING AHEAD

You will need colored pencils, crayons, or paint, in addition to paper for tomorrow's devotion.

November 12

READING THE BIBLE TOGETHER

Read Deuteronomy 5:12-14a.
(This is a more difficult passage—you may want an adult to read it.)

TELL US MORE

When God delivered the Hebrew people out of their slavery in Egypt, Moses was called to the top of Mount Sinai to receive instructions from God about how the people were to live together. Among those instructions were ten statements—which we call the Ten Commandments. One of those commandments, the fourth, tells the people how important it is that they take time to rest one day every week. The word *sabbath* comes from a Hebrew word meaning *rest*, and refers to the seventh day of the week.

SHARING TOGETHER

What comes to mind when you hear the word *rest*? How do you feel when you hear the word? What does *rest* look like? Use colored pencils, paints, or crayons to draw a picture of rest. Then share with one another what helps you to rest.

SINGING TOGETHER

Sing or say the words to this song called "I've Got Peace like a River."

I've got peace like a river;
I've got peace like a river,
I've got peace like a river in my soul.
(Repeat)

I've got joy like a fountain . . .

I've got love like an ocean . . .

PRAYING TOGETHER

Pray this prayer quietly and repeat it four or five times. As you repeat the prayer, let it follow the rhythm of your breathing.

We rest in you, (inhale) **O God** (exhale).

November 13

READING THE BIBLE TOGETHER

Read the fourth commandment together as you find it in Deuteronomy 5:12. (A parent can read a phrase at a time while others echo the words.)

TELL US MORE

God gave Moses and the Hebrew people Ten Commandments to help them love God and live well together. The fourth commandment is God's instruction to the Hebrew people to rest every week (Deut. 5:12-15). One of the reasons for that instruction is found as a part of that same commandment: The Hebrew people had been slaves in Egypt, and now they were free. Therefore, they should no longer have to work all the time, as though they were still slaves!

How do you feel when someone is always telling you what to do? That's how it was for the people of Israel when they lived in Egypt as slaves—they were told go here, go there, work harder, work longer. They had no freedom to choose their own way of life. Their lives never became easier, only harder.

Then God said to them, "You are to have a time of rest because now you are free people."

SHARING TOGETHER

When do you have to work hard? When do you rest?
What about the work in your house—is it shared in a fair way or does one person have to do more work than the others?

What about your schoolwork or your job? How can you balance these with other important things in your life?

Is there time both for satisfying work and freedom to rest from that work?

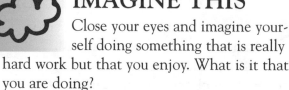

IMAGINE THIS

Close your eyes and imagine yourself doing something that is really hard work but that you enjoy. What is it that you are doing?

Now imagine that you are resting, enjoying yourself, and having free time. Where are you, and how are you resting?

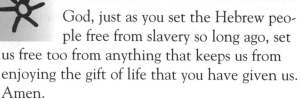

PRAYING TOGETHER

God, just as you set the Hebrew people free from slavery so long ago, set us free too from anything that keeps us from enjoying the gift of life that you have given us. Amen.

November 14

READING THE BIBLE TOGETHER

Read Exodus 20:11.

TELL US MORE

If you read about the fourth commandment yesterday, you know that it talks about the importance of taking a day of rest or sabbath every week. In Deuteronomy, the reason given for this is that God's people, who had once been slaves, were now free. In Exodus, where the Ten Commandments are found, we find another reason for keeping the sabbath. That list explains that when creating the world, God rested on the seventh day. Therefore, since God rested from work, we should rest too and regard the seventh day as special.

A long time ago the church began observing the sabbath on the first day of the week (Sunday) rather than the seventh day (Saturday). This change came about because Jesus was raised from the dead on the first day of the week. Sunday became the church's day of rest and worship.

SHARING TOGETHER

What do you think it is like for God to rest? Does your family take a sabbath day of rest every week? Is Sunday a day of rest and worship for your family, or is it filled with busyness?

Consider planning a rest/sabbath day for this week or the next. Try to consider one another's needs in planning your family's time of rest. One person may find reading restful, another not. One may find simple tasks or physical work at home restful, while another may think these are chores. Four things that allow us to rest are time with God, time with nature, play, and creative endeavors.

- Time with God may include quiet prayerful times, singing hymns or songs, attending worship, and reading the Bible or a favorite Bible storybook.
- Time in nature is restful for many people. This might include taking a walk, watching the stars, or feeding ducks in a park.
- Another good activity is imaginative play (without the help of electronics). Making

up skits, building things, playing games, or doing a puzzle—these can all be restful.

- Finally, using the sabbath to be creative through arts, crafts, baking, handwork, making music, or creating cards and gifts can provide rest for a family.

Rest is as much about leaving certain things out of our sabbath time as it is about including other things. Try to leave out the busyness of everyday schedules—errands, shopping, paperwork, television, telephones, and computers. Remember that rest is about cultivating an awareness of God's presence in our midst.

PRAYING TOGETHER

Be silent together as a family and allow yourselves to rest in that silence for as long as it continues. Or share the prayer from November 12:

We rest in you, (inhale) **O God** (exhale).

LOOKING AHEAD

During November 15–20 we will be talking about bread and harvest themes. Consider making a simple centerpiece of wheat or other grains for the place where you gather for devotions.

November 15

CONSIDER THIS

One day, some of Jesus' friends, called disciples, asked him to teach them how to pray. Jesus taught them a prayer, known to us as the Lord's Prayer. In the very middle of that prayer is a sentence asking God to provide us each day with enough to eat: *Give us each day our daily bread* (Luke 11:3).

Most of us have pantries or refrigerators where we store food. When we shop, we buy groceries that will last for several days, and we don't have to worry about what we will eat tomorrow. Yet in some parts of the world, each day's food is still gathered that day—just as it was by the Hebrews in the wilderness. And in every city and town and in every country some people are so poor that they don't know where their next meal will come from.

The way Jesus taught the Lord's Prayer makes it a prayer for all of us together, not just for one person. It doesn't say, *Give* me *each day* my *daily bread*. It says, *Give* us *each day our daily bread*. Part of what we mean when we pray this prayer is, Let the day come when all people everywhere have enough to eat. And let me do my part to make it so.

SHARING TOGETHER

Discuss ways your family can be involved in feeding the hungry, either directly (such as volunteering in a food pantry or soup kitchen) or indirectly (such as contributing canned goods or collecting money to be donated to a hunger relief ministry).

PRAYING TOGETHER

Close with this version of the Lord's Prayer, including the phrase added below. A leader can read each line, with others repeating it.

> Our Father in heaven,
>   hallowed be your name,
>   your kingdom come, your will

be done,
  on earth as in heaven.
Give us today our daily bread.
Let the day come when all
  people everywhere have enough to eat.
And let me do my part to make it so.
Forgive us our sins
  as we forgive those who sin against us.
Save us from the time of trial
  and deliver us from evil.
For the kingdom, the power, and the
  glory are yours now and forever.
Amen.

⭐ OPTIONAL ACTIVITY

See page 267.

November 16

📖 READING THE BIBLE TOGETHER

Read Luke 13:20-21.

Sometimes Jesus told stories to help people understand the kingdom of God. The kingdom of God is one way we talk about God's ways in the world. This story is simple and short; with just a few words it says a lot, but it raises lots of questions too.

SHARING TOGETHER

Three measures of flour is a lot of flour—enough to feed fifty people! Why do you think the woman was planning to make so much bread? A story in Genesis, chapter 18, tells about Abraham and Sarah being visited by three strangers. The meal they prepared for these three strangers included *three measures of choice flour* — once again, enough to feed fifty people!

Remember a time when bread was baking in your oven or when you walked by a store where bread was baking. How did it smell?

When you saw dough before it went into the oven, what did it look like? As the fresh, hot loaf came out of the oven, how did it look?

What does yeast do to bread? What would the bread be like if the baker left the yeast out? How do you think the kingdom of God is like yeast in dough?

PRAYING TOGETHER

God, you are like someone baking bread with yeast in the flour, dough in the oven, and bread enough for the whole world! Amen.

OPTIONAL ACTIVITY

See page 267.

November 17

READING THE BIBLE TOGETHER

Read Luke 14:15-24.

SHARING TOGETHER

Those invited to the great dinner had lives that were already full and busy. They had no time to attend even a special dinner. How do you think the host felt when no one could come? Have you ever had a special party, gathering, school program, or game, and someone special was unable to come? If so, how did you feel?

Jesus told this story as a way of letting us know about God's ways in the world. The master persisted in finding others to come to the dinner. Do you think God is that persistent in finding people to be a part of this great feast of life?

How do you find ways to include those who are forgotten or have special needs?

SINGING TOGETHER

Sing this "This Little Light of Mine."

This little light of mine,
 I'm gonna let it shine.
This little light of mine,
 I'm gonna let it shine,
This little light of mine,
 I'm gonna let it shine,
let it shine, let it shine, let it shine.

PRAYING TOGETHER

God, you find us wherever we are, young or old, ready or not, and invite us to a great dinner—life lived together in your love. To your invitation, we say *yes*! Amen.

LOOKING AHEAD

You'll need some rocks along with plastic or paper snakes tomorrow.

November 18

When setting the table for the meal just before your family devotions, put rocks and plastic snakes on each plate. Let the Bible reading explain later what you were up to.

READING THE BIBLE TOGETHER

Read Matthew 7:7-11.

SHARING TOGETHER

If you were to ask God for certain things, really important things, what would they be? Start by thinking about what is important for the whole world. Then think about your city or community.

What important requests would you make for your church or for your family?

And finally, what really important things would you ask God to provide you with?

TELL US MORE

Imagine that you are really hungry. You sit down expecting a delicious meal, but instead you're served a rock! Or what if you were hiking and you got really thirsty, but when you asked for a drink, someone handed you a snake?

Sometimes Jesus can be pretty funny, and this story is pretty funny if you think about it. Of course Jesus knows that parents give their children the best things—or at least try to. All the more, Jesus says, our Father in heaven gives good things to us when we ask for them.

CONSIDER THIS

Before praying, try memorizing Matthew 7:7-8. One person in the family can read the verses aloud while the others begin to say them in unison. Then pass the Bible around to the next reader, letting him or her read while everyone else recites along with the reading. Finally, try reciting the verses together without referring to your Bible. Have fun!

PRAYING TOGETHER

The prayer below mentions some of the good things God wants to give us. Choose two readers to read it in alternating lines.

God, you are kind and loving,
  kind and loving let us be.
God, you are wise and knowing,
  wise and knowing let us be.

God, you are strong but gentle,
  strong but gentle let us be.
God, you see all things clearly,
  all things clearly let us see.

God, you are always near us,
   always near you let us be. Amen.

SINGING TOGETHER

If you know the tune, sing this song together, called "God Is So Good." If you don't know the tune, let one person say the words, with everyone else echoing them.

God is so good,
God is so good,
God is so good,
[God's] so good to me.

November 19

READING THE BIBLE TOGETHER

Read Mark 4:2-9.

IMAGINE THIS

One of the most exciting ways to study the Bible is to act out its stories, and the story of the sower and the seed is one of the best. (See Dramatizing a Bible Story on page 12.)

Move to a room where there's plenty of space. Decide on the four different places where the seed will be sown. Someone can be the sower, another the seed, another a bird, and so forth. If necessary, one person can play

more than one part. It may help to have one narrator the first time but feel free to act out the story more than once, changing roles as you go.

Warning: This can really get silly, but that is perfectly okay. After all, isn't it already funny that Jesus told this whole story about soil and roots and earth and grain while he was sitting in a boat on the water?

PRAYING TOGETHER

Let one person pray this prayer phrase by phrase, with others repeating the words and gestures after the leader.

Dear God,
Teach us to listen for your Word in all
   its goodness and wisdom,
(Slowly bring your hands to your heart.)

so that it may be planted in our ears
   and minds and hearts.
(Place your hands on your ear, your
   forehead, your heart.)

Then, may we be like good soil, growing good things inside of us.
(Slowly bring your hands from your
   heart upward and outward like a growing plant.)
Amen.

LOOKING AHEAD

Tomorrow you will need construction paper and crayons or markers.

November 20

READING THE BIBLE TOGETHER

Read again the story Jesus told about a sower and seed in Mark 4:2-9.

SHARING TOGETHER

Several things in the Bible story—birds, rocky ground, scorching sun, and thorns—prevented the seeds from growing and making grain. What things in your family prevent God's goodness from growing in your lives and friendships? Take turns sharing how your family can be good soil, open to God's love and goodness.

A STORY

Rick and Juan were neighbors and friends. They liked to play together at each other's home. When they were together, though, it was easy to sit down at the computer and play video games until it was time to go home, leaving them little time to talk or play other games. When Juan's mom suggested one day that the boys not play computer games, at first they scoffed and complained. But gradu-

ally they began discovering other fun stuff to do, like biking, playing games in the yard, and talking. Soon they were leaving the computer off more and more of the time. For Juan and Rick, the computer had become like shallow soil for their friendship. In time, they had begun to find deeper soil in other activities.

SHARING TOGETHER

Gather construction paper and crayons or markers. Draw pictures of things that are like rocky soil, birds, sun, and thorns in your family, such as shopping, TV, meetings, etc. Cut these out and glue them together in one picture, surrounding them with lots of healthy, growing wheat stalks.

PRAYING TOGETHER

Let one person pray this prayer phrase by phrase, with others repeating words and gestures after the leader.

Dear God,
Teach us to listen for your Word in all
 its goodness and wisdom
(Slowly bring your hands to your heart.)
so that it may be planted in our ears
 and minds and hearts.
(Place your hands on your ear, your
 forehead, your heart.)
Then, may we be like good soil, grow
ing good things inside of us.
(Slowly bring your hands from your
 heart upward and outward as a grow
 ing plant.)
Amen.

OPTIONAL ACTIVITY

See page 268.

November 21

READING THE BIBLE TOGETHER

Read Genesis 1:31a.

TELL US MORE

When God had finished creating the world, the Bible tells us that God had one last look at everything and decided that it was all very good. Actually, the phrase *God saw that it was good* has already appeared five times in the creation story before we come to today's verse. (If you want to read about the creation, and find these words, you can look up Genesis 1:1-31, or read from a storybook version of creation.)

SHARING TOGETHER

Take a walk, go to the park, or simply step outside and notice the creation around you. What in nature might God have seen so long ago and thought was very good? How many colors do you see in God's creation?

Sometimes people say that the world is a mean or dangerous or bad place to live, but the Bible teaches us that God made the world beautiful and that God still loves the world very much. Someone once said that God's signature is on every blade of grass, every tree trunk, every night sky. What do you suppose that means?

SINGING TOGETHER

Read the following words or sing this song called "This Is My Father's World."

This is my Father's world,
    And to my list'ning ears,
All nature sings, and round me rings
    The music of the spheres.
This is my Father's world;
    I rest me in the thought
Of rocks and trees, of skies and seas;
    His hand the wonders wrought.

PRAYING TOGETHER

Thank you, God, for the wonderful world of nature—trees, grass, and sky; stones, plants, and animals; people, places, and things. Give us eyes to see the world as you see it—very good—and hearts to love it as you do. Amen.

LOOKING AHEAD

Tomorrow you may want to meet in a room with space to move around.

November 22

READING THE BIBLE TOGETHER

Read Psalm 145:13c-16.
Stand in a circle and ask one person to read the passage again one phrase at a time. Think of a movement or gesture to describe each

phrase and use this gesture. Then read the verses a third time using all the gestures.

A STORY

One morning Blue Jay woke up hungry. She hadn't eaten for two days, and the baby birds in her nest were also growing hungry. The yards and fields where she normally looked for worms and bugs had been picked over by many birds and other insects.

As she looked out over the rooftop from the tree where she had her nest, she saw a family bringing out shovels, work gloves, and a tall, skinny tree wrapped at the bottom in a ball of burlap. They began to dig a big hole right in the middle of their yard—and to make a big pile of dirt! Then they placed the tree in the hole they had made and began covering it back up with dirt. After watering their newly planted tree, they gathered up their gloves and shovels and went back inside.

Blue Jay flew straight down to the spot where the tree was. She knew that where there is freshly shoveled dirt, there are usually worms! Sure enough, she found plenty of worms to feed her family and herself for days. Blue Jay made many happy trips to the wonderful feeding spot in the dark dirt circle of the newly planted tree.

TELL US MORE

The Bible sometimes speaks about how all creatures and things—nature, people, stars, the heavens—look to God in praise and to find their place in creation. God provides for every living thing.

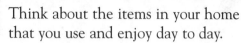

SHARING TOGETHER

Think about the items in your home that you use and enjoy day to day. Choose one item, such as the food you have eaten today, the clothes you wear, the books on your shelf, or the furniture in the room.

See if you can name some of the elements and people who may have been a part of providing those items for you and your home. (For example, the food you have eaten today required soil, water, sun, farmers, harvesters, canners, bakers, truckers, stockers, grocery clerks, those who cooked, served, and so forth.)

PRAYING TOGETHER

Offer a prayer or litany of thanks that includes some of those items, people, and processes you've named. You might begin:

Thank you, God, for . . .

When everyone has had a chance to name something, join together and say:

We thank you, God, for everything. Amen

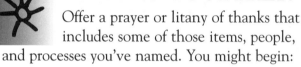

November 23

READING THE BIBLE TOGETHER

Today read chapter 1 in the Book of Ruth. Let all the family members who can read take turns reading verses 1-5, 6-14, 15-18, and 19-22.

CONSIDER THIS

The first chapter of Ruth tells the story of a woman named Naomi and her husband, Elimelech, who left their home in Bethlehem to live in a foreign country named Moab. While they were there, Elimelech died. Their two sons grew up and married Orpah and Ruth, two women from the land known as Moab. But in time, the two sons died also. Naomi decided to return to Bethlehem and encouraged Orpah and Ruth to stay in Moab where they had family to care for them. Ruth refused, insisting on traveling with her mother-in-law back to Bethlehem. They arrived just in time for the yearly barley harvest.

SHARING TOGETHER

How do you think it felt for Naomi to lose first her husband and then both her sons? How did it feel for Orpah and Ruth to lose their husbands? How would Ruth's devotion to Naomi and Naomi's care of Ruth help to heal that sorrow?

Grief is what we feel when a person dies but also when a pet dies or when we move to a new home or when we leave our old school. Remember a time when your family experienced grief or loss. Who helped you through that time?

SINGING TOGETHER

A song that has helped many through sad times is called "Kum Ba Yah." Notice the way it moves from sadness to singing. You can sing it together as a family.

Kum ba yah, my Lord, Kum ba yah.
Kum ba yah, my Lord, Kum ba yah.
Kum ba yah, my Lord, Kum ba yah.
Oh, Lord, Kum ba yah.

Come by here, my Lord, come by here .
(Sing 3 times)
Oh, Lord, come by here.
Add other verses using the following words:
Someone's crying, Lord . . .
Someone's praying, Lord . . .
Someone's singing, Lord . . .

PRAYING TOGETHER

Thank you, God, for Ruth and Naomi whose lives went from hardship to hopefulness because of their love for each other and for you. Thank you for those people in our lives who help to heal our sadness and sorrow. Amen.

November 24

READING THE BIBLE TOGETHER

Read chapter 2 of the Book of Ruth today. (If you haven't done so earlier, be sure to read chapter 1 also today.)

TELL US MORE

In this chapter we hear how hard Ruth worked to glean what was left over from the barley harvest. Gleaning is the practice of going in after the first harvesters have

finished their work and gathering up leftover grain. It is based on a law in the Bible (see Lev. 19:9-10; 23:22) that requires farmers to leave part of their harvest for the poor.

SHARING TOGETHER

Boaz observed the law of his faith by leaving some barley in the field for poor people to glean. But then he went beyond what the law required with his kindness toward Ruth. How did Boaz show kindness toward Ruth?

At different times in our lives, we either receive or give kindness. Besides the customary ways of donating money or food to help the poor, how could we show kindness to such people? Is there a particular person or family with special needs to whom your family could show special care?

PRACTICING WHAT JESUS TAUGHT

Gleaning is still practiced in our country. Groups like The Society of St. Andrew organize volunteers to glean food crops and donate them to food banks for distribution to hungry people and families. Consider being a part of a gleaning project, if such is available where you live. Otherwise, you might want to contribute some food or time to a local food pantry, shelter, or Meals on Wheels. Your church staff can help you with more information.

PRAYING TOGETHER

Is there someone who has shown you kindness beyond what was expected? Offer a prayer thanking God for this person; if more than one name is mentioned, thank God for each person.

READING THE BIBLE TOGETHER

For today, read Ruth 3:1-5, 14-18; and 4:13-17.

If time allows, read all of chapters 3 and 4. (If you haven't done so earlier, begin by reading Ruth, chapters 1 and 2.)

TELL US MORE

In chapters 3 and 4 we read a rather involved story about how Ruth took Boaz as her husband. Though by law Boaz followed certain rules to ask Ruth to be his wife, it was she, with the help of her mother-in-law, Naomi, who decided this was what she wanted. Then, with courage and determination, Ruth and Naomi worked to bring this about. Once Boaz and Ruth were married, they had a child. As an indication that the community members of Bethlehem had accepted Ruth, who was originally an outsider, they helped to name the child.

Though she was born in another country and was a stranger to the people in Bethlehem, Ruth gradually became one of their own. This happened in part because of her determination and in part because the people of Bethlehem willingly accepted her after they saw how Ruth loved and cared for Naomi.

SHARING TOGETHER

Why do you think Naomi and Ruth were so determined for Ruth to marry Boaz? When have you worked hard on something until it was finished? Who offered support for your efforts?

PRAYING TOGETHER

O Lord, you know each one of us as you knew Ruth.

You know our stories of disappointment, frustration, and hurt…and our hopes, dreams, and joy.

You know where we have failed to love you or to love our neighbor or ourselves, and you know when we have been kind and loyal.

We delight in being your children, known so well by you.

How our hearts yearn to know you and to love you too. Amen.

CONSIDER THIS

Set up a scene where the story of Ruth could be played out with dolls, stick figures, or puppets. (See Dramatizing a Bible Story on page 12.)

November 26

READING THE BIBLE TOGETHER

Read Luke 9:16.

TELL US MORE

Offering thanks for food that is about to be shared and eaten is an ancient custom. In the story of Jesus' feeding thousands of hungry people, Jesus said a blessing over the loaves and fish. Jesus was continuing a tradition he learned from his own family and their ancestors. In today's devotion, you can look at some common mealtime prayers or table graces that your family may use at home.

A common mealtime prayer reminds us of the fact that everything we eat involves work on the part of others:

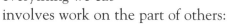

Bless this food and the hands that have prepared it, in Jesus' name. Amen.

Another, from Charles Dickens's novel *A Christmas Carol* is offered by Tiny Tim. It is like a big tent covering everybody:

God bless us every one!

Another prayer reminds us that our food is a gift and that eating it is a way of receiving that gift:

For these gifts we are about to receive, and for all your bounty, we are thankful. Amen.

Some children's graces use rhyming words, such as this simple prayer:

Thank you for the world so sweet,
Thank you for the food we eat,
Thank you for the birds that sing,
Thank you, God, for everything. Amen.

SHARING TOGETHER

Perhaps there are mealtime prayers that your family has prayed together. Share with your family a prayer you may have learned in another place—a mealtime blessing from camp, church gatherings, or other settings. Some of these may be sung rather than spoken. Parents may remember a prayer that they prayed with their families when they were growing up.

CONSIDER THIS

If you would like to keep one or more of these prayers for use at mealtimes in the future, have someone write them down on paper or index cards, and keep them in a handy spot. Soon they may be memorized.

SINGING TOGETHER

If you know the tune, sing together this mealtime prayer song:

For health and strength and daily food,
We praise thy name, O Lord.

PRAYING TOGETHER

Dear God, bless our family. Bless our home. Bless our table spread. And bless the prayers we offer, that they may express our thanks and honor you. Amen.

November 27

READING THE BIBLE TOGETHER

Have one person read Psalm 106:1; then let the entire family say the verse again in unison.

Repeat the verse seven times, emphasizing these different words each time: *praise, thanks, Lord, good, love, endures, forever.* Think about each particular word as you emphasize it.

A STORY

Once, over a period of weeks, a pastor was visiting a woman named Delle who was near death. A brain tumor had left Delle with less and less ability to move and speak. The last few days before she died, Delle was confined to her bed and could say only two words: *Thank you.* When someone entered the room and came to her bedside, she would say, "Thank you." When she was asked any question, she would answer, "Thank you." When someone prayed with her or wiped her forehead with a cool cloth or simply held her hand, she said, "Thank you." Delle left this world speaking over and over what are perhaps the most basic, most important words we can ever learn: *Thank you.*

TELL US MORE

Again and again, the Bible invites us to give thanks to God. Those who wrote the books of the Bible knew that we are made to recognize goodness in our lives and that we need to have somebody to thank.

SINGING TOGETHER

Say the words to or sing together the song called "Praise the Lord Together."

Alleluia, alleluia, alleluia . . .
(Repeat several times.)

90

PRAYING TOGETHER

Yesterday we spoke of graces that were written or sung by others for us to recite in thanksgiving. Today, try praying a prayer of thanks spontaneously, that is, a prayer that comes from your own present thoughts and feelings. Try the litany below with everyone taking a turn to complete the phrase. Then close with amen.

Thank you, God; thank you, God;
thank you, God, for . . . (First person names something.)
Thank you, God; thank you, God;
thank you, God, for . . . (Second person names something.)

OPTIONAL ACTIVITY

See page 268.

November 28

READING THE BIBLE TOGETHER

Read Exodus 35:4-10, 20-21, 29 and 36:2-7.

TELL US MORE

When it was time for the Hebrew people to build a tabernacle, that is, a place to gather for worship, Moses asked the people to bring materials to help build it. They were to bring only what they felt led to bring. The people brought earrings and other jewelry, fine linens, wood, and items from their own personal possessions. The response was so great that Moses had to tell the people to stop bringing their offerings!

A STORY

When Mary Ellen heard about her church's plans to send a team in mission to Central America, she immediately felt a call to join the team. But she knew that she could not afford the trip. Word went out around the church for contributions that would allow Mary Ellen and others to go on the trip. Gifts came from the choir, Mary Ellen's Sunday school class, the women's group, Mary Ellen's own grown children, and other individuals. The church's response was extremely generous. Before she knew it, Mary Ellen had more than enough money to pay for her trip! What was she to do now? During the mission trip, she decided to use the extra money to buy chairs for the kindergarten in the village where the church's mission team was at work. When she returned to her church, she told them how much their gifts had done for the village and for her.

SHARING TOGETHER

Have you ever experienced a time when there was a special need, and in response people gave more than enough?

What is God asking you to give right now, either of your money, your time, or your skills?

What would it mean for you to give generously from your heart to a special need that you know of?

91

PRAYING TOGETHER

Dear God, you have given us so much. Give us one thing more: hearts for sharing from the abundance in our lives in ways that show your love in the world and honor you. Amen.

LOOKING AHEAD

You will need a bowl or basket in addition to your paper and pencils.

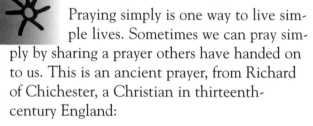

November 29

READING THE BIBLE TOGETHER

Read Mark 12:41-44.

TELL US MORE

Jesus may have highlighted this woman's gesture of giving for many reasons: to point out the unfairness of the system that kept her poor, to speak about generosity to the point of sacrifice, or maybe to observe simplicity enacted in a such beautiful way. Perhaps Jesus was looking at this woman as an example of living simply and giving freely.

SHARING TOGETHER

Discuss the following questions. Give everyone a chance to share their thoughts.

- What does simple living mean?

- What is a simple life like?
- How does being generous lead us there?

Decide as a family one step you can take toward simple living, such as sharing a simple meal one night this week. Your meal might include bread, fruit, and cheese, or beans and rice.

Play charades or pantomime games. Pass out slips of paper, and let each person write or draw an example of living simply and/or giving freely. Fold these up and place them in a basket or bowl. One person draws a slip, chooses a partner, and together they act out the words or picture while others try to guess it.

PRAYING TOGETHER

Praying simply is one way to live simple lives. Sometimes we can pray simply by sharing a prayer others have handed on to us. This is an ancient prayer, from Richard of Chichester, a Christian in thirteenth-century England:

O most merciful Redeemer, friend, and brother,
may we know you more clearly,
love you more dearly,
and follow you more nearly, for your own sake.
Amen.*

*The United Methodist Hymnal , #493.

November 30

READING THE BIBLE TOGETHER

Read Mark 13:37.

⊙ TELL US MORE

These words from Mark are part of a story about someone who has gone on a journey and is expected home any time. Since nobody knows what time it will be, everyone must watch all the time. During Advent, candles can be a symbol of waiting and watching for God. A lighted candle is a way of showing that we are searching and keeping watch, much like a porch light left on for the last person home or a lantern on a walk in the woods at night.

🏠 A STORY

In Maria's attic are boxes with special things for Advent and Christmas. Every year, when Advent draws near, Maria and her dad climb into the attic and find the Advent box. But they would never venture into the attic without one special tool—a good flashlight.

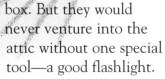

Without the flashlight, Maria and her dad would have no way of seeing their way to the right box. So up they go into the darkness of the attic, and on goes the flashlight, as they search for that one special box they need. The flashlight—and the searching that goes with it—are always a part of Maria's family's getting ready for Christmas.

☀ PRAYING TOGETHER

Light a candle and share this prayer:

Light of the world, come and warm us
  by your light.
Light of the world, come and illumine
  the world's darkness.
Light of the world, come and wake us
  from our sleeping.
Light of the world, come and live
  among us forever. Amen.

DECEMBER

December 1

Attending worship together each Sunday is an important part of Advent activities.

READING THE BIBLE TOGETHER

Read 1 John 4:7-9.

One person can read the following verse one line at a time; the rest of the family will echo each line.

Reader: God sent his only Son
All: **God sent his only Son**
Reader: into the world
All: **into the world**
Reader: so that we might live
All: **so that we might live**
Reader: through him
All: **through him.**

SHARING TOGETHER

Advent is here. It is time to get ready once again for the baby Jesus' birth. Can you remember when a new baby was coming into your family or a friend's or relative's family? We make a place for a new baby. We clear out a room or part of it. We put some different things in that space, things the baby will need and like.

We get ready for the baby Jesus by making a place for him in our hearts. We try to clear out things that keep us from focusing on Jesus or being ready to receive him again. We try to make our hearts a loving place for the baby Jesus. Sometimes we don't do this very well, but God knows we are trying and God always loves us.

Christmas is coming! The baby Jesus will soon be here, God's best gift of all!

IMAGINE THIS

Pretend a baby (biological, adopted, or foster) is coming into your family. Imagine a family meeting to plan for the baby's arrival. What does a family do to get ready for a baby? Which of those activities apply to getting ready for the baby Jesus?

Next, take turns naming everything you think of when you hear the word *Christmas*. Which of those activities have nothing to do with the baby Jesus?

Think about getting your heart ready for the baby Jesus. You may want to share changes you would like to make.

PRAYING TOGETHER

Loving God, thank you for the baby Jesus. Help us to remember during all of December that Christmas is coming because—and only because—of Jesus' birth. Amen.

PRAISING GOD TOGETHER

Together say or sing this praise song to the tune of the chorus of "The First Noel."

Praise God! Praise God!
Praise God! Praise God!
Eternal Holy One, we love.

OPTIONAL ACTIVITY

See page 268 about creating an Advent wreath for the family.

December 2

READING THE BIBLE TOGETHER

Read 1 John 4:7-9.

One person can read the following verse one line at a time; the rest of the family will echo each line. This is the same verse we read for December 1.

Reader: God sent his only Son
All: **God sent his only Son**
Reader: into the world
All: **into the world**
Reader: so that we might live
All: **so that we might live**
Reader: through him
All: **through him.**

TELL US MORE

The church season when we prepare a place for Jesus in our hearts is called Advent. It begins four Sundays before Christmas. Advent is so important that the first day of Advent is the first day of the Christian year.

All during Advent, we are encouraged to prepare our hearts for Jesus' birth. But

December is a very busy month. Calendars become crowded, and to-do lists grow longer. We are busy at work, at school, and at church. We rush to prepare for Christmas. But how much of our busyness actually has anything to do with the baby Jesus?

Let's remember that Jesus was born in a quiet stable and lay on hay in a simple manger. It is not in our rushed busyness but in our quiet moments alone and as a family that we truly prepare for Christmas.

SHARING TOGETHER

What are some of the things that make December so busy? What can your family change to make this season a simpler, quieter, and more holy time together as you prepare for the birth of the baby Jesus?

PRAYING TOGETHER

Loving God, thank you for the baby Jesus. Forgive us when we get trapped in the rush of Christmas. Help us to focus on preparing our hearts for the birth of the baby Jesus. Amen.

PRAISING GOD TOGETHER

Together say or sing this praise song to the tune of the chorus of "The First Noel."

Praise God! Praise God!
Praise God! Praise God!
Eternal Holy One, we love.

LOOKING AHEAD

Tomorrow during this time together, try to repeat 1 John 4:9b from memory so that you can always have it with you.

December 3

READING THE BIBLE TOGETHER

Try to repeat together 1 John 4:9b from memory:
God sent his only Son into the world so that we might live through him.

Look at Matthew 1:20.
- What are the first four words the angel said to Joseph after saying his name?

Look at Luke 1:13.
- What are the first four words the angel said to Zechariah?

Look at Luke 1:30.
- What are the first four words the angel said to Mary?

Look at Luke 2:10.
- What are the first four words the angel said to the shepherds?

TELL US MORE

Advent wreaths are one sign of the Advent season. Angels are another. Angels appeared to Joseph, Zechariah, Mary, and the shepherds. Each time the angel said the same thing: "Do not be afraid."

Often fear is used to get us to do what others want us to do. People who want to sell items use fear to get us to buy them. People on news programs use fear to get us to watch their broadcasts. People running for political office use fear to keep votes from other candidates. Sometimes people at school or work use fear to get us to do what we know we shouldn't do. No wonder we sometimes feel afraid!

Each time we see an angel on a card or in a decoration during Advent, let's remember the Christmas angels' message: "Do not be afraid."

SHARING TOGETHER

Take turns sharing a time when you felt afraid. Have you ever done something you didn't want to do because you were afraid? Has fear ever kept you from doing something you wanted to do? When is fear helpful? When is fear hurtful?

PRAYING TOGETHER

Loving God, thank you for the angels' Christmas message. When we feel afraid, help us to remember that you are with us. Amen.

PRAISING GOD TOGETHER

Together say or sing this praise song to the tune of the chorus of "The First Noel."

Praise God! Praise God!
Praise God! Praise God!
Eternal Holy One, we love.

December 4

READING THE BIBLE TOGETHER

Try again to say 1 John 4:9*b*
from memory so that you can always
have it with you.

You may also want to repeat the verse on fear
Do not be afraid, especially if someone in the
family is struggling with fear. Read Luke 2:8-
12. Repeat the following verse in echo style.

Reader: I am bringing you good news
All: **I am bringing you good news**
Reader: of great joy
All: **of great joy**
Reader: for all the people.
All: **for all the people.**

TELL US MORE

It may surprise us to learn that candy
canes are also a sign of this season. They
symbolize a shepherd's staff. Many years
ago a man in Germany made candy canes by
shaping sticks of sugar in the form of a staff.

Each time you eat a candy cane or see one
on a tree, think of the good news of great joy
which the shepherds heard from the angel–the
joyful news about the birth of Jesus.

SHARING TOGETHER

Name some ways your life would be different without Jesus' birth. Name some
ways our world would be different.

CONSIDER THIS

If you have a Christmas tree, you may
want to hang some candy
canes on it to
remind you of
the shepherds
hurrying to the
manger. Candy
canes may also
remind you to take
time to be with Jesus
in prayer.

Or you may want
to make some sugar
cookies in the shape of
candy canes to give to a
friend or neighbor, explaining that the cookies represent
the shepherds' staffs. You may
also want to tell them that you
will pray for them that night. (If
you say it, don't forget to do it!)

PRAYING TOGETHER

Try this echo prayer with a person
reading one line at a time and the rest
of the family echoing that line together.

Loving God,
thank you for the good news
of your love
that Jesus brought us.
Help us today
to treat people
at school, work, and home
in a way that shows your love.
Amen.

PRAISING GOD TOGETHER

Together say or sing this praise song to the tune of the chorus of "The First Noel."

Praise God! Praise God!
Praise God! Praise God!
Eternal Holy One, we love.

December 5

READING THE BIBLE TOGETHER

Say 1 John 4:9b from memory and repeat the verse about fear. Read Luke 2:13-14.

TELL US MORE

Various versions of the Bible use different words in these verses. For example, some versions use the phrase *praising God and singing*; other versions use the word *saying* instead of *singing*. Today we want to talk about singing.

Caroling is a sign of the season. Saint Francis of Assisi started this tradition when he led his people to outdoor nativity scenes where they sang Christmas hymns.

A STORY

A Russian youth choir was singing hymns in Moscow's Red Square. At the same time a demonstration was going on. Carrying signs of protest, angry adults marched around the square.

As the youth began to sing, the marchers slowed down. Some lowered their signs. Gradually, many drifted nearer to the youth choir to hear better. Soon the demonstration stopped, and the marchers circled round the choir, smiles replacing the anger on their faces. The youth continued to sing their praise to God.

SHARING TOGETHER

One way we praise God is through singing. Plan a caroling party with some other families. Or, if possible, listen to carols when you have dinner together. What other ways can you show your praise for God?

PRAYING TOGETHER

Loving God, thank you for the gift of music and for the special songs of this season. Help us to remember today to make our actions a song of praise to you. Amen.

PRAISING GOD TOGETHER

Together say or sing this praise song to the tune of the chorus of "The First Noel."

Praise God! Praise God!
Praise God! Praise God!
Eternal Holy One, we love.

December 6

READING THE BIBLE TOGETHER

Read Luke 2:13-14. Repeat the following verse in echo style.

**Glory to God
in the highest,
and on earth
peace, good will
toward [all].**
(Luke 2:14, KJV).

A STORY

Peace and goodwill are signs of Advent. As we prepare our hearts for the baby Jesus, we try to have peace and goodwill toward others.

Katie showed goodwill when she played the board game Candyland with her grandmother. Katie's grandmother landed on a square that would keep her there until she drew a yellow card .

Katie looked through the stack until she found a yellow card, handed it to her grandmother, and said, "Here, Grandmom. Now you can move." Later, Katie drew the card that let her cross into the castle and win the game. But first she swooped back with her red gingerbread boy and scooted her grandmother's blue one along with it. "See, Grandmom. We can both win."

In a way, we play Candyland with people everyday. When we look behind us at school or work and see someone stuck along the way, what do we do? Do we brag about being ahead? Do we race on, trying even harder to beat the person? Do we ever try to help someone who is behind? When we are about to win, do we ever scoop up another and share the victory?

In our daily lives at home, school, and work, our words and actions can help bring peace and goodwill. It is a matter of choice.

SHARING TOGETHER

Take turns telling about a time when you brought peace or goodwill to someone. How did that feel? Talk about a time when you could have brought peace or goodwill to someone and did not. How did you feel then?

CONSIDER THIS

As a family or individually, think about Christmas messages you want to send to a grandparent or an older family friend.

PRAYING TOGETHER

Loving God, thank you for family gatherings and the good memories we make. Please forgive us for the times we have hurt someone in order to win. We pray for those who have done that to us. Help us to bring peace and goodwill today. Amen.

PRAISING GOD TOGETHER

Together say or sing this praise song to the tune of the chorus of "The First Noel."

Praise God! Praise God!
Praise God! Praise God!
Eternal Holy One, we love.

LOOKING AHEAD

Tomorrow you will need construction paper, markers and pens to make a Christmas card.

December 7

If you are using an Advent wreath with large candles, you may want to light the appropriate candle(s) for this time together. Family church experiences are also an important Advent activity.

PRAYING TOGETHER

Loving God, thank you for this family time together when we think about you, about the words of the Bible, and about your gift of Jesus. Amen.

READING THE BIBLE TOGETHER

Read Luke 2:14.

SHARING TOGETHER

Christmas cards are a sign of the season because they are a way to share the good news of Christ's coming birth with friends. Peace and goodwill are common themes of Christmas cards.

Take turns telling about a time when someone at home, school, or work showed goodwill toward you or helped bring you peace.

Think of something that reminds you of Advent. Take turns sharing your thoughts. Take a few minutes to create a Christmas card

that shows what Advent means to you. It could be about peace and goodwill, waiting for Jesus' birthday, or about hope. It may contain a prayer for you and your family for this Advent season.

Let each person's Christmas card be a gift for the baby Jesus. If you are using an Advent wreath or a nativity scene or some other special worship center, put your cards there. If not, a Bible can be placed on a table or a shelf, and these cards placed around it.

PRAISING GOD TOGETHER

Together say or sing the closing praise to the tune of the chorus of "The First Noel."

> Praise God! Praise God!
> Praise God! Praise God!
> Eternal Holy One, we love.

December 8

READING THE BIBLE TOGETHER

Read Luke 2:15-16.

CONSIDER THIS

Shepherds are another sign of the season. Luke tells us that as soon as the shepherds received the good news, they hurried to see the baby Jesus.

They didn't pick up a pencil and write *go to the manger* on a to-do list. They didn't say, "I'll go as soon as I finish…(playing or working or shopping or cleaning the house or washing the car or making some phone calls)." No, they ran with their shepherd staffs in hand and their robes flying.

We can be so busy getting ready for Christmas that we don't ever make it to the manger to see the baby Jesus. The shepherds help us to remember to focus on the Christ child in all that we do during this busy season.

IMAGINE THIS

Pretend that you are the shepherds. What do you see when you get to the stable? What do you hear? What do you smell? How do you feel when you see the baby Jesus?

SHARING TOGETHER

If you ran to the manger today to see the baby Jesus, think about what would not get done.

- How much of what would not get done is really important?
- What could you stop doing to give you more time to center on the Christ child?
- What could you start doing that would help you to focus on Jesus?

PRAYING TOGETHER

Loving God, thank you for the shepherds who taught us to put the manger first. Help us to remember the Christ child in all we do today. Amen.

PRAISING GOD TOGETHER

Say or sing this praise song to the tune of "Joy to the World."

Glory to God, the Holy One!
We praise your name, O God!
O how we adore you!
O how we adore you!
We sing our praise to you;
we sing our praise to you;
we sing,
we sing our praise to you.

December 9

If you have been using an Advent wreath for your devotions, please continue to do so until Epiphany, January 6.

READING THE BIBLE TOGETHER

Read Luke 2:15-20.

SHARING TOGETHER

Christmas stories are a sign of Advent. Of course, the most important Christmas story is about the birth of Christ and is found in the Bible. Many people have created other stories, poems, songs, movies, and TV programs for this season. Can you think of some of them? What are some of your family's favorites?

A STORY

Your family can create a Christmas story also. Let a grown-up read the following paragraph that begins the story. Someone else takes it up and then stops, giving the next person a turn, and so on. The parent who reads the beginning of the story finishes it after everyone in the family has had a chance to add to it.

Our family was in a spaceship for a Christmas trip. We accidentally went through a time warp. And suddenly there we were looking up at the head angel and a great throng of the heavenly host. They were all praising God and singing. Off to the side were the shepherds running as fast as they could to see the baby Jesus. Then...

You may want to write this story down after it is finished. Someone else may want to draw pictures to go with the story. If you decide to do this, put the story and pictures in the special place with other Advent items.

PRAYING TOGETHER

Loving God, thank you for Christmas stories. Thank you for giving us imaginations so that we can create our own Christmas story. Help us to think about the real Christmas story as we go about our daily activities. Amen.

PRAISING GOD TOGETHER

Say or sing this praise song to the tune of "Joy to the World."

Glory to God, the Holy One!
We praise your name, O God!
O how we adore you!
O how we adore you!

We sing our praise to you;
we sing our praise to you;
we sing,
we sing our praise to you.

READING THE BIBLE TOGETHER

Read Luke 2:1-7.

TELL US MORE

Nativity scenes are another sign of Advent. Perhaps your church or your family has one. They usually include the baby Jesus, Mary and Joseph, the shepherds and some animals, and the wise men with their gifts.

Nativity scenes remind us that everyone has a place and a part in the Christmas story. The Christmas story calls all people together. Jesus is not alone but with his family. The angel did not speak to one shepherd but to all the shepherds. Even the angel who appeared to them was not alone but with *a multitude of the heavenly host.* It was not a wise *man* but the wise *men* who came from the East. God gives each one of us a place and part in living out the Christmas story, which is the beginning of the Christian story.

Usually a nativity scene includes a stable. It is likely, however, that Mary and Joseph were in a cave; caves were commonly used to shelter animals. Jesus' bed, the manger, was probably a trough carved of stone where the animals were fed. Mary and Joseph probably put hay in the trough to make a soft bed for the baby Jesus.

IMAGINE THIS

Pretend that you are one of the wise men who went to see the baby Jesus. Imagine that you are kneeling before him as he lies in the manger. What do you see? What do you hear? What do you smell? What do you feel with your hands and with your knees as you kneel? Take turns sharing together what each of you imagined.

PRAYING TOGETHER

Pray as an echo prayer:

Loving God,
thank you for the baby Jesus.
Thank you for what he taught us.
Help us to do the things
we know you want us to do. Amen.

PRAISING GOD TOGETHER

Say or sing the closing praise to the tune of "Joy to the World."

Glory to God, the Holy One!
We praise your name, O God!
O how we adore you!
O how we adore you!

We sing our praise to you;
we sing our praise to you;
we sing,
we sing our praise to you.

December 11

READING THE BIBLE TOGETHER

Read 2 Corinthians 8:13-15. Let someone read this scripture line by line, and have everyone echo each line.

A STORY

Magdelena lives in Prague in the Czech Republic. One afternoon when her friend Pat from the U.S. was visiting, Pat noticed that Magdelena played happily with her doll the whole afternoon. Magdelena loves her doll. It is the only one she has and the only one she needs.

Pat, on the other hand, has so many toys that none is special. Toys fill the closet, shelves, and three bins—piled high and spilling over. Pat cannot remember which ones were gifts or who gave them. She enjoys a new toy briefly, then replaces it with a newer toy. The old toy is soon forgotten.

All of Pat's toys put together do not bring as much joy as Magdelena's one special doll.

SHARING TOGETHER

Unfortunately, Christmas has become a time when buying things seems too important. Many TV commercials try to get us to buy something new rather than take care of something we already have. Advertisers try to persuade us that buying new items will make us happy. They encourage us to be greedy.

But it is hard for greedy people to be happy because no matter how much they have, it will never be enough. Also, they do not share what they have with people in need.

Buying something can make us happy in the moment, but does having a lot of things make us a happy person? Think about times when you feel very happy. Take turns sharing what you think brings that happiness.

CONSIDER THIS

In some families, each person receives three gifts in remembrance of the wise men who brought three gifts for the baby Jesus. You may also want to buy three gifts to donate to people who are in need. Discuss the possibility of adopting one of these practices in your family.

PRAYING TOGETHER

Loving God, we are thankful that Jesus taught us about true happiness. Forgive us when we buy too much and share too little. Help us today not to confuse what we want with what we need. Amen.

PRAISING GOD TOGETHER

Say or sing the closing praise to the tune of "Joy to the World."

Glory to God, the Holy One!
We praise your name, O God!
O how we adore you!
O how we adore you!

We sing our praise to you;
we sing our praise to you;
we sing,
we sing our praise to you.

December 12

READING THE BIBLE TOGETHER

Read 2 Corinthians 8:15.

TELL US MORE

Christmas stockings are another sign of Advent. They remind us of the spirit of Advent. For the spirit of Advent is not about getting, not about making our wish list or expecting more gifts. The spirit of Advent is kept by giving and sharing with others, as Jesus shared with others.

SHARING TOGETHER

A common question heard during the season is this: "What do you want to get for Christmas?" Suppose the common question, instead, was "What do you want to give for Christmas?" If that were the question in your family, what would change?

Make a simple Christmas stocking out of felt and glue the edges. Put some wrapped candy canes, nuts, or raisins in it. Leave it as a secret gift on a neighbor's door—and don't tell!

CONSIDER THIS

Think back to last Christmas. Do you remember what gifts you received or who gave them to you? Try to remember a special gift you gave to someone last year. How do you feel when you give someone a gift?

One child had five dolls (or trucks) and gave one away. Another child had two dolls (or trucks) and gave one away. Which child gave the most? How do we measure our giving?

PRAYING TOGETHER

Loving God, thank you for Jesus, the best gift of all. Please forgive us when we hoard things. Help us to be generous today and each day during this Advent season. Amen.

PRAISING GOD TOGETHER

Say or sing this praise song to the tune of "Joy to the World."

Glory to God, the Holy One!
We praise your name, O God!
O how we adore you!
O how we adore you!
We sing our praise to you;
we sing our praise to you;
we sing,
we sing our praise to you.

December 13

READING THE BIBLE TOGETHER

Read 2 Corinthians 8:13-15.

Read the following shortened version and then repeat it:
In order that there may be a fair balance. . . .
"The one who had much did not
have too much,
and the one who had little did
not have too little."
(2 Cor. 8:13*b*, 15).

A STORY

Once there were two children. They were the same age and went to the same school. Both made good grades. Both had loving parents. Both were equally loved by God.

But on Christmas morning, one received many new toys while the other did not receive any toys. The difference on Christmas morning was because one child's parents had plenty of money while the other child's parents had very little. It is easy to see that we do not have a fair balance, as described in the Bible reading, in our world, our country, our community, or even our church family. Some people have more than they need; others need more than they have.

SOMETHING TO CONSIDER

Perhaps during this Advent season we could practice a new pattern: To get something is to give something. Each time we start to buy anything new, we can also decide what we are going to give away. For example, if we buy a new toy, we would give a toy away; if we buy new shoes, we would give a pair away.

We still end up with the same amount of stuff, but it keeps the balance from tipping too far one way. The one who has too much does not continue to add more but instead makes things available for the one who has too little.

SHARING TOGETHER

Take turns sharing what it would mean to adopt this practice: When I get something, I give something. Do you want to commit to trying this during Advent? Talk about ways you can lovingly help one another keep this commitment.

PRAYING TOGETHER

Thank you, God, for what we have. We pray that people who have more than enough will give more away, so that people who have less than enough can receive more. Today help us to do a better job of sharing what we have. Amen.

PRAISING GOD TOGETHER

Say or sing this praise song to the tune of "Joy to the World."

Glory to God, the Holy One!
We praise your name, O God!
O how we adore you!
O how we adore you!
We sing our praise to you;
We sing our praise to you;
We sing,
We sing our praise to you.

December 14

PRAYING TOGETHER

Loving God, we are thankful for this time together when we read from the Bible and think about what it means to follow Jesus' teachings. Because of the love in our family, we can better see what your love for us means. Help us as we continue to prepare our hearts for the coming of the baby Jesus. Amen.

READING THE BIBLE TOGETHER

Read 1 Corinthians 13:8-13.

A STORY

Once upon a time a boy received a gift from his grandfather. The present was wrapped in shiny green paper, and the boy couldn't wait to open it. Hoping it was the soccer ball he had asked for, he yanked off the red bow and tore open the box. But when he looked inside, he saw nothing. He looked at his grandfather questioningly. Was this a bad joke?

"You think that box is empty," the grandfather said. "But the best gifts are things we cannot see."

"I don't understand," the boy said. "How can getting nothing be better than getting something?"

"A soccer ball would last until it wore out or you lost it. Invisible gifts are with you forever—gifts like faith, hope, and love. You can't see faith. You can't touch hope. You can't hold love in your hands. But you know what these things are and how sad you feel when

one is missing," his grandfather said.

That was true. The boy could remember sad times when he wondered if he was loved.

"God gives us many wonderful, invisible gifts. We feel them the strongest when we share them with others," the grandfather said. "Now do you understand?"

"I think so," the boy said.

"Invisible gifts are about life together—giving love, offering hope, sharing faith. Invisible gifts become visible when we live them out," the grandfather said.

Suddenly the boy smiled. "I get it. The box really isn't empty. It's filled with invisible gifts."

"Right," the grandfather said with a twinkle in his eye. "And since you have the gift of hope, you can still hope to find that soccer ball under the tree Christmas morning!"

SHARING TOGETHER

Love cannot be put in a box, wrapped up, and opened. But what are some of the ways we give the gift of love to someone? Hope cannot be put in a box, wrapped up, and opened. How can we give the gift of hope and encouragement? What invisible gift would you like to give a friend or family member?

PRAYING TOGETHER

Thank you, God, for gifts we cannot see. Help us to share these gifts with others today. Amen.

PRAISING GOD TOGETHER

Say or sing this praise song to the tune of "Joy to the World."

Glory to God, the Holy One!
We praise your name, O God!
O how we adore you!
O how we adore you!
We sing our praise to you;
We sing our praise to you;
We sing,
We sing our praise to you.

OPTIONAL ACTIVITY

See page 268.

December 15

Attending worship together with your family each Sunday is an important part of Advent activities.

READING THE BIBLE TOGETHER

Read Luke 1:46-49.

TELL US MORE

Joy is a sign of Advent. During this season, we often hear the Song of Mary read from the Bible and sung by choirs. Another name for the Song of Mary is the Magnificat. Mary's Song begins with her rejoicing and declaring the Lord's greatness.

A FAMILY LITANY

During today's time together, create a spontaneous family litany, your own Magnificat. Take a moment for the family to think about some things that bring joy: (1) something in the universe, (2) a plant, (3) an animal, (4) a person. Also, practice the family's line: *We rejoice in you, O God.*

Parent: We declare your greatness, O Lord, for you have created the whole universe. (Each person names something in the universe that brings joy.)
All: **We rejoice in you, O God.**
Parent: We declare your greatness, O Lord, for you have created all the earth and all the plants. (Each person names a special plant—for example, a kind of flower, tree, fruit.)
All: **We rejoice in you, O God.**
Parent: We declare your greatness, O Lord, for you have created all the animals. (Each person names a special animal.)
All: **We rejoice in you, O God.**
Parent: We declare your greatness, O Lord, for you have created the people we love. (Each person names someone loved.)
All: **We rejoice in you, O God.**
Parent: We declare your greatness, O Lord, for your many gifts this season. (Each person names something in Advent that brings joy.)
All: **We rejoice in you, O God.**

PRAYING TOGETHER

Loving God, thank you for the Song of Mary. Help us today to be mindful of your greatness and to rejoice in your many gifts. Amen.

PRAISING GOD TOGETHER

Say or sing this praise song to the tune of "Silent Night."

Holy God, Loving God,
Praise to you,
Praise to you.
Holy God, Loving God,
Holy God, Loving God,
How we praise your name,
How we praise your name.

December 16

READING THE BIBLE TOGETHER

Read Luke 1:50.

TELL US MORE

Mary's Song is not talking about being scared of God. Some versions of the Bible use the words *worship* or *reverence* instead of fear. Mary is talking about showing God reverence, worshiping God, being in awe of God, and honoring God.

CONSIDER THIS

Evergreen branches and trees are signs of Advent. Perhaps you have an Advent wreath or door wreath made of evergreen, or an evergreen garland or Christmas tree. Because evergreens do not turn brown and lose their foliage in the fall, they are a symbol of eternal life.

Sometime during this season, many of us gather with extended family (like grand-parents, aunts, uncles, and cousins). Often, we share Christmas memories that seem important to us, and we talk about special people who no longer sit around the table with us.

Some of the family stories make us laugh; some make us sad. Some of them point to courage, and others show a lack of it. Some give us a sense of pride; others do not. Just as we learn our family stories by sharing them from generation to generation, we learn about God's mercy and love through the stories from generation to generation in the Bible.

SHARING TOGETHER

Let each family member share a story about someone he or she loved who has died. Then talk about why the stories are important to you.

IMAGINE THIS

Pretend that someday in the future family members are telling stories about you. What would you want them to say? Take turns sharing that. Think quietly for a few minutes about whether you are living your life in a way that tells the story you want it to tell.

PRAYING TOGETHER

Dear God, thank you for loving us from generation to generation. Help each of us to make today's page in our life story one that is pleasing to you. Amen.

PRAISING GOD TOGETHER

Say or sing this praise song to the tune of "Silent Night."

Holy God, Loving God,
Praise to you,
Praise to you.
Holy God, Loving God,
Holy God, Loving God,
How we praise your name,
How we praise your name.

LOOKING AHEAD

If you have any kind of bell, bring it to tomorrow's devotion time.

December 17

READING THE BIBLE TOGETHER

Read Luke 1:51 from the Song of Mary. Some versions of this Bible passage use *arrogant of heart and mind* or *high and mighty* instead of the word *proud*.

CONSIDER THIS

Bells are a sign of the season. We hear bell choirs at church. Some carolers use jingling bells while singing. Long ago, towns had a big bell to call people together. It clanged when leaders were proud of something, and it also rang to warn of a fire or attack. Just as those bells could bring good news or bad, our pride can be good or bad. We

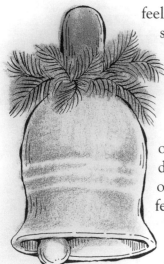

feel proud when we do something well. A sense of pride brings us joy, and we ring our pride bell.

But pride can grow too big and begin to rule our hearts. We may decide not to help someone at school or work, fearing the person may become as good at something as we are—or maybe even better.

Pride can also cause us to see ourselves as better than some people and to judge them. At those times, the pride bell needs to clang a warning. Mary's song reminds us to praise God for favors we receive and for things we do well.

SHARING TOGETHER

Name something you feel good about that brings you pride. Begin with "I thank God for...." If you can, share a time when you acted in a way you shouldn't have because of too much pride.

Now divide into pairs. One acts out being a person who is too prideful. The other rings the pride bell when he or she thinks the actor has crossed the line.

You may want to keep the pride bell handy. If a family member acts too proud, arrogant, or high and mighty, someone may ring it as a reminder to praise God—not ourselves. (Remember to ring unto others only as you would have them ring unto you!)

PRAYING TOGETHER

Loving God, thank you for your gifts that bring us pride. Forgive us when we let pride get out of hand. Help us today to remember to give thanks and praise to you when we feel proud. Amen.

PRAISING GOD TOGETHER

Say or sing the closing praise song to the tune of "Silent Night."

Holy God, Loving God,
Praise to you,
Praise to you.
Holy God, Loving God,
Holy God, Loving God,
How we praise your name,
How we praise your name.

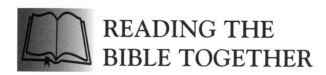

December 18

READING THE BIBLE TOGETHER

Read Luke 1:52a from the Song of Mary.

TELL US MORE

Purple is a sign of Advent.

Considered a sign of royalty, purple symbolizes Jesus because Jesus was descended from King David's line. During Advent, we see purple candles in Advent wreaths, purple stoles on pastors, and purple vestments on altars and pulpits. As a symbol of royalty, purple reminds us of power.

CONSIDER THIS

Each of us has at least some power.

Even a baby has the power to cry—power that brings grownups or a big sister or brother running to help.

One kind of power comes through our possessions. Our toys, clothes, and food are examples. Jesus taught us to use our possessions to help others by sharing with them. He said that if we have two coats, we should share with anyone who has none (Luke 3:11).

Another kind of power may come through our work at home, school, or job. Jesus told tax collectors and soldiers not to use their power in a way that harms people (Luke 3:12-14). We could sum up his word as "Don't cheat people, threaten them, lie to them, or be greedy." If we follow Jesus' teachings, we will use our personal power in a way that helps others.

SHARING TOGETHER

What do you have the power to do? How can you use your power to help another person?

Take some time to find words using the letters in the word *power*. Then look at three of the words that can be found in power.

Pow—Someone can use power to hurt others.
Owe—Someone can use power to help others, but then feel that the person helped owes a debt that he or she should repay.
Rope—Someone can use power like a rope to bind another or use the rope to save another, as when rock climbing.

PRACTICING WHAT JESUS TAUGHT US

Sometime today, use your power in a way that helps someone else. Be ready to tell about it tomorrow.

PRAISING GOD TOGETHER

Say or sing this praise song to the tune of "Silent Night."

Holy God, Loving God,
Praise to you,
Praise to you.
Holy God, Loving God,
Holy God, Loving God,
How we praise your name,
How we praise your name.

PRAYING TOGETHER

Pray this prayer echo style:

Loving God,
thank you for your many gifts.
Forgive us when we have cheated,
lied, threatened someone,
or been greedy.
Help me today to use my power
as Jesus taught me.
Amen.

December 19

SHARING TOGETHER

If family members used their power to help someone else yesterday, begin by letting each person share what happened.

READING THE BIBLE TOGETHER

Read Luke 1:52 from the Song of Mary. Some versions of the Bible use the word *humble* instead of *lowly*.

111

TELL US MORE

Sheep are a sign of Advent. Sheep were around the stable where Jesus was born and in the fields when the angel appeared to the shepherds, who were seen as lowly because they didn't have money or power. Often, like young David, the shepherds were children. Shepherds took care of sheep, and sheep learned to follow the shepherd—as we learn to follow Jesus, the "Good Shepherd."

But anyone, no matter what age, can be a shepherd.

A STORY

During worship one Sunday, a pastor named Dennis baptized a baby. While he was still holding the baby, he invited the children of the church to come forward to see their new baby brother in the church. They made a circle around the baby and prayed for him, repeating Pastor Dennis's words.

Another pastor was also there to preach that Sunday. While the children were still gathered, Pastor Dennis invited the visiting pastor to sit in their midst. This time the children made a circle around the pastor, touching him, and praying for him as they had for the newly baptized baby.

Pastor Dennis reminded the children that they too are ministers. We are all ministers. We can all pray for others. We can all bless others. We can all touch others' lives and have the joy of lifting up other persons.

IMAGINE THIS

Pretend you are a shepherd and the people in your class or workplace are sheep. Isn't that a funny thought? But if you were their shepherd, you would want to take good care of them. Imagine what you could do to make things better for some of them. You may want to tell what you imagined.

PRAYING TOGETHER

Loving God, thank you for opportunities to lift up other persons, to pray for and bless them with our actions. Help us today to see others through your eyes and to hear them through your ears. Amen.

PRAISING GOD TOGETHER

Say or sing this praise song to the tune of "Silent Night."

Holy God, Loving God,
Praise to you,
Praise to you.
Holy God, Loving God,
Holy God, Loving God,
How we praise your name,
How we praise your name.

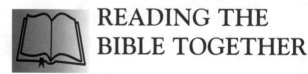

December 20

READING THE BIBLE TOGETHER

Read Luke 1:53-55 from the Song of Mary.

CONSIDER THIS

Good smells are a sign of the season— cookies and candy, cinnamon and cider. *Wassail* (an old word which means *to bless with good health*) is the name of an apple drink that smells good. Long ago people served wassail after caroling.

Sometimes when we smell good smells, we feel hungry. Maybe our stomachs even growl. Hunger is not a worry when we have food in the house or money to buy it. But hunger is a worry for many families. Many people do not have enough food available to fill their stomachs and keep them healthy. If we have extra food, we can share it with those who don't have enough. If all the people in the world who have money and food would share with those who don't, no one would have to worry about food.

SHARING TOGETHER

What good things do we hunger for besides food? How can we fill these kinds of hunger? How can we help others fill these kinds of hunger?

PRAYING TOGETHER

Dear God, one of the good things we hunger for is love. Help us today to show your love to others by loving them. Amen.

PRAISING GOD TOGETHER

Say or sing this praise song to the tune of "Silent Night."

> Holy God, Loving God,
> Praise to you,
> Praise to you.

Holy God, Loving God,
Holy God, Loving God,
How we praise your name,
How we praise your name.

December 21

READING THE BIBLE TOGETHER

Read Isaiah 9:2 and John 1:1-5

Repeat the following verses from these two readings echo style:

> The people who walked in darkness
> have seen a great light.
> The light shines in the darkness,
> and the darkness
> did not overcome it.

CONSIDER THIS

Christmas lights are a sign of the season. Bright lights decorate trees, houses, and shop windows. They remind us that the light of Christ shines even in the darkness.

Children and sometimes even adults feel afraid of the dark. The words of Isaiah and John comfort us when we are afraid of the dark, for no darkness can overcome the light of Christ.

So far during this season of Advent, the sun has risen later and set earlier each day. We have lived with longer and longer nights and shorter and shorter times of daylight. Now, the winter solstice has come, the shortest day of the year. It tells us that the birth of the baby Jesus is near. Christmas is almost here. The light of Christ's love is with us, offering to help heal us from whatever we fear.

 ## SHARING TOGETHER

Eat tonight's dinner by candlelight, with the candles representing the light of Christ that shines in the darkness. Or go outside and look up at the stars. Every time we see the stars, we can remember that they twinkle with God's love for us.

 ## PRAYING TOGETHER

Hold hands as a one person prays.

Dear God, thank you for the light of love that shines even in the darkness. Help us to remember that you know when we are afraid and that, especially in those times, you hold us in your loving arms. Amen.

PRAISING GOD TOGETHER

Say or sing the closing praise to the tune of "Joy to the World."

Glory to God, the Holy One!
We praise your name, O God!
O how we adore you!
O how we adore you!
We sing our praise to you;
We sing our praise to you;
We sing, we sing our praise to you.

 ## READING THE BIBLE TOGETHER

Read Luke 2:1-5.

TELL US MORE

Bethlehem is a sign of Advent. We sing about it in carols and read about it in the Christmas stories in the Bible. Bethlehem means *house of bread* because the town was surrounded by grainfields. The Christ Child, born in the house of bread, became the Bread of Life.

A STORY

Mary and Joseph had to go to Bethlehem to be registered. (It was like taking the census.) The trip was nearly 100 miles. That doesn't sound very far today. But without a car, bus, plane, or train, it was a long journey. Mary and Joseph left their home in Nazareth, which was in the country of Galilee, and traveled through the country of Samaria, and on into Judea.

We can imagine that sometimes the wind blew sand in their faces. Sometimes rain poured down and soaked their clothes. Sometimes they worried about their safety. They were probably afraid in Samaria because Jews and Samaritans did not get along. They may also have been afraid of bandits that hid in the hills. Yet they trusted God.

When they finally arrived in Bethlehem, they were very tired and eager to rest, especially Mary who was expecting a baby.

SHARING TOGETHER

When you take a trip, do you ever get tired? Do you ever ask, "How much farther?" Have you ever felt uneasy on a trip because you didn't know anyone? Have you ever had trouble finding a place to stay?

PRAYING TOGETHER

Loving God, thank you for being with us, especially during hard times. Help us to remember that you are with us when we are uneasy, especially when we are in a strange place. Amen.

PRAISING GOD TOGETHER

Say or sing the closing praise to the tune of "Silent Night."

Holy God, Loving God,
Praise to you,
Praise to you.
Holy God, Loving God,
Holy God, Loving God,
How we praise your name,
How we praise your name.

READING THE BIBLE TOGETHER

Read Luke 2:6-7.

TELL US MORE

Door wreaths are signs of the season. They are formed in a circle. A circle symbolizes the eternal because a circle has no ending and no beginning. A wreath on the door is a way of saying welcome to our guests.

A STORY

Let's go back in time and be guests at the inn when Mary and Joseph arrive.

Mary and Joseph see no wreath on the innkeeper's door. Instead of welcoming them, he turns them away. Some of the guests in the crowded inn see Mary and Joseph standing there. Even though Mary is expecting a baby and needs to rest after the long journey, no one offers to give up space for her.

We see Mary and Joseph too. Because we know they are the Holy Family, we would gladly give up our room for them. But on that day, no one in the inn knew they were the Holy Family. And we would not have known it either.

PRACTICING WHAT THE BIBLE TAUGHT

Let three family members act out being the innkeeper and Mary and Joseph. If there are more family members, they can be the guests who have space in the inn.

SHARING TOGETHER

Do you make room for someone outside your circle of friends? for someone who is from another place? for someone whose beliefs are not like yours? Is it easier to make room for some people than others? Take turns sharing your answers.

CONSIDER THIS

Everyone we know is a child of God and, therefore, could be considered part of the Holy Family. Each of us has opportunities to welcome another or turn the person away. Our actions today show whether we would have shared our space with Mary and Joseph—or turned them away.

(Parents should be sure that children understand that kindness to strangers in a safe place is different from the reasonable and necessary teaching of stranger danger.)

PRAISING GOD TOGETHER

Say or sing the closing praise to the tune of "Silent Night."

> Holy God, Loving God,
> Praise to you,
> Praise to you.
> Holy God, Loving God,
> Holy God, Loving God,
> How we praise your name,
> How we praise your name.

OPTIONAL ACTIVITY

December 24

READING THE BIBLE TOGETHER

Read Luke 2:1-20.
Ask the family to listen carefully, and try to see in their minds all the people and the places, to hear the sounds, to smell the scents, and to feel the textures, air, and excitement.

Read Luke 2:1-7.
Wait patiently for answers to give everyone time to imagine the scene.
What could you see? What could you hear? What could you smell? Could you touch or taste anything?

Read Luke 2:8-14.
What could you see? What could you hear? What could you smell? Could you touch or taste anything?

Read Luke 2:15-20.
What could you see this time? What could you hear? What could you smell? Could you touch anything? Taste anything?
This would be a good time to share the things you have put on the special table during Advent. Share with one another the happy memories of this Advent season.

PRAYING TOGETHER

Hold hands and let each person who wants to take a turn praying.

If you have an Advent wreath, light all the candles for this time together, including the Christ candle.

See page 269.

116

December 25

A FAMILY LITANY

Before you begin, take a moment to practice the family's line: The Lord is present!

All: **The Lord is present!**
Parent: Let hope flood over us! (With palms up, raise your arms like water splashing over you.)
All: **The Lord is present!**
Parent: Let faith strengthen us! (Use praying hands gesture.)
All: **The Lord is present!**
Parent: Let love renew us! (Do a family group hug.)
All: **The Lord is present!**

READING THE BIBLE TOGETHER

Read Psalm 98:1*a*.
O sing to the LORD a new song,
for he has done marvelous things.

Take turns naming a marvelous thing God has done.

Read Psalm 98:4.
Make a joyful noise to the LORD, all the earth;
break forth into joyous song and sing praises.

A parent may lead the family in familiar words or song to praise God.

Read Psalm 98:5-6.
Sing praises to the LORD with the lyre,
with the lyre and the sound of melody.
With trumpets and the sound of the horn
make a joyful noise before the King, the LORD.

If possible, a family member can play a Christmas carol on a musical instrument, or you may want to sing a carol together.

Read Psalm 98:8-9*a*.
Let the floods clap their hands;
let the hills sing together for joy
at the presence of the LORD.

Take turns sharing times during Advent when you felt the presence of God.

PRAYING TOGETHER

Take turns saying a short prayer on this holy day when we celebrate the birth of Jesus. Wish one another a merry Christmas, offering a hug and words of love for each person.

December 26

PRAISING GOD TOGETHER

Say or sing the closing praise to the tune of "The Twelve Days of Christmas."

On the first day of Christmas
we celebrate God's gift:
in the presence of the dear Christ child.

TELL US MORE

We have been in the season of Advent for the four weeks before

Christmas until Christmas Day. Now we are in the season of Christmastide, which will end on Epiphany, January 6. This twelve-day time is sometimes referred to as *The Twelve Days of Christmas*. Some Christians celebrate Christmas on January 6 instead of December 25.

READING THE BIBLE TOGETHER

Read John 1:10-13.

Repeat the following verse in echo style:

> To all who received him,
> who believed in his name,
> he gave power
> to become children of God (John 1:12).

A STORY

In *Circle of Wonder, A Native American Christmas Story* by N. Scott Momaday, Tolo's parents have the honor of bringing home the statue of the Christ Child following midnight mass on Christmas Eve and keeping it during the twelve days of Christmas.

Tolo cannot talk, and he has been very lonely since his grandfather died. He falls asleep at church and dreams of seeing his grandfather and following him into the mountains. Tolo hears his own voice—clear and beautiful—call out to the animals, which join him in a circle of wonder around the gift of the fire.

When Tolo awakens on his warm pallet on the earthen floor at home, he sees a soft glow from the candle shining on the head of the Christ child, and his heart is full of joy.

SHARING TOGETHER

What would change in your family if the baby Jesus were coming to live with you during the twelve days of Christmas? What would it be like to awake and find him in your home? How would your family care for him? Remember—Jesus can always be with us in our hearts.

Take turns sharing ways your life would be different if Jesus had not been born—the books you couldn't read, the stories you would not know, the activities you couldn't do, and the places you couldn't go.

PRAYING TOGETHER

Dear God, thank you for Jesus. Thank you for the difference he makes in the world. Thank you that he can live in our hearts and make a difference in our lives. Amen.

December 27

PRAISING GOD TOGETHER

Say or sing praise for God's gifts to the tune of "The Twelve Days of Christmas."

> On the second day of Christmas
> we celebrate God's gifts:
> two Testaments
> and the presence of the dear Christ child.

118

READING THE BIBLE TOGETHER

In your Bible, find the first and last verses of the Old Testament printed below.

In the beginning when God created the heavens and the earth (Gen. 1:1). He will turn the hearts of parents to their children and the hearts of children to their parents, so that I will not come and strike the land with a curse (Mal. 4:6).

Find the first verse of the New Testament. *An account of the genealogy of Jesus the Messiah, the son of David, the son of Abraham (Matt. 1:1).*

Find the last verse of the New Testament. *The grace of the Lord Jesus be with all the saints. Amen (Rev. 22:21).*

TELL US MORE

The Bible is divided into two parts: The Hebrew Scriptures (commonly called the Old Testament), which were written before Jesus was born; and the New Covenant (commonly called the New Testament), which is about Jesus.

A STORY

Natasha grew up in a country where it was unlawful to be a Christian. People could not gather for worship. They could not own a Bible, read it, or talk about it.

Natasha was among some very brave Christians who did not want to forget what the Bible said. They gathered regularly in homes, even though it was a great risk. With no

Bibles, they had to depend on verses from memory. They could not share these verses aloud because they feared that government agents might have put listening devices in their homes.

Natasha and her friends sat in silence together. Each one wrote a Bible verse from memory and passed it around the circle. That is how they kept the Bible alive without having one to read.

SHARING TOGETHER

Pretend your family lives in a place like Natasha and that you are among the brave Christians. Take turns sharing a Bible verse from memory.

PRAYING TOGETHER

Dear God, thank you for the Bible. We pray for people who lack the freedom to go to church and to read your Word. Help us to show with our lives what the Bible teaches. Amen.

OPTIONAL ACTIVITY

See page 269.

December 28

PRAISING GOD TOGETHER

Say or sing praise for God's gifts to the tune of "The Twelve Days of Christmas."

On the third day of Christmas
we celebrate God's gifts:
three wise men
two Testaments
and the presence of the dear Christ child.

READING THE BIBLE TOGETHER

Read Matthew 2:1-6.

Repeat the following verse in echo style:

We saw his star
when it came up in the east,
and we have come
to worship him. (GNT)

A STORY

The magi or wise men were very different from Mary and Joseph. They were from a different country. They had different beliefs and traditions. They didn't have the same religion as the Holy Family. Yet, they followed the star.

Their long journey from the East was difficult. Unlike people today, they couldn't go by plane or car. There were no fast-food restaurants along the way where they could grab a hamburger. No cell phone, radio, or CDs to play. No motels at the end of each day with a bath and a warm bed. Yet, they followed the star. They wandered along, swaying on dirty camels, smelling sweat and tasting dust. Yet, they followed the star.

SHARING TOGETHER

What do you do to get ready for a trip? What do you think the wise men did to get ready for their journey? What would it be like to follow a star instead of a map?

We do not have a star to follow, but what are some things that help guide people to Jesus today?

IMAGINE THIS

Act out the journey of the wise men.

PRAYING TOGETHER

Dear God, thank you for the magi, who had the courage to follow the star to the stable. Help us to have the courage to follow you, even when it is hard. Amen.

December 29

PRAISING GOD TOGETHER

Say or sing praise for God's gifts to the tune of "The Twelve Days of Christmas."

On the fourth day of Christmas
we celebrate God's gifts:
four Gospel books,
three wise men,
two Testaments,
and the presence of the dear Christ child.

READING THE
BIBLE TOGETHER

Read John 1:14-18

Repeat the following verse in echo style:

> The law indeed
> was given through Moses;
> grace and truth
> came through Jesus Christ. (John 1:17)

CONSIDER THIS

The Gospels are the first four books in the New Testament: Matthew, Mark, Luke, and John. The words Jesus spoke are in them. Some Bibles show Jesus' words in red print.

The word *love* is used in forty-four verses of the Gospels: three verses in Mark, and ten verses each in Matthew and Luke. In John, which is sometimes called the Gospel of Love, the word is used in twenty-one verses.

Look at the Gospels in your Bible. Which one has the most chapters? Which one has the fewest? If your Bible uses red print to show when Jesus speaks, flip through it to see his words.

SHARING TOGETHER

 Why do you think the word *love* is used so often in the Gospels? If you have a favorite verse that Jesus said, take turns sharing it. What does that verse mean to you in your daily life?

PRAYING TOGETHER

 Dear God, we thank you that we can read Jesus' words and know how he wants us to live. Help us today to remember his words and follow them. Amen.

December 30

PRAISING GOD TOGETHER

 Say or sing praise to the tune of "The Twelve Days of Christmas."

> On the fifth day of Christmas
> we celebrate God's gifts:
> five loaves of bread,
> four Gospel books,
> three wise men,
> two Testaments,
> and the presence of the dear Christ child.

 READING THE
BIBLE TOGETHER

Read Matthew 14:15-21.

A STORY

 Tracy sat down beside Pat in the school cafeteria. Both were responsible for making their own school lunches.

Tracy pulled out a peanut butter and jelly sandwich and began to eat it, feeling Pat's hungry eyes watching each bite. "Don't you have a sandwich?" Tracy asked.

"I didn't have time to make one," Pat said.

Tracy wanted to tell Pat to get up earlier instead of staring at someone else's sandwich. But before school that morning Tracy's family had read together the story of the loaves and fishes. Now Jesus' words seemed to echo through the lunchroom: "You give them something to eat." With a sigh, Tracy tore the sandwich in half and offered it to Pat.

Pat downed it quickly. Then Pat offered Tracy one of the two cookies she had grabbed before running out the door to catch the bus.

"Thank you," said Tracy, thinking that maybe that is how the story of the loaves and fishes had worked. Maybe everyone there who brought food had shared it.

SHARING TOGETHER

How would this story be different if Tracy hadn't shared? If Pat hadn't shared?

When have you shared what you had with another person? How did that feel? When have you chosen not to share what you had with another? How did that feel?

PRACTICING WHAT JESUS TAUGHT

One thing the story of the five loaves teaches us is to share what we have with others instead of being selfish. Especially during Christmastide, the days from Christmas Eve till after New Year's Day, let's look for ways to share that help someone else.

PRAYING TOGETHER

Loving God, we pray for those who have little to share. Help us today to remember the story of the five loaves of bread and to share what we have. Amen.

December 31

PRAISING GOD TOGETHER

Say or sing praise to God to the tune of "The Twelve Days of Christmas."

On the sixth day of Christmas,
we celebrate God's gifts:
six days creating
five loaves of bread
four Gospel books
three wise men
two Testaments
and the presence of the dear Christ child.

READING THE BIBLE TOGETHER

Read Genesis 1:14-18.

TELL US MORE

There are two creation stories in Genesis. The first story speaks of the six days of creation, and says that *God saw everything that he had made, and indeed, it was very good* (Gen. 1:31).

The second story does not mention the length of time for creation.

A STORY

On New Year's Eve, a while before midnight, a mother and her two children walked to the beach. The moon that God created lit the white sand like snow and made the waves sparkle on the waters.

The family of three had a party, eating snacks and watching the fireworks they had brought. The mother would walk out a short distance in the sand, light a fuse, and run quickly back to her children. Once, she fell in the soft sand and stood up again, chuckling. Dots of purple, blue, green, red, and white from the fireworks burst across the sky God created.

The children's happy laughter sounded like tinkling bells in the night. The three of them created a good memory of saying good-bye to the old year and hello to the new one.

more memories. Perhaps we have also grown spiritually.

When did you most feel God's love in your family this year? What have learned this year about how to love and serve God?

God created the sky and the earth and us. We create the way we use time, the way we treat others, our visions and dreams, and our attitude. We can also create good memories. Perhaps your family would like to plan some special family times in the new year, times that will create good memories for all of you.

CONSIDER THIS

This is the last day of the year. All of us have grown in some ways. Children are bigger. Children and parents know more than they did this time last year. We have

PRAYING TOGETHER

Invite each person to pray, thanking God for some of the things he or she is most grateful for during this past year.

JANUARY

January 1

New Year's Day offers an opportunity to reflect on what Sunday school and worship mean to each of us and to make or renew our commitment to attend church together.

PRAISING GOD TOGETHER

Light a candle, join hands, and repeat the following in echo style (one person reads a line, and the others echo it):

We praise you, Loving God,
for new beginnings.

READING THE BIBLE TOGETHER

Read Genesis 2:1-3.

CONSIDER THIS

We call the seventh day that God blessed the sabbath. As Christians, we celebrate the sabbath on Sunday, the first day of the week, because Jesus rose from the dead on the first day of the week. The sabbath is a time to rest and to reflect on whether we are centering on God in our daily living. It is a day that offers us a new beginning.
New Year's Day is also a time of new beginnings. Many people make New Year's resolutions—decisions about changes they want to make in their lives. Today is a good time to think about changes we can make that will help us begin to live as Jesus wants us to live. Of course, we are not perfect, and we will fall short. But we don't have to wait until next New Year's Day to begin again. Each new day offers us a new beginning. As Christians, we go from one beginning to another beginning.

SHARING TOGETHER

Take turns sharing some new beginnings in your lives such as starting school or a new job, moving to a new home, baptisms, and birthdays.
Decide on three changes you would like to make this year. Be realistic, but do give yourself a bit of a challenge. Each Sunday, think about these changes and reflect on how you are doing. Each morning, ask God to help you make the changes just for that day.

PRAYING TOGETHER

Dear God, thank you for this new year and the new beginning it brings. Thank you for this new beginning in our family journey. Help us to face toward you in our journey together this year. Amen.

OPTIONAL ACTIVITY

See page 269.

LOOKING AHEAD

Before tomorrow's session, find something that reminds you of a new beginning. Bring it with you tomorrow and tell about it. You will also need a candle tomorrow.

January 2

PRAISING GOD TOGETHER

If you followed yesterday's suggestion and found something that reminded you of a new beginning, take turns showing it and telling about the new beginning it represents for you.

Light a candle, join hands and repeat the following in echo style:

We praise you,
Loving God,
for new beginnings.

READING THE BIBLE TOGETHER

The teachings of Jesus in Matthew 5:3-10 are called The Beatitudes. Take turns reading the verses below, one section at a time.

Read verses 3-4. We have all mourned or felt sad about the death of someone we love or perhaps a pet. Jesus promises us comfort in our sadness. Have you ever felt God's presence when you were sad? If so, take turns sharing.

Read verses 5-6. Sometimes we feel an empty space inside of us. It is as if we feel hungry—but not for food. We feel thirsty—but not for water. We long for something else. That something is God. We want assurance that God loves us. When we feel that love, we also yearn to do what is right in God's eyes, to be better people. How do you feel when you know inside yourself that God loves you?

Read verses 7-8. There are times when we are kind to others who hurt us in some way. We show them mercy even though we may feel they don't deserve it. Have you ever done that? If so, take turns talking about it. (Parents, make sure your children understand that showing mercy does not mean tolerating abuse.)

Read verses 9-10. There are times when we try to bring peace at home or school or work. Perhaps we try to end fights instead of making them worse. When have you tried to be a peacemaker?

The Beatitudes remind us that we are blessed with God's presence.

PRAYING TOGETHER

Take turns praying, thanking God for a particular blessing you feel.

SINGING TOGETHER

Hold hands and sing "Jesus Loves Me."

LOOKING AHEAD

You will need a candle and paper and crayons for tomorrow's devotion.

125

January 3

PRAISING GOD TOGETHER

Light a candle, join hands, and repeat the following in echo style:

We praise you, Loving God,
for new beginnings.

READING THE BIBLE TOGETHER

Read Galatians 5:22-26.

CONSIDER THIS

We are like fruit trees. A fruit tree reaches down through its roots to the soil to receive nourishment, and it reaches out for the water around it. But the tree cannot bear good fruit unless it also reaches up toward the light of the sun.

In the same way, we reach down into our family roots for the nurture we need, and we reach out to others—giving and receiving care. But when we reach toward the light of God's love, we can bear the fruit of the Spirit.

The Apostle Paul tells us that when we let the Spirit—the spirit of God's love—guide us, we will bear the fruit of the Spirit. These fruits are a way of living; we show love, joy, peace, patience, kindness, generosity, faithfulness, gentleness, and self-control.

None of us always does these things. But we are more likely to grow in showing these fruits when we let the Spirit guide us through

the day. Praying, reading the Bible, and sharing in this family time together help us to remember that the Spirit is our guide.

SHARING TOGETHER

Take turns talking about which of the fruits of the Spirit (love, joy, peace, patience, kindness, generosity, faithfulness, gentleness, and self-control) are visible in your life. Which ones are least visible?

Draw and color some pieces of fruit. On each piece, write one of the fruits of the Spirit that is important to each of you. Place the fruits in a basket in the center of your table to remind you of the fruits of the Spirit.

PRAYING TOGETHER

A parent begins, then each person takes a turn praying for one or two of the fruits of the Spirit: to be more loving or joyful or peaceful or patient or kind or generous or faithful or gentle, or to have more self-control.

Dear God, thank you for the fruits of the Spirit. Help me to . . . .

(Close after all have finished:)
Help us to let the Spirit guide us today. Amen.

OPTIONAL ACTIVITY

See page 269.

LOOKING AHEAD

You will need a candle for tomorrow.

January 4

PRAISING GOD TOGETHER

Light a candle, join hands, and repeat the following in echo style:

We praise you, Loving God,
for new beginnings.

READING THE BIBLE TOGETHER

Read Exodus 20:3, 4-6.

These first two commandments tell us not to put any god before our Ever-Living, Ever-Loving Creator. This is harder than it sounds. It means that we are to put God *first*. It is easy for us to let other things take first place in our lives. Perhaps money is most important. Or friends. Or our job. Or our home. Or our place at school. If anything becomes more important to us than God, it becomes an idol for us.

Using different readers (if possible), read each of the remaining commandments one at a time: Exodus 20:7, 8-11, 12, 13, 14, 15, 16, 17. Pause after each one to share together what it means to you. Don't worry about whether anyone has the right meaning. What is important during this time together is sharing what the commandment means to each family member.

TELL US MORE

The Ten Commandments are found in the Hebrew Scriptures, which we know as the Old Testament. In the New Testament, Jesus said that the greatest commandment is to love God and the second is to love your neighbor as yourself.

PRAYING TOGETHER

Loving God, forgive us when we do not keep your commandments. Help us to put you first today. Amen.

LOOKING AHEAD

You will need a candle for tomorrow.

January 5

PRAISING GOD TOGETHER

Light a candle, join hands, and repeat the following in echo style:

We praise you, Loving God,
for new beginnings.

READING THE BIBLE TOGETHER

Read Matthew 10:1-4.

IMAGINE THIS

A parent reads, pausing long enough after each sentence to give time for imagining. Pretend that Jesus named you as one of the twelve apostles, and …

- Imagine how it would be to dress in robes and sandals like people in those days did.
- Imagine walking along dirt paths with Jesus.
- Imagine listening to Jesus' voice as he tells stories.
- Imagine talking to him.
- Imagine eating at the same table with him.
- Imagine sitting beside him.
- Imagine touching his hand.
- Imagine that he asks you to do something for him.

SHARING TOGETHER

Take turns sharing what you imagined and how you felt. In which imaginary situation did you feel closest to Jesus?

CONSIDER THIS

We do not know how Jesus' voice sounded, but we can hear it through the voice of others who read and tell his stories. We can talk to him in our prayers. We can invite him, through our mealtime prayers, to be with us at the table. Just as Jesus sat beside the apostles, he is also with us. We cannot reach out and touch his hand, but we can feel his presence with us. We know what he asks of us because the Bible tells us. We sometimes disappoint him, but he continues to love us anyway, just as he did the apostles.

PRACTICING WHAT JESUS TAUGHT

Today practice being what every Christian is—one of Jesus' disciples!

PRAYING TOGETHER

Loving God, help us remember to try to be Jesus' true disciples, and not ones who betray him. Thank you for forgiving us when we disappoint you. Thank you for loving us always. Amen.

OPTIONAL ACTIVITY

See page 269.

LOOKING AHEAD

Since Epiphany, January 6, has to do with light, you may want to light several candles tomorrow.

January 6

PRAISING GOD TOGETHER

Light one or more candles, join hands, and say or sing this praise to the tune of "Jesus Loves Me," without the refrain.

Follow, follow the Lord's light.
Follow, follow the Lord's light.
Praise God! Praise God for the light.
Praise God! Praise God! We praise God!

READING THE BIBLE TOGETHER

Read Matthew 2:7-12.

TELL US MORE

On Epiphany we celebrate the visit of the wise men, also called the magi. Their visit is a sign that Jesus offers hope for all people.

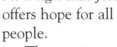

The magi were different from Mary and Joseph. They were not the same race. They didn't have the same religion, beliefs, or traditions as the Holy Family.

We don't know much about the magi. We don't even know for sure how many wise men there were. We assume there were three because there were three gifts: gold, frankincense, and myrrh. What we do know is this:

- They followed the star seeking Jesus.
- They were overwhelmed with joy when they found him.
- They knelt down before him.
- They offered him gifts.

The celebration of Epiphany reminds us to do what the magi did:

- To follow the light, seeking Jesus.
- To remember that joy is part of our faith.
- To kneel before Jesus in humility and gratitude and in obedience to his teachings.
- To offer our gifts in his name.

SHARING TOGETHER

When you think about Jesus, what brings you joy? Which of his teachings do you have a hard time following? What gifts can you offer?

PRAYING TOGETHER

Pray this prayer echo style, with one person reading a line and everyone else repeating it:

Thank you, Loving God,
for the family journey
we are making together.
Thank you for joy
on our faith journey.
Help us to be
like the magi,
always following your light.
Amen.

LOOKING AHEAD

You will need a candle for tomorrow's devotion.

Reminder: Family experiences at church influence children's spiritual growth.

January 7

PRAISING GOD TOGETHER

Light a candle, join hands, and say or sing this praise to the tune of "Jesus Loves Me," without the refrain.

Follow, follow the Lord's light.
Follow, follow the Lord's light.
Praise God! Praise God for the light.
Praise God! Praise God! We praise God!

READING THE BIBLE TOGETHER

Read Luke 2:52.

A STORY

A little boy stood at the window watching the clouds gather over the mountains. "The clouds are sitting on top of the mountains, Mommy," he said. "Why?"

"Clouds often do that," she said. "Maybe they like the mountains."

"They are getting bigger. Why?"

"They are going to bring rain," she said. "Why?"

"To make things grow."

Later raindrops began to fall, and the little boy went outside. When his mother saw him standing in the rain, she called to him, "You'll get all wet! What are you doing?"

"I want to grow!" he said.*

SHARING TOGETHER

What are some of the ways you want to grow? Luke tells us the ways Jesus continued to grow from the time he was twelve. One of those ways was *in favor with God*. In other words, Jesus grew spiritually. That is one of the ways we can also grow. We can grow spiritually by going to Sunday school and church and by sharing in this family time. We can grow spiritually by reading the Bible and praying together, talking about our faith, and listening to one another.

Since beginning this family time together, are you becoming more aware of God's presence in your lives? Are you becoming more aware of God's love for you?

Individually and as a family, how do you respond to God's loving presence? When do you feel reverence and joy?

Are you sometimes tempted to hurry through this time like a duty to be checked off the list? If so, would it help to change the time of day you gather? Is one day of the week so hectic that it would be better to skip this time altogether that day? Or, since that day is so hectic, is it even more important to find time to pray and talk about your faith together? Remember that your commitment to this time should be something to celebrate, not something to make you feel guilty when you are unable to find the time.

PRAYING TOGETHER

Take turns thanking God for something you find meaningful in this family time together.

*This story was told by Tomas Gonzalez in the "Children's Moments" during the worship service at St. John's United Methodist Church, Santa Fe, New Mexico, March 19, 2000.

LOOKING AHEAD

You will need a candle and matches for tomorrow.

January 8

PRAISING GOD TOGETHER

Light a candle, join hands, and say or sing the opening praise to the tune of "Jesus Loves Me," without the refrain.

Follow, follow the Lord's light.
Follow, follow the Lord's light.
Praise God! Praise God for the light.
Praise God! Praise God! We praise God!

READING THE BIBLE TOGETHER

Read Isaiah 57:14-15.

CONSIDER THIS

Two girls were walking around the playground at school. One was looking at the other and stumbled over a rock that she hadn't seen. Have you ever stumbled over something you didn't see?

Isaiah tells us to move out of the way the things that cause us to stumble. But Isaiah was not talking about rocks on the playground or about stumbling physically. He was talking about the things that cause us to stumble in our spiritual growth.

SHARING TOGETHER

What are some of the *rocks* you stumble over in your spiritual growth—things that get in your way as you try to grow in your love for God? Are there rocks inside yourself—thoughts and feelings that get in your way as you try to grow in showing God's love?

IMAGINE THIS

Imagine that God, the Holy One, is coming here to be with you during your family devotion time. Imagine what that would be like.

Look around you at the place you gather. What would you do to prepare it for that special visitor? Do you see some things that help

you feel this is a holy space for family sharing, a place that welcomes the Holy One everyday? Are there some symbols of faith you would like to add? Are there some things you would like to clear away from this space? Look at Preparing the Place on page 9. Decide together on any ways you would like to change your family worship space.

Remember! The Holy One is always with you—today, tomorrow, and every day.

PRAYING TOGETHER

Take turns thanking God for something you find meaningful about sharing this time with your family.

LOOKING AHEAD

In order to be prepared for tomorrow's session, you may want to look at Reading the Bible Together on page 10, giving special attention to how you can help children enter the scene and to the importance of repetition.

January 9

PRAISING GOD TOGETHER

Join hands and say or sing the opening praise to the tune of "Jesus Loves Me," without the refrain.

Follow, follow the Lord's light.
Follow, follow the Lord's light.
Praise God! Praise God for the light.
Praise God! Praise God! We praise God!

IMAGINE THIS

Pretend that the chapters in the New Testament of the Bible are like very old letters written to you that you have just discovered. Each one comes from another place, another time, another culture. Imagine that each one begins, *Dear* (use parent's name) or *Dear* (repeat using each child's name).

Imagine holding these letters carefully in your hands.

Imagine what the letters are saying to you as you live in this place, in this time, in your own culture.

Imagine taking these very old letters seriously as you become aware of their love and wisdom, and as you apply their insights to your own life.

READING THE BIBLE TOGETHER

Read Acts 27:18-20, 39-44.

Try using your senses as you hear the scene described in the Bible. As one person reads the scripture, let everyone try to enter fully into the shipwreck scene—seeing it, hearing it,

smelling it, touching the planks, maybe even tasting the water. Then share together:

- What did you see?
- What did you hear?
- What did your hands and feet touch?
- What did you smell?
- What did you taste?

Read the scripture and repeat the last sentence together several times.

SHARING TOGETHER

Think about a time that your family or some members of your family had a scary experience like Paul in the storm and shipwreck, but all came through safely.

Maybe you had an accident or an angry disagreement with someone or a pet was almost hurt. How did you feel when it was over and you were safe once more? Share together if you wish.

PRAYING TOGETHER

Dear God, thank you for the Bible and its stories. Thank you for staying with us in the scary, stormy times until we are brought safely to land. Help us to see the words of Jesus in the Bible as personal letters written to each of us. Amen.

OPTIONAL ACTIVITY

See page 269.

January 10

READING THE BIBLE TOGETHER

Read 1 John 2:7-11.

Repeat in echo style:
>Anyone who claims
>to live in God's light
>and hates a brother or sister
>is still in the dark. (THE MESSAGE)

TELL US MORE

When this scripture speaks of a brother or sister, it includes family members. But it also means others. Since all of us are God's children, we are all brothers and sisters.

CONSIDER THIS

The sun sleeps a lot during the midwinter month of January in the northern part of the earth. Darkness snatches more than its share of time. Yet some of the most beautiful sights we see are in winter. Rolling hills and rooftops are often white with snow. Roads are like narrow ribbons winding through a white-cloud world. Icicles hang from barren branches, glinting in the light like sparkling fruit. It is as though God's love shines even brighter in the dark times.

IMAGINE THIS

Pretend that you are out in a cold, dark winter night. Imagine that clouds completely hide the moon and stars. The electricity is off, so there are no streetlights or house lights or city lights.

Pretend that you are the one who can bring light; you have a bright-burning candle. Pretend that you go to each sister and brother you love and light a candle from your candle. Can you see the little lights coming on?

Imagine all of them do the same thing for all the people they love. Then those people do the same. Can you see how bright the world is becoming?

SHARING TOGETHER

Take turns sharing your feelings as you imagined the little lights coming on. Who are some of the people whose candles you lit?

PRACTICING WHAT JESUS TAUGHT

Let us remember, especially in the dark times, that hate snuffs out the light and causes us to stumble in the darkness. When we live in love, that love lights the world.

PRAYING TOGETHER

Sing as a prayer "This Little Light of Mine," or close with a brief spoken prayer.

OPTIONAL ACTIVITY

See page 270.

January 11

READING THE BIBLE TOGETHER

Read 1 Peter 1:8-9.

A STORY

After a winter storm in January, a family made a snowman. First they rolled a huge ball of snow and then a slightly smaller one to place on top of it. Next, on the very top, they put a smaller one, the right size for his head. He was a tall snowman!

The family grew cold and stopped to drink some hot chocolate before finishing their snowman. Then they used licorice to shape black eyebrows and walnut shells for his eyes. A radish served as his nose. They cut a red pepper into strips for smiling lips, put a navy-blue stocking cap on his head and a green wool scarf around his neck. The family stood back, admired their snowman, and decided to name him Clem.

SOMETHING TO CONSIDER

What if we could see things from Clem's point of view? The people were shaping him the way they wanted him to be—without bothering to consider what he might like to be. Maybe he didn't feel like smiling. Maybe he didn't like the old clothes they dressed him in. And what if he didn't want to be called Clem?

If we look at something through another person's eyes, it may not look the same!

SHARING TOGETHER

Have you ever felt that someone was trying to shape you into what he or she wanted you to be, instead of appreciating who you are? If so, how did you feel? Have you ever done that to someone else?

Has anyone ever told you to smile when you didn't feel like it or not to cry when you could hardly hold back the tears? If so, how did you feel? Have you ever done that to someone else?

Has anyone ever called you a name you did not like? If so, how did you feel? Have you ever done that to someone else?

PRACTICING WHAT JESUS TAUGHT

When we love one another, we try to see with eyes of love. Of course, we do not do this perfectly. But every time we try, we are practicing what Jesus taught. Let's try to see with eyes of love today.

PRAISING GOD TOGETHER

Sing to the tune of "Brother John":

Are you seeing? Are you seeing,
child of God, child of God?
With new eyes we're seeing.
With new eyes we're seeing.
Thank you, God. Thank you, God.

Now repeat the song, perhaps faster and faster, or sing it as a round.

January 12

READING THE BIBLE TOGETHER

Read 2 John 5.

SHARING TOGETHER

Use the same family members for both of the role-plays below. You will need two people: a student and classmate. Or you can simply discuss the situations together.

Situation 1: A teacher asks to speak to you alone. Later, a classmate asks, "What did the teacher want?" You feel that this classmate cares about you and hopes you aren't in trouble. How do you answer?

Situation 2: The same thing happens, except that this time you feel the classmate doesn't really care about you and maybe even hopes that you are in trouble. How do you answer?

Take turns sharing what you would have said and done in these two situations. Parents can substitute a supervisor at work and colleague for the teacher and classmate.

If your response in the first situation was warm and kind, how do you think your classmate felt? Do you think your response helped your friendship grow stronger?

If your response in the second situation was cool or rude, how do you think your classmate felt? Do you think your response made it even harder to become friends?

SOMETHING TO CONSIDER

These two situations describe decisions about the ears with which we listen. In the first situation, we listened with ears that expected friendship.

Suppose that in the second situation we decided to listen with new ears and responded in a warm, kind way. How might the classmate feel? Could our decision open the possibility of friendship?

Remember: It takes two people to make a friendship. But even one can keep a relationship from getting worse.

PRACTICING WHAT JESUS TAUGHT

To hear with new ears, ears that listen with love, doesn't mean that we suddenly trust everyone. But we try to respond to others, even those people we find it hard to like, with kindness. If we practice, we can learn to hear through ears of love. Let's try to listen with new ears today.

PRAISING GOD TOGETHER

Sing to the tune of "Brother John":

Are you hearing? Are you hearing,
child of God, child of God?
With new ears we're hearing.
With new ears we're hearing.
Thank you, God. Thank you, God.

January 13

The Basilique Notre-Dame-de-Fourvière in Lyon, France, is a very large basilica (or church) at the top of a high hill overlooking the city. It has an oblong shape, and four square towers rise above the roof, one at each corner. Because of its shape, some of the local people joke that it looks like an upside-down elephant.

READING THE BIBLE TOGETHER

Many of Jesus' teachings sound *upside down* because Jesus spoke with a new tongue. He said to love our enemies and to pray for people who hurt us. Read Matthew 5:38-41, 43-44 and Matthew 6:19-20 to hear his upside-down words.

SHARING TOGETHER

How do you feel about these upside-down sayings?
Which is hardest for you to follow?
What are some things you would not say anymore if you tried to speak with a new tongue?

PRACTICING WHAT JESUS TAUGHT

When we love one another, we try to speak with a new tongue, using words that show our love. No one is always able to speak in a loving way, but every time we try, we are practicing what Jesus taught. Today let's try to speak with kind and loving words.

PRAISING GOD TOGETHER

Sing to the tune of "Brother John":

Are you speaking? Are you speaking,
child of God, child of God?
With new tongues we're speaking.
With new tongues we're speaking.
Thank you, God. Thank you, God.

You may want to sing the seeing and hearing verses again also (from Jan. 11 and 12).

January 14

READING THE BIBLE TOGETHER

Read Romans 12:1-2.
Read the verses again and repeat together: *Be transformed by the renewing of your minds.*

A STORY

Adolph Gottlieb did a series of paintings known as *Bursts* and *Blasts*. He once began a lecture with this story about a child's painting:

A little girl was painting a picture. A person looked over her shoulder, watched a moment, then asked the common question, "What are you painting?"

She did not give a common answer. She replied, "I think, then I draw around my think."*

PRACTICING WHAT JESUS TAUGHT

To renew our minds means that we look deeper than common answers. We think about God's love and Jesus' teachings, and we know there are uncommon answers, better ones, upside-down ones. We apply them to how we live. First we think, then we act around our think.

We cannot always think with this new mind. But every time we try, we are practicing what Jesus taught. Let's try to think with a new mind today.

SHARING TOGETHER

Role-play something that commonly happens at school or work and how you or another student or a coworker generally reacts.

Role-play the same event again, but this time think with a new mind and apply that uncommon thinking of Jesus' teachings.

PRAISING GOD TOGETHER

Sing to the tune of "Brother John":

Are you thinking? Are you thinking,
child of God, child of God?
With new minds we're thinking.
With new minds we're thinking.
Thank you, God. Thank you, God.

You may want to sing the seeing, hearing, and speaking verses (Jan. 11, 12, and 13).

*From a brochure published by the Dallas Museum of Art, Dallas, Texas.

January 15

A STORY

There is a riverside café in France where people enjoy giving bits of bread to the graceful swans in a nearby lake. One evening, some of the bread pieces floated over the small dam at the end of the lake. The swans had plenty to eat within reach and did not need the bread that got away. But two swans chased after it anyway—and fell over the dam into the water below!

With their long necks, they could see over the dam where they used to be. They watched the other swans float around above them, eating the tossed bread. The two looked for a way to get back over the dam. They swam around and around. But they couldn't find a way.

The swans spread their wings to fly but were afraid to try. They were also afraid to leave the other swans behind and paddle downstream. They simply swam back and forth, back and forth, peering up over the dam but not solving their problem.

SHARING TOGETHER

Probably all of us know what it is like to have all of something that we need, but to try to get more of it anyway (perhaps more food, money, toys or other possessions, love, prestige, or honors). So we do greedy things and, like the two swans, often end up causing ourselves trouble. Take turns sharing a time when you did something greedy and ended up with a problem.

Sometimes we envy other people, especially if they have something we once had. Have you ever watched a group of people from a distance and envied them? Or envied an individual? If so, take turns telling about it. Do you sometimes want to risk doing something to solve a problem, but you are afraid to try? If so, take turns sharing.

How can others in your family help you be aware when you do something that may be based on greed? Or envy? Or fear? Do you need to be more generous to others in your words and actions? If so, what will help you do that?

READING THE BIBLE TOGETHER

Read Psalm 149:1.

PRAYING TOGETHER

Dear God, help us to end our old song, our song of greed for what another has. Help us to sing a new song, a song of thanks to you for the gifts we already have. Help us to sing a new song, a song of courage. Help us to sing a new song, a song of faith. Amen.

OPTIONAL ACTIVITY

See page 270.

January 16

READING THE BIBLE TOGETHER

Read Matthew 6:25-31.

A STORY

A family was on a backpacking trip in the Rocky Mountains in Colorado. The parents and four children each carried a backpack. Even the family dog carried a pack over her back that held her dog food. When the family began planning their trip, they thought of many things they wanted to take along. They knew that if they took too much, the packs would be too heavy. They could only take what they really needed: food; a couple of pots for cooking and boiling water; plastic plates and silverware; a tin cup each; soap, toothbrushes, toothpaste, and towels; two tarps and a rope and clothespins to make a tent; sleeping bags; warm coats; an emergency kit; a pocket knife; and a change of clothes. Planning that trip taught the family what they really needed.

CONSIDER THIS

Pretend you are going on a backpacking trip. Make a list of all the things you would want to take. Then look at each item on your list and ask whether you would really need that thing. Would you be willing or able to carry it for several days? What's left on your list after you cross off the things you don't really need?

SHARING TOGETHER

Do you have more things than you really need as you walk through the daily journey of your life? If so, would you like to give some things away to someone who has less than he or she really needs?

PRACTICING WHAT JESUS TAUGHT

Jesus taught us to give generously. In places, the Bible talks about giving a tithe or a tenth. What would it mean to you to give to the church one-tenth of your allowance or your salary? It may sound radical and impossible. But if we give generously based on our income, after a while we will find it is not a dreaded duty but a great joy.

PRAYING TOGETHER

Loving God, forgive us for getting more when we already have enough. Help us to know when enough is truly enough. If we have more than we really need, help us to be generous enough to give away the extra. Amen.

January 17

READING THE BIBLE TOGETHER

Read Psalm 18:1-3.

A STORY

A little boy was helping his mom clean house one Saturday morning. He worked fast because they had planned a trip to the zoo as soon as the work was finished. The kitchen came last, and the mom asked the little boy to get the broom.

"No," he said. "I don't want to get it."

The mother frowned. "Why not?"

"It's dark in the closet," he said. He paused, then admitted, "I'm afraid."

"You don't need to be afraid. God is with you even in the dark."

The boy walked to the closet, took a breath, and turned the knob slowly. He opened the door a few inches, staying behind it and reaching his hand around. "God," he said, "if you're in there, please hand me the broom."

CONSIDER THIS

Some doors we can see, like closet doors, bedroom doors, front and back doors. But we also experience doors to our lives—times when new possibilities are open to us. For example, we miss a lot when we are afraid to open up and let others into our lives. Maybe we are afraid to open the door to people who are different from us in the way they look or act, the school they attend, the area where they live, their age, or their economic group. Sometimes we are afraid to open our lives to certain people because we have a stereotype of them. We think we know what someone is like, and we don't get close enough to discover our view isn't true. We miss opportunities to know all kinds of people. And we cheat ourselves.

Sometimes we fear opening our door to those who are different from us because we are afraid of what other people will think or say about us. Again, it is ourselves whom we cheat.

SHARING TOGETHER

Think about a person or group with whom you have avoided contact or conversation. If you would like, take turns sharing whom you thought of and what you fear about contact with this person or group.

Draw a picture of a door. Draw yourself standing outside the door. On the inside draw a person you think would not feel comfortable opening the door to you. Talk about why.

PRAYING TOGETHER

Pray together using the echo style:

Loving God, thank you for people
who are different from us.
Help us to open the door
of our lives to them
and to remember
that all people are your children.
Help us to practice that today. Amen.

January 18

READING THE BIBLE TOGETHER

Read Galatians 3:26-28.

A STORY

The first African-American woman poet, known as Phillis Wheatley, arrived in Boston in 1761—but not by choice. When she was about eight years old, she was kidnapped from Senegal, Africa, and held in the overcrowded darkness of a slave ship on the long, long voyage to America. The horrible conditions on the slave ship caused health problems that plagued her for the rest of her life. The terrified little girl wanted her parents. But she would never see them again, and they would always wonder what happened to her.

John Wheatley bought her as a slave to help his wife. They could not understand her words, nor she theirs. She felt very lonely. They even called her by an unfamiliar name—Phillis.

In time, the Wheatleys became fond of her. Slaves could not go to school, but the Wheatleys educated Phillis in the classics, astronomy, geography, and history. She learned quickly. The Bible was one of her favorite books. The Wheatleys attended Old South Meeting House, which made an exception to its rule against slaves being baptized into the church. Phillis became a member of that church at age sixteen.

IMAGINE THIS

Pretend you are taken away from your family. (Adults were also kidnapped from Africa.) Imagine how that might feel.

Pretend you find yourself in a foreign land, surrounded by strangers. You can't understand their words, and they can't understand yours.

Pretend you are owned by people who can boss you around any way they like. Imagine how that feels—even if the people are kind to you.

SHARING TOGETHER

Take turns sharing some of your feelings as you imagined those things. When you see a stranger—someone new in class or at work or church—how do you treat that person?

If someone speaks with a different language or accent—do you try to understand? Or do you expect that person to try to talk like you? Do you boss anyone around? Do you expect anyone to do what you want all the time? How is that similar to treating someone like a slave?

PRACTICING WHAT JESUS TAUGHT

We wish we could undo cruel things that have been done to people. We can't undo those things, but we can keep from doing mean things ourselves. We can remember what Paul said—that we are all *one* in Christ Jesus.

☀ PRAYING TOGETHER

Take turns praying for those who are hurt by the cruelty of others.

January 19

READING THE BIBLE TOGETHER

Read Hebrews 11:1-3.

🏠 A STORY

(*If you missed yesterday's devotional time, you may want to look back at* A Story *to learn more about Phillis Wheatley.*)

The first African-American woman poet, known as Phillis Wheatley, was only thirteen years old when her first poem was printed. Seven years later, a book of her poetry was published. Poetry linked her with many famous people—George Washington, John Hancock, Ben Franklin, the Reverend George Whitefield, King George III, and the Lord Mayor of London. Jupiter Hammon, the first African-American male poet, addressed a poem to her.

Once Phillis visited London with a member of the Wheatley family. She was to be honored by being presented at court to the royal family. However, she was still a slave and was called home because Mrs. Wheatley was ill.

Phillis became a freed woman in 1773, shortly before the Revolutionary War. That was a difficult time, and after her marriage she lived in extreme poverty. Much of her poetry was published after her death.

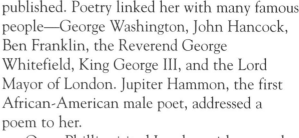 TELL US MORE

Phillis Wheatley lived more than 200 years ago, but her words can still be heard through her poetry. Though she experienced the ugliness of slavery, she could still see beauty; and when it wasn't before her eyes, she turned inward to her imagination. A few lines from her poem, "On Imagination," give us an example:

Though Winter frowns to Fancy's raptur'd eyes
The fields may flourish, and gay scenes arise;
The frozen deeps may break their iron bands,
And bid their waters murmur o'er the sands.*

🪑 SHARING TOGETHER

Have you ever turned inward to your imagination when you didn't like what was going on around you? If so, take turns talking about it.

Think about a place where you do not feel comfortable. Go to that place in your imagination and change it to the way you wish it were. Take turns sharing.

CONSIDER THIS

When we can imagine something better than it is, we can begin to hope for it to be that way. When we hope for something, we can begin to work toward bringing it about. When we begin to work toward bringing something about, maybe in time it will happen. Abolishing slavery is an example of something many people worked to make happen.

PRAYING TOGETHER

Dear God, thank you for our imagination. Thank you for faith, and for our belief and trust that reach beyond what we can see. Amen.

PRAISING GOD TOGETHER

Sing to the tune of "Mary Had a Little Lamb":

We praise God for hope and faith,
hope and faith, hope and faith.
We praise God for hope and faith
and for our inner eyes.

*From "On Imagination" published in *Poems on Various Subjects, Religious and Moral* by Phillis Wheatley.

January 20

CONSIDER THIS

Have you ever seen violent videos, TV shows, or movies? Have you ever played video games that are violent? These can be scary, but we know that they are just pretend. But in some places in the world, real bombs and missiles are exploding.

A STORY

Just before Christmas, a Palestinian Christian boy named Faisal stood beside the remains of his home in Beit Jala near Bethlehem. His grandfather had spent twenty-five years building this home. Now Faisal's big brother walked carefully on the bombed roof, looking for clay roof tiles that could be saved. Inside, his mother held the baby, and his grandmother cried as she looked at the walls with gaping holes from missiles.

Three generations had lived in that home together, including fifteen children—Faisal's brothers and sisters and cousins. All his life they had laughed and played, eaten and slept within those walls. Now there were only memories and tears.

And remnants of shells (marked USA) remained. They were used by the Israeli military, who heard gunshots near Faisal's house and retaliated with missiles and bombs.

SHARING TOGETHER

Do your best to imagine what it would be like to be Faisal or one of his parents. Share some of the feelings you might have about not being safe, about losing your home, about those who destroyed it and those who made the missiles.

READING THE BIBLE TOGETHER

Read 2 Corinthians 5:16-17.

PRAYING TOGETHER

Loving God, forgive us for forgetting that we are all your children and that your family is one, though living in many nations. Help our leaders to be wise about selling weapons that might make children elsewhere unsafe. Help us, in our own lives, to replace the old way of the love of power with Christ's new way of the power of love. Amen.

January 21

A STORY

Robert, an eighteen-month-old baby, had a number of physical challenges. His arms ended above the elbows, and his legs ended above the knees. He was also blind.

Robert could use his forearms and thighs very well to play with toys and scoot across the floor. And he could hear his name.

A visitor picked up a yellow rubber duck, sat down on the floor, and said Robert's name. He smiled and scooted toward her. He sat on the visitor's lap, and they played with the squeaking duck. Robert's wonderful laugh rang through the room.

SHARING TOGETHER

What is the most important thing that you notice about the story of Robert? Do you know a child or adult who has physical challenges similar to the ones he faced? Talk together about the ways that you are different from that person. Now identify the ways in which you are alike. What did you learn? You probably found that there are many more ways you are alike than ways you are different!

Today at school or work, be aware of classmates or coworkers who have special needs. Try to get to know them better.

READING THE BIBLE TOGETHER

Read Mark 9:36-37.

PRAYING TOGETHER

Pray this prayer echo style:

Loving God, thank you for Robert
and all persons with special needs.
Help us to remember
to treat all persons
with love and respect.
Amen.

PRAISING GOD TOGETHER

Sing to the tune of "Mary Had a Little Lamb":

We praise God for hope and faith,
hope and faith, hope and faith.
We praise God for hope and faith
and friends with special needs.

January 22

READING THE BIBLE TOGETHER

Read Romans 5:1-5.

A STORY

Tony Melendez sat barefoot on a small platform, his guitar in front of him on the floor. Nearby was the stage where Pope John Paul II would greet the crowd.

Tony was born without arms, and sometimes when he was a little boy he felt sad and wondered how he could make it. But his mother always encouraged him; she believed that God had created Tony with something wonderful in mind.

That night, Tony was introduced to the pope as a man with a special gift. Tony's gift was music, but he also represented courage, self-motivation, and family support. Tony sang and strummed his guitar with his toes—as he always had. But that night was an amazing opportunity for him—he sang and played for the pope, celebrating the presence and power of God in each of us.

The pope kissed Tony and told him that he was giving the gift of hope to all people. Tony realized that it was true that he could give hope to others. Perhaps this was the special purpose that God had in mind for him—just as his mother had always believed.

CONSIDER THIS

Perhaps the most important lesson in Tony Melendez's book, A *Gift of Hope*, is this statement: *You could play the guitar with your feet if you were willing to practice hard enough.**

Tony wanted to sing and play the guitar. Since he didn't have hands and fingers, he figured out another way.

God creates each of us with a special purpose. We are never too old or too young to discover what that may be. It may be something big or something small, but as each of us fulfills the particular purpose God has for us, we become a gift to others.

SHARING TOGETHER

What do you think your special purpose might be? What gift can you give others by fulfilling that purpose?

Is there something that makes it hard for you to fulfill your purpose? Can you find a way to fulfill your purpose, even if it is hard?

Listen as each family member tells what special purpose he or she may have.

PRAYING TOGETHER

Take turns expressing your thanks to God for giving you a special purpose—even if you are not yet sure what it is.

PRAISING GOD TOGETHER

Say these words or sing them to the tune of "Mary Had a Little Lamb":

We praise God for hope and faith,
hope and faith, hope and faith.

We praise God for hope and faith
and for the special ones.

*From Tony Melendez, A *Gift of Hope* (Rensselaer, Ind.:
Angelus Media Publications, 1996), 3.

January 23

READING THE BIBLE TOGETHER

Read Psalm 61:1-2.

CONSIDER THIS

Some older people suffer severe memory loss as a result of Alzheimer's disease. Perhaps you have a family member or a friend or acquaintance who has this disease. A person with Alzheimer's may not even recognize family members when they visit. Yet that person still needs to know that he or she is loved.

A STORY

Molly loved her grandmother very much. She spent a week with her each summer. They had fun together playing all sorts of games. One year they wrote pretend letters to each other, with Molly pretending to be a princess and her grandmother pretending to be a queen.

While Molly was in college, her grandmother got Alzheimer's and didn't know Molly anymore. But Molly still went to see her. One time her grandmother showed Molly a wedding picture and said proudly, "That's my daughter."

Molly said, "It's my mother too."

"Really?" Her grandmother smiled, surprised and pleased.

Molly still has her grandmother's letters and the wonderful memories—and her love for her grandmother, which holds fast, even in this painful situation.

SHARING TOGETHER

Things change in families. People grow older, move away, become ill. Yet nothing can separate us from the love of God in Christ Jesus; and, in that love, nothing can separate us from our love for one another —even when things change.

If your family is facing the illness of a loved one, you may want to share your feelings about this. Perhaps you long for things to be the way they once were. Perhaps it is difficult now to know how to show your love. Perhaps you feel angry that things have taken this turn. It is all right to feel angry. Remember that God weeps with us when painful changes occur.

PRAYING TOGETHER

Thank you, God, for good memories, especially when things change and we can no longer be with someone we love the way we once were. Help us to make good memories each day. Amen.

PRAISING GOD TOGETHER

Sing to the tune of "Mary Had a Little Lamb":

We praise God for hope and faith,
hope and faith, hope and faith.
We praise God for hope and faith
and for our memories.

January 24

READING THE BIBLE TOGETHER

Read 2 Corinthians 11:23-28.
Much was required of Paul in his ministry,
and he said *Yes!*

A STORY

One of the bravest Methodists in history was Deaconess Anna Eklund who served in St. Petersburg, Russia, from 1908 through 1931. She remained in St. Petersburg during the terrible hardships of the Communist Revolution and the years following it. When all of the clergy left St. Petersburg, Sister Anna remained and was put in charge of the Methodist work. Because of her, the life of that congregation was never interrupted. She even protected the church building. This was not easy because wooden structures were being torn down and used for firewood in the bitter cold.

Sister Anna experienced the assassination of Tsar Nicholas and the formation of the Soviet Union, world war and civil war, famine and purge, and the death of Lenin. She lived in severe hunger, was imprisoned, and watched eighteen of her friends die of starvation. During all those years of extreme hardship in St. Petersburg, the security of Sister Anna's home in Finland was only a day's ride away. She could have escaped, but Sister Anna said *Yes!* to God's call to stay in St. Petersburg.

SHARING TOGETHER

What sacrifices would you be willing to make for your church? Unlike Sister Anna, we don't face starvation and imprisonment in our efforts to keep our congregation going. But what can we do? What gifts do we have that we can offer? How do we say *Yes!* to God's call?

PRAYING TOGETHER

Pray this prayer in echo style:

Dear God,
thank you for Saint Paul
and faithful people like Sister Anna.
Help us to have the courage today
to say *Yes* to your call!
Amen.

PRAISING GOD TOGETHER

Sing to the tune of "Mary Had a Little Lamb":

We praise God for hope and faith,
hope and faith, hope and faith.
We praise God for hope and faith
and for the brave Christians.

January 25

READING THE BIBLE TOGETHER

Read 1 Peter 2:9-10.

A STORY

Mininjtjimuli is a beautiful aboriginal painting of a plant with purple flowers, which has the same name. The artist lives in the northern area of Australia in the Nauiyu Nambiyu community.

Many artists live in that community. Most of them are women. The great-grandmothers, grandmothers, mothers, and daughters sit together in a circle and tell stories. Ranging in age from eighteen to eighty, they keep the ancient stories alive through their art. The younger ones, who listen and learn the stories, are like new leaves growing on the branches. And the branches are always attached to the ancient vine and roots from the past.

IMAGINE THIS

Pretend that people from your church are gathered in a circle, telling stories. Imagine that everyone has a turn to tell some story about the church— either from a long time ago or from today. Pretend that it is your turn to tell a story. What will you tell? Take turns sharing the story you would tell about your church.

How much do you know about your church's history? Would you like to know more?

SHARING TOGETHER

Invite your pastor or an older member of your church to tell you some of the stories about the beginnings of your church. You may want to invite that person to your home for a meal or for cookies and hot chocolate. When you learn these stories, don't forget them. Someday you can pass them along to the generation that comes after you.

PRAYING TOGETHER

Thank you, God, for the old stories. Help us to write new stories that are pleasing to you. Most of all, thank you that when we tell our stories we are connected to you and to other people. We are new leaves on the vine of your love and strength. Amen.

PRAISING GOD TOGETHER

Sing to the tune of "London Bridge":

We are leaves that praise our God!
Praise our God! Praise our God!
We are leaves that praise our God
    and Christ Jesus!

January 26

READING THE BIBLE TOGETHER

Read Proverbs 12:15-18.

CONSIDER THIS

Just as there are many kinds of people, there are many kinds of families. Some families have one child; some have many children. Some children are born into their families; some have been chosen by their families through adoption.

Some families have two parents; some have one. Some children live with grandparents or with both a parent and a grandparent. Some families have stepparents and stepchildren, stepbrothers and stepsisters, or half brothers and half sisters. Some families are made up of foster parents and foster children. Some parents are young; some are older.

Even though families are different, they have three things in common: All families are loved by God. All families do their best to love one another. And all families have misunderstandings, that can result in arguments and conflict.

Joan Chittister gives us some good advice. She says a misunderstanding is "an ordinary call to do some extraordinary listening."* Shouting our own point of view louder and louder does not help end a misunderstanding. To turn misunderstanding into understanding, we use our ears instead of our mouths and try very hard to hear what the other is saying—even when we don't want to!

SHARING TOGETHER

Share together some common misunderstandings in your family. Listen carefully to one another. Maybe you can turn misunderstanding into understanding. Discuss these misunderstandings in a soft voice, gently—not in a blaming way. If you find yourselves blaming one another, take a breath and apologize.

Take turns telling each person in the family one or two things you especially appreciate about him or her.

PRAYING TOGETHER

Pray this prayer in echo style:

Thank you, God, for our family.
Help us to listen to each other,
especially when we disagree.
Help us to listen to others
instead of judging them. Amen.

PRAISING GOD TOGETHER

Let each family member offer a simple thank you to God for a special blessing.

*From Joan Chittister, *The Psalms: Meditations for Every Day of the Year* (New York: Crossroad Publishing Company, 1996), 23.

January 27

CONSIDER THIS

Words! Words! Words!
So many words!
Words in the car. Words at the table.
Words on the phone. Words on the Web.
Helpful words. Hateful words.
Kind words. Mean words.
Spoken words. Shouted words.
Soft words. Sung words.
Scribbled words. Secret words.
Savage words. Sacred words.
What does God do with all these words!

TELL US MORE

There are so many words. No wonder there are misunderstandings! Think of some words you like to hear—for example, *I love you*. Take turns sharing them.

Think of some words you do not like to hear and take turns sharing them.

There is an old saying we often use in childhood when someone calls us a name:

Sticks and stones may break my bones,
but words can never hurt me.

That isn't true, is it? Words can hurt us. And we can hurt others with our words.

SHARING TOGETHER

Pretend that you are making a family flag to hang by your door. Decide together what words you would want to put on it. What words would you like people to think of when they think about your family? You may want to make a small paper flag to put on your worship center to remind you each day of what your family wants to become.

READING THE BIBLE TOGETHER

Read Psalm 46:1-5, 10.

PRAYING TOGETHER

Let us chase words from our minds, be silent, and simply rest in the oneness of God's love. Appoint a family member to end the time of silence after a few minutes with these words: *Be still, and know that I am God!*

January 28

READING THE BIBLE TOGETHER

Read Psalm 103:8-14.

TELL US MORE

A long time ago (about 350 years after Jesus), a man named Evagrius Ponticus listed the major problems inside ourselves:

- wanting too much of something
- being greedy
- being habitually sad
- wanting something so much we do bad things to get it
- being angry
- being bored and sloppy
- being dependent on praise
- being prideful or arrogant.

He did not call these problems "sins" and judge us for them. He considered them to be habits of the heart that needed to be healed. All of us have some of these habits.

CONSIDER THIS

Today when we think of these habits, we might say that we need a big-time attitude adjustment. We know that when one of these habits gets the best of us, it is as though we cast shadows over other people.

It helps to be aware of these behaviors in

ourselves. It helps to say what is going on within us. It helps to heal these habits of our hearts so that we don't hurt other people.

God's love is like the sun. When the sun is straight above us, we walk under it without casting a shadow. But when the sun is at the far edges of the earth, we cast long shadows. In the same way, when we keep God's love at the center of our lives, it is as though we walk directly under God's love, and we don't cast shadows on others. But as we draw farther away from that center, we cast longer and longer shadows.

SHARING TOGETHER

Though Evagrius lived hundreds of years ago, we still struggle with the behaviors he named. Think about some problems today that you can connect to poor habits of the heart. (Some possibilities: materialism, competition, pollution, abuse of tobacco, alcohol and other drugs, peer pressure, gambling, stealing.) As you name them, think about which habit of the heart each problem is related to. Which of the habits Evagrius named do you have difficulty with?

We have developed undesirable habits of the heart over time and through experience. They can be changed, but it takes time and trust in God's love. Be patient with yourself!

PRAYING TOGETHER

Take turns praying for God to help you with poor habits of the heart that hurt others.

PRAISING GOD TOGETHER

Sing to the tune of "London Bridge":

We praise God for healing hearts!
Healing hearts! Healing hearts!
We praise God for healing hearts
   and for loving!

January 29

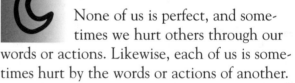

READING THE BIBLE TOGETHER

Jesus spoke often of forgiveness. For examples, read Matthew 6:14-15; Mark 11:25; and Colossians 3:13.

CONSIDER THIS

None of us is perfect, and sometimes we hurt others through our words or actions. Likewise, each of us is sometimes hurt by the words or actions of another.

Either way, it is as if night has come. After we hurt someone in our family, we feel bad and need to know that we are forgiven. When others hurt us, they need our forgiveness, and we feel sad until we forgive them. Waiting for forgiveness is like waiting in the night, wanting the dawn to break and light to come again.

A STORY

A long, long time ago, a Seeker asked a Wise One: "When will the dawn come? Will it come when I can tell a sheep from a dog?"

"No," said the Wise One. "It will not come when you can tell a sheep from a dog."

"Will it come when I can see the difference between a fig tree and another kind of tree?"

"No," said the Wise One. "It will not come when you can see the difference between a fig tree and another kind of tree."

"Then when will the dawn come?"

The Wise One answered, "The dawn will come when you can see that each person is your beloved sister or brother."*

TELL US MORE

Forgiving each other is essential in a family. It brings the dawn.

Mealtime is a good opportunity to ask forgiveness. Mealtime can be like a family Communion as we drink and eat together. We remember that when we participate in Communion at church we are to be in love and charity with our neighbors. Likewise, at family meals, it is good to be in love and charity with one another. We could stop for a time right after our mealtime prayer to create an opportunity to forgive one another, when it is needed.

SHARING TOGETHER

Take turns asking forgiveness of a family member for something you have done. Focus on your own need to seek forgiveness, not on what others have done to you.

PRAYING TOGETHER

Take turns praying for God's forgiveness for something you have done. You may pray aloud or silently. Experience the joy of being forgiven and the joy of forgiving. Hug one another!

*This story was told by Dr. Evelyn Laycock, Bishops and Laity Weekend, Mount Sequoyah, Arkansas, June 23, 2000.

January 30

READING THE BIBLE TOGETHER

Read the parable of the Good Samaritan in Luke 10:29-37.

CONSIDER THIS

People see things differently, depending on the glasses they look through. Let's put on some pretend glasses of the various people involved in the story and see how they might have viewed the situation.

• The robber: *I needed that money worse than he did. He probably won't even miss the money! And I wouldn't have hurt him if he had just handed it over. It's his own fault he got hurt.*

Have you ever taken anything that belonged to someone else or cheated anyone? If so, why did you do that? If not, why do you think people do that?

• The priest or the Levite: *The robbers might be hiding, and I might get robbed myself. I must hurry on. I have to get to my sick friend's home before it's too late.*

Poor man! But I can't touch a Samaritan! If I do I won't be able to go to the Temple! It's his own fault. He should have been more careful. Why should I bother?

Are there ever good reasons not to help someone? Sometimes we are afraid to help. Why? Are you ever so busy that you don't notice someone who might need your help?

- The man who was robbed, after he was well again: *What could I expect! Getting robbed is just the way life is. People cheat you and hurt you. It isn't my fault I have no money so I shouldn't have to help myself. Someone else should take care of me from now on.*

Do you generally expect bad things or good things to happen? When something bad happens to you, do you think it's someone else's responsibility to fix it or do you try to help yourself?

TELL US MORE

One of the things this parable can help us learn is that there is more than one way to look at a situation. People see things in different ways, and all of us tend to think our view is the right one. It is important to remember that others may feel just as strongly that their view is the right one.

This story is about being a good neighbor. One way we do that is not to judge others too harshly when they don't see things the way we do or do what we think they should do. It is helpful to try to look at a situation the way they see it—to borrow their glasses, so to speak.

PRAYING TOGETHER

Pray this prayer echo style:

Dear God,
when I think someone is wrong,

help me not to be too sure I'm right until I have traded glasses with the other. Amen.

SINGING TOGETHER

Sing or say to the tune of "I Know the Lord":

O, I know the Lord,
I know the Lord,
I know the Lord
   has laid his hands on me.

OPTIONAL ACTIVITY

See page 270.

January 31

READING THE BIBLE TOGETHER

Read 1 Corinthians 4:20-21.

A STORY

During the children's sermon, a little boy began to disturb the others around him. He made loud noises and stepped on the other children to get out of the circle. Then he began wandering around the altar area. His daddy came forward.

What would the father do? Scold the child? Force him to sit down and be quiet? Take him back to his pew? Out of the sanctuary?

The daddy walked up to the altar area and put his arm lovingly around his child, moving him back into the circle. Then without saying a word to the child, the daddy sat down beside him, waiting patiently. His presence helped the child behave better, and he no longer disturbed others.

CONSIDER THIS

Jesus sometimes used the word *Abba* to address God. This word is somewhat like Daddy, a closer, less formal word than Father. It is like the difference between Mommy and Mother. We are children of this kind of God, a close and loving God.

Sometimes we disturb others in some way or are disrespectful of them. Sometimes we say things before we've listened enough to know what we're talking about. Sometimes we step on people and shove them around to get what we want and where we want to be. Sometimes we just wander around, not even realizing we are on sacred ground, for all ground is sacred.

And God comes forward. What do we think God will do? Give up on us? Punish us? Take away our freedom? Instead, God sits down beside us and enfolds us in love. We feel the power of God's loving presence, and that helps us do better.

PRAYING TOGETHER

Pray this prayer in echo style:

Thank you for being with us.
Thank you that nothing can separate us from your love.
Help us to be loving toward others.
Amen.

FEBRUARY

February 1

FAMILY LITANY

One person reads, and everyone joins in the response.

Reader: A moment may not seem important, but moments add up to days, weeks, months, and years.

All: **Give us meaning in these moments together.**

Reader: Create special memories to cherish and look back upon.

All: **Give us meaning in these moments together.**

Reader: Once a moment slips away, we cannot bring it back again.

All: **Give us meaning in these moments together.**

Reader: No one else can live our moments for us.

All: **Give us meaning in these moments together.**

Reader: Each moment is a special gift from God.

All: **Give us meaning in these moments together.**

Reader: Spend them with those you love. Spend them giving love. Spend them learning about God's love.

All: **Give us meaning in these moments together.**

Reader: Begin now. Begin with this moment.

SHARING TOGETHER

What are some of the most meaningful moments you have had? What made them special? How did you feel at the time? If you could relive an experience of your life over again, which one would it be? Why?

READING THE BIBLE TOGETHER

Read Psalm 118:24, 28-29.

SINGING TOGETHER

Sing to the tune of "When the Saints Go Marching In" or say the words. One person can sing or say each line and let the family repeat it. Clap as you sing or recite the lines.

This is the day. This is the day.
This is the day the Lord has made.
Oh, let's rejoice and be glad in it.
It's the day that the Lord has made!

Fill it with love. Fill it with love.
This is the day the Lord has made.
Oh, let's rejoice and be glad in it.
It's the day that the Lord has made!

Give thanks and praise. Give thanks and praise.
This is the day the Lord has made.
Oh, let's rejoice and be glad in it.
It's the day that the Lord has made!

PRAYING TOGETHER

Pray this prayer echo style with one person saying each line and the family repeating it.

> For each moment,
> **For each moment,**
> For each hour,
> **For each hour,**
> For each day,
> **For each day,**
> For the gift of life,
> **For the gift of life,**
> We thank you, God.
> **We thank you, God.**
> Amen.

February 2

READING THE BIBLE TOGETHER

Read 1 Corinthians 13.

SHARING TOGETHER

Think about the scripture you just read. Each family member can share words or phrases to complete "Love is...." The response could be something you do or say, the name of a person or a group, or other words that describe love. Let a family member record the responses and put them away to look at and possibly add to later.

Here are some things you may want to include:

Love is...a hug, a smile, a gentle touch, a pat, a squeeze of the hand, outstretched arms.
Love is...a kind word, a prayer, a special gift, a selfless act, something shared, taking time to care, laughing and playing together, walking side by side.
Love is...family, friends, and all those people who give special meaning to our lives.
> God is love.
> Love is the greatest gift of all!
> Yes! Love is!

PRAYING TOGETHER

Let someone read a line saying the letter first, and others echo it.

Dear God, help me to love. Help me to . . .

L – Let go of hatred, resentment, prejudice, and envy.

O – Open my heart to your guidance.

V – Value my relationships with others.

E – Encourage compassion, caring, and kindness.

Amen.

OPTIONAL ACTIVITY

See page 270.

February 3

IMAGINE THIS

What is God's love like? Do you have an idea? Let's think about this today! God's love is like:

- An anchor—It gives us something to hold onto and keeps us steadfast.
- A compass—It points us in the right direction. It shows us the way to go.
- A lighthouse—It guides us.
- A bridge—It connects us with others.
- A steel beam—It is strong, lasting, and gives us support.
- Glue—It will not let us go!
- The universe—It never ends.
- The air—We cannot see it, but we can feel it and know that it is there.
- Water—It helps to wash away feelings of prejudice, jealousy, resentment, and hatred.
- The sun—It makes us feel warm and good inside.
- A flower—It causes us to grow and blossom.
- An eraser—It removes our sin.
- A healing ointment—It eases our pain and suffering.

SHARING TOGETHER

Let each family member take a minute to look around your home and find an object with which to compare God's love. If possible, bring the object back to the place for your devotions to share or just tell the others about it.

READING THE BIBLE TOGETHER

Read Psalm 34:1-6.

PRAYING TOGETHER

Dear God, thank you for the gift of your love. Help us to share this precious gift of love with others. Help us all to see your love at work in our lives. Amen.

February 4

READING THE BIBLE TOGETHER

Read Romans 8:28, 38-39.

A STORY

In the classic children's book *The Runaway Bunny*, by Margaret Wise Brown,* a little bunny thinks he wants to run far, far away from his mother. He imagines all kinds of things he would become and places he would go. As the bunny tells each idea to his mother, she responds by letting him know that she would find a way to be with him. Finally the little bunny decides where he really wants to be is at home in the loving arms of his mother.

CONSIDER THIS

Wherever we go, whatever we do, or whatever happens to us, God will never be far away from us. Nothing can separate us from God's love. God's love is always there for us.

SHARING TOGETHER

Let the children in the family pretend to be reporters. The reporters' assignment is to interview the parents and ask them, "What has God's love meant in your life? How have you felt God's love?"

A FAMILY LITANY

Children repeat, "God's love is there for me." Parents say the other lines, and include additional ones if they wish.

Parents: When I am sad and lonely,
Children: God's love is there for me.
Parents: When I am afraid,
Children: God's love is there for me.
Parents: When I am hurting,
Children: God's love is there for me.
Parents: When I am trying something new,
Children: God's love is there for me.
Parents: When I need to make a decision,
Children: God's love is there for me.
Parents: When I am helping someone,
Children: God's love is there for me.
Parents: Whether I am awake or asleep, near or far away, wherever I go, whatever I do, and whatever happens,
Children: God's love is there for me.
All: **Thank you, God! Amen!**

*Margaret Wise Brown, *The Runaway Bunny* (New York: HarperCollins Children's Books, 1974).

February 5

READING THE BIBLE TOGETHER

Read Matthew 7:24-27.

SINGING TOGETHER

Sing to the tune of "Row, Row, Row Your Boat." Form hands into fists and hit the top of one fist with the bottom of the other in rhythm to the words.

Build, build, build your house.
Build it on a rock.
Build it wisely. Build it strong.
Build it on a rock.

Build, build, build your house.
Build it on a rock.
Where rains and floods and winds that come can never make it fall.

Build, build, build your house.
Build it on God's love.
Build it wisely. Build it strong.
Build it on God's love.

SHARING TOGETHER

In our Bible passage today, Jesus uses the illustration of building a house to help us see that each of us needs a strong foundation of hearing God's word and acting on it. Families also need a strong foundation in God's love. We need this to grow together in faith and love and to face the daily challenges and difficult circumstances that come our way.

Often we hear families who have been through difficult times say, "We don't know what we would have done without our faith. We don't know how we would have survived without God's love." One of the greatest gifts

family members can give is to help one another grow in faith. Doing so builds a foundation that will last forever!

IMAGINE THIS

Imagine that you are gathered together to develop plans for building a strong foundation for your family. Close your eyes and imagine what kind of foundation it will be. What will you use as your guide? What materials will you rely on to build it strong? Who else can help your family grow in love? When should you begin? How long do you think this project will take? Share your thoughts with each other.

PRAYING TOGETHER

Parents say and lead the actions. Children give the response.

Parents: Clap your hands. Shout for joy!
Children: God's love will make us strong.
Parents: Clap your hands. Lift them high!
Children: God's love will make us strong.
Parents: Clap your hands. Stomp your feet!
Children: God's love will make us strong.
Parents: Clap your hands. Give a hug!
Children: God's love will make us strong.
Parents: Clap your hands, all say "Amen!"
All: **Amen!**

February 6

READING THE BIBLE TOGETHER

Read Matthew 19:13-15.

SINGING TOGETHER

Sing to the tune of "Joshua Fought the Battle of Jericho" or recite the words. Parents do a verse and children echo it. Clap and sway in rhythm to the words.

Verse 1
People brought their children, children, children.
People brought their children
so that they might be blessed.
Verse 2
Keep the children by your side, by your side, by your side.
Keep the children by your side,
the disciples cried to them.
Verse 3
Let the children come to me, come to me, come to me.
Let the children come to me.
Jesus called, "Yes, come!"
Verse 4
For it is to such as these, such as these, such as these,
for it is to such as these
that the kingdom of heaven belongs.
Verse 5
Then Jesus laid his hands on them,
hands on them, hands on them.
Then Jesus laid his hands on them,
and love shone all around!

SHARING TOGETHER

Parents, use this time to tell your children the special qualities you love about them and how much they mean to you.

PRAYING TOGETHER

Think about children all over the world. Think about children in your area and children you know personally. Think about children in all kinds of situations with many different needs. Pray aloud for these children. Let each family member add to the prayer. Begin your prayer this way:

Dear God, we come to you in prayer for the children. We pray for children everywhere. We pray that you would wrap your loving arms around them and hold them close. We pray for… (name individual children or groups of children).

(Parents, close the time of prayer with thanks to God for your own children.)

OPTIONAL ACTIVITY

See page 270.

LOOKING AHEAD

Have one or more hand mirrors available for tomorrow.

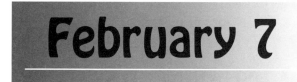

February 7

READING THE BIBLE TOGETHER

Read Matthew 19:16-19.

CONSIDER THIS

In Matthew 19:19, Jesus tells us to "Love your neighbor as yourself." But many people do not really love themselves as God wants us to love. They find all kinds of reasons why they are unlovable, and they feel no one could possibly love them. But when we do not know how to love ourselves, it keeps us

from being able to love our neighbors fully. It keeps us from being all that God created us to be!

FAMILY LITANY

One person reads the responsive lines; everyone else repeats, "Love yourself!"

Reader: You are made in God's image.
All: **Love yourself!**
Reader: You are a child of God.
All: **Love yourself!**
Reader: You are unique, one of a kind.
All: **Love yourself!**
Reader: You are blessed with special gifts.
All: **Love yourself!**
Reader: So that you can love others.
All: **Love yourself!**
Reader: So that you can be all God created you to be!

SHARING TOGETHER

Distribute the mirror(s) to family members. Give each person the opportunity to study himself or herself in the mirror and think about qualities (special gifts, abilities, physical attributes) that he or she feels blessed to have. Each family member can then tell other family members at least five things that he or she likes about themselves.

SINGING TOGETHER

Sing to the tune of "He's Got the Whole World in His Hands" or say the words. Parents sing a verse and children echo it.

Yes! God made a very special me. (Sing 3 times.) For no one else is quite like me!

Yes! God's own image is in me. (Sing 3 times.) Wow! That makes an awesome me.

Yes! I am sure that God loves me. (Sing 3 times.)
What a great feeling inside me.
Yes! I look in the mirror and what do I see?
(Sing 3 times.)
Someone's happy I'm the me I see!

Sing alleluia, praise to God! (Sing 3 times.)
Give thanks for the gift of life!
Yes! (Shout together and give yourself a hug!)

PRAYING TOGETHER

Lord, help me to love myself. Help me to love others. Help me to love you. Amen.

February 8

READING THE BIBLE TOGETHER

Family members take turns reading the verses from Luke 10:25-37.

A STORY

As one person reads the story below, the others make stepping sounds by hitting knees with hands each time the reader says, "Step, step, step."

A man was going down from Jerusalem to Jericho. It was a treacherous road to travel. It was dark and dangerous.
Step, step, step, step . . .
A thief attacked the man. He robbed, beat him, and left him to die.
Step, step, step, step . . .
A priest soon came along the road. He glanced at the man but did not stop. He passed by on the opposite side.

Step, step, step, step . . .
A Levite came to the place where the man lay. He turned his head and pretended not to see. He too passed by on the opposite side.
Step, step, step, step . . .
A Samaritan traveled on the road. He drew near and stayed with the suffering man. He dressed the man's wounds and helped him.
Step, step, step, step . . .
The Samaritan got his animal and gently placed the man on it. He brought him to an inn. He cared for him and paid for him to stay.
Step, step, step, step . . .
Jesus comes to us today. He speaks in our hearts saying, "Like the Samaritan who showed mercy, go and do likewise."
Step, step, step, step . . .
We go to love, love, and love again! We go for Jesus. We go for our neighbor.

SHARING TOGETHER

Invite each family member to tell a personal Good Samaritan story. Talk about a time when someone helped you when you really needed it. Then tell of a time when you came to the aid of someone. Share the feelings you had.

SINGING TOGETHER

Sing to the tune of "Jacob's Ladder" or recite the words.

I shall love the Lord my God, (Sing 3 times.)
With all my heart.
I shall love the Lord my God, (Sing 3 times.)
With all my soul.
I shall love the Lord my God, (Sing 3 times.)

With all my strength.
I shall love the Lord my God, (Sing 3 times.)
And my neighbor as myself.

PRAYING TOGETHER

Lord, help me to be a Good Samaritan. Help me to love my neighbor as myself. Amen.

February 9

READING THE BIBLE TOGETHER

Family members take turns reading 1 John 3:17-18; Proverbs 14:31; and Proverbs 31:8-9.

A STORY

*The Shoemaker's Dream** is a wonderful children's book that people of all ages can enjoy. The book tells the story of a Russian shoemaker named Martin who has a dream that Jesus will come to visit him the next day. Martin loves Jesus, and he excitedly anticipates Jesus coming to see him. The following day passes by, but Martin does not feel that he has seen Jesus.

In a second dream, Jesus shows Martin the many people in need whom Martin had helped that day. When Martin wakes from the dream, he understands that by showing love to those in need, he has shown love to Jesus.

* English text by Mildred Schell, *The Shoemaker's Dream* (Valley Forge, Penn.: Judson Press, 1948).

CONSIDER THIS

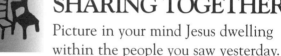

In *The Shoemaker's Dream*, no one forced Martin to be loving. Martin chose to do so. Just as in Martin's experience, people come into our lives who need help, but we can choose to help or not. We have a choice to give love or withhold it, to obey or disobey God.

Now close your eyes and think about the past several days. Did you see or meet anyone who had a special need? Did you see pictures of people who could use your help? Did a family member or friend need you? Did you choose to respond to the needs of these people in any way, or did you ignore them for some reason? What was the reaction of the people you helped? What do you think Jesus' reaction is to an expression of love from someone?

SHARING TOGETHER

Picture in your mind Jesus dwelling within the people you saw yesterday. How does this change the way you feel about them or what you might do or say to them? Gather as a family to share your thoughts.

PRAYING TOGETHER

Dear Jesus, open our eyes to see the needs of others all around us. Open our ears that we may hear the cries for help from those who are hurting. Open our arms to embrace the lonely and outcast of this world. Open our mouths to speak words of love to one another. Open our hearts to be filled with the Holy Spirit. Amen.

LOOKING AHEAD

Place a basket in the area where your family gathers for this time of prayer and devotions.

February 10

📖 READING THE BIBLE TOGETHER

Read John 6:1-14.

☁ IMAGINE THIS

Jesus and his disciples are traveling one day near the Sea of Galilee. As they walk, they hear the sound of footsteps following closer and closer. When they reach the top of a mountain, they turn to look and see a large crowd of people pressing toward them.

Pretend that you are in the crowd too. You are very excited to see Jesus. You have heard much about this man of Nazareth.

Jesus then speaks to his disciples and says, "I am tired and hungry, and I am sure this crowd is too."

The disciples shake their heads. "What can we do? There is not enough money to buy such a huge quantity of bread."

Suddenly one of the disciples points at you and says, "Look, Jesus, there is a person with a basket filled with five barley loaves and two fish."

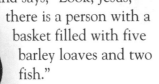

Then Jesus turns, looks directly at you, and kindly asks, "Will you please share what you have with these people today? Will you share what you have with me?" You think about what you have and what Jesus is asking you to do. You respond to Jesus by saying....

🪑 SHARING TOGETHER

Family members complete this story by telling how they would feel and what their response would be.

〰 PRACTICING WHAT JESUS TAUGHT

Select a family in need, a local food pantry, or other organization to which your family will donate food. You could also invite another family over to share a meal with you. Write what your family wants to do and place it in the basket now as an offering to Jesus.

☀ PRAYING TOGETHER

Dear Jesus, we offer what we have to you....(Family members name gifts.) Help us to realize that however small these gifts may seem, when placed in your hands, their blessings are greatly multiplied. Amen.

👉 LOOKING AHEAD

Gather keepsakes, cards, or gifts sent to you during a difficult time for tomorrow.

February 11

🏠 A STORY

The Downing family has a very special box they will always cherish and keep close at hand. When you look at this box, you see that the lid is completely covered with pictures of angels that children have drawn. The edges of the box are tattered and worn from use and have begun to split from the bulging contents inside. What this box holds is priceless. The family calls the box, "Scottie's Box."

Do you have any idea what it might contain? Let's carefully remove Scottie's Box from its shelf and gently remove the lid to discover what is inside.

On the very top is a birth certificate that reads: James Scott Downing, born March 5, 1979. Scottie was born with a severe form of a disease called spina bifida. Scottie lived just one month before he went to heaven to be with God. It was a very sad time for the Downing family.

But Scottie's Box is filled with many cards expressing love to Scottie's family and letting them know that people were praying for them and thinking about them during this difficult time. Also in the box is a list of people who donated money to their church in memory of Scottie and another list of families who brought them food. The box includes letters, prayers, special scripture passages, and other words of comfort. Scottie's Box is a box filled with love—God's love. Each time the Downings look through it, they are reminded of how God hurts for us when we are hurting and gives us love through others to ease our pain. Perhaps you know of a family who is hurting and who needs to feel God's love.

SHARING TOGETHER

Parents, share with your children a time when you felt God's presence through the love of others. Share any special keepsakes or reminders that people sent to you during that time. Talk about the meaning these keepsakes have for you.

PRAYING TOGETHER

Dear God, teach us to listen and hear the needs of others. Teach us to respond to those needs and to be messengers of your love. Amen.

READING THE BIBLE TOGETHER

Read 1 Corinthians 13:7 and Galatians 6:7-9.

February 12

READING THE BIBLE TOGETHER

Read 1 Corinthians 12:4-11.

A STORY

The teenagers at a large Methodist church have a very special ministry of music through their youth choir. The choir's mission is to help others know

Jesus and to feel God's love for them.

Every Sunday morning, the congregation is blessed by the music of this choir. Throughout

163

the year, the youth choir travels to other places to spread their message of love. Wherever they are, the light of Christ shines brightly through them and for others!

SHARING TOGETHER

Imagine your family as a special mission team whose goal is to spread the message of Christ and God's love. What ministries need help at your church? What community or world needs can your family respond to? How can your family help, even in what seem like small ways?

FAMILY LITANY

Someone reads the responsive lines. All repeat the other lines.

All: **Lord, help me to open my heart and make room for Jesus**
Reader: that I may be filled with the love of Christ.
All: **Lord, help me to open my heart and make room for Jesus**
Reader: that I may receive all of the blessings you have for me.
All: **Lord, help me to open my heart and make room for Jesus**
Reader: that I may listen to and follow your loving guidance.
All: **Lord, help me to open my heart and make room for Jesus**
Reader: Help me to let the love of Jesus in!
All: **Lord, help me to open my heart and make room for Jesus**
Reader: that I may live my life by the example of your Son.
All: **Lord, help me to open my heart and make room for Jesus**
Reader: that I may show your love in all I do and say.

All: **Lord, help me to open my heart and make room for Jesus**
Reader: that I may help others learn about you and your love.
All: **Lord, help me to open my heart and make room for Jesus. Amen.**

February 13

CONSIDER THIS

Take a moment to really examine your hands. Did you ever think about what a precious gift your hands are? Did you ever consider all the ways you can use your hands to touch others with God's love?

Hands can hold or gently squeeze someone else's hands, pat a crying baby, wipe away a tear, place a bandage on a scraped knee, help to give a hug, point the right direction for someone, give a high five.

Hands can write a letter or type an e-mail, paint a picture, create a gift for someone, pick flowers to give, play an instrument for others to hear, help make cakes and cookies to share, knock on a friend's door, and dial a phone number to say "we care."

Hands can turn on a light, open a window, put things in place, pick something up, wipe an area clean, plant a seed, and feed the birds.

Hands can open Bibles, be folded in prayer, give an offering, be placed on someone who is being baptized, give and receive the bread and cup for Communion, and reach out to welcome another. Hands are one of God's many loving gifts to us. We show God our thanks by using our hands as loving gifts to others.

SHARING TOGETHER

Each family member can talk about special ways he or she can use their hands to reach out to others. Then discuss how the hands of others have helped you.

SINGING TOGETHER

Sing the words below to the tune of "Jesus Loves Me."

Lord, I give my hands to you.
Hold them, guide them, let them be
hands that move to show I care,
hands that move to spread your love.
Lord, take my hands. (Sing 3 times.)
And use them as you will.

READING THE BIBLE TOGETHER

Read Romans 12:3-13.

PRACTICING WHAT JESUS TAUGHT

During the upcoming week, ask God each day to show you a special way you can use your hands to reach out to someone and share God's love. Then commit to doing these things.

LOOKING AHEAD

Collect and prepare valentines you have received or plan to give for tomorrow. Address one to a person who may need to feel loved.

February 14

A STORY

Saint Valentine was a priest who lived in Rome during the third century C.E. At the time, Rome was ruled by Emperor Claudius, who was disliked by many people, including Saint Valentine.

Claudius wanted to have a huge army, and he expected the men to volunteer for service. When the men refused because they didn't want to leave their families, it made Claudius very angry! Then he decided that if the men remained single they would be more willing to join his army. So Claudius created a law prohibiting marriage. The people did not like this new law one bit, and Saint Valentine did not support it.

As a priest, Saint Valentine's favorite thing to do was to marry couples. When Claudius's law went into effect, Saint Valentine secretly continued to perform marriage ceremonies. One night, however, Saint Valentine was caught marrying a couple. The couple escaped, but Saint Valentine was put in jail and sentenced to death.

Saint Valentine was very brave and tried to remain cheerful. Many young people visited the jail and threw notes and flowers to Saint Valentine through his jail window. They wanted to let him know they shared his belief about love. One young girl, the daughter of a prison guard, visited Saint Valentine every day. She helped to lift his spirits.

On February 14, 269 C.E., the day Saint Valentine was to be put to death, he left a note for this girl to thank her for her friendship. He signed the note, *Love from your Valentine*.

This began the tradition of exchanging messages of love on February 14, Valentine's Day. The day is also a reminder that love is strong and cannot be taken away!

SHARING TOGETHER

Name some of the good qualities that you see in Saint Valentine. Think about people in your life or people in the news whom you admire who seem to possess similar qualities. What people are saints to you? Share the valentines you have received.

READING THE BIBLE TOGETHER

Read 1 John 4:7-8, 11, 15-16.

PRAYING TOGETHER

Read words of Psalm 150 as your prayer.

February 15

READING THE BIBLE TOGETHER

Read Proverbs 11:17; 14:21; and Ephesians 4:31-32.

SHARING TOGETHER

Think about all the kind things you can do for others and some of the ways other people have been kind to you. Remember these as you play this game together called the ABCs of Kindness. For this game, family members take turns naming an alphabet letter and an act of kindness that begins with that letter. Begin with the letter A and go through the entire alphabet. If a family member gets stuck on a letter, others may help. Here are some suggestions to get you started:

A – Ask a friend to visit.
B – Bake cookies for someone.
C – Collect clothes for a needy family.
D – Donate food to the hungry.
E – Empty the trash.
F – Forgive someone.
G – Give a hug!

SINGING TOGETHER

Say the words together or sing them to the tune of the chorus for "Go Tell It on the Mountain."

Be kind to one another,
Each hour of every day.
Be kind to one another,
Wherever you might be!

Be kind to one another,
Each hour of every day.
Be kind to one another,
And help someone in need!

Be kind to one another,
Each hour of every day.
Be kind to one another,
And love will follow you!

PRAY TOGETHER

Lord, help me to be kind to others wherever I might be, each and every day. Amen.

LOOKING AHEAD

Do something kind for someone this week without letting anyone know you did it!

CONSIDER THIS

Persons who attend worship services on Sunday look forward to this time for many reasons. Church is a place where we can gather with fellow believers, give praise and thanks to God, receive Communion, study God's word, and grow in our faith. At one church in Tennessee, the congregation always anticipates the greeting of their senior pastor. As they sit in the sanctuary, the pastor comes to stand before them and, with outstretched arms, greets them by saying, "Hello, beautiful people!" These words help to set the tone for the rest of the service and let everyone know they are welcome! What a way to begin! What power our words have!

What words do you choose to say each day? Do they encourage or do they discourage? Do they build someone up or tear someone down? Do they comfort or hurt? Do they instill hope or create despair? Do they draw people closer or push them away? Try praying before you speak. Remember: The words you choose to say each day cannot be taken back!

READING THE BIBLE TOGETHER

Read 1 Corinthians 13:1-3. (Repeat several times, letting different family members read.)

SHARING TOGETHER

Talk about a time when the words someone spoke made you feel loved and accepted or gave you encouragement and hope. Then create a *Word Bank*. Family members share as many words and phrases as they can that express kindness. Deposit them into a Word Bank by recording them on paper or storing them in your mind!

SINGING TOGETHER

Say the words below or sing them to the tune of "Jesus Loves Me":

Words of kindness, words of care,
Words of comfort, words of hope,
Let me speak with words of love.
Let me speak as Jesus would.
Lord, guide and help me. (Repeat twice.)
Use words of love each day.

A STORY

A certain family had a wonderful way of letting one another know they care. Members of this family left surprise notes containing messages of love for one another. A note might pop up any place, anywhere, or anytime! No matter what the note actually

167

said, the message was clear: You are loved!

When Julie, the daughter in the family, was in elementary school, her mom would tuck notes inside her lunchbox. Years later, when Julie's parents took her to college many miles away, they came home to find special messages from Julie all over the house!

What a great feeling it was to come upon a note with the words, *I miss you, Have a happy day, You're the best, So-o-o proud of you,* or simply *Love you!*

 ## SHARING TOGETHER

Has your family ever left messages of love for one another? If so, share how it feels to give and receive such notes. If not, commit as a family to try this special tradition. Distribute paper and pencils to each family member. Parents, write a message of love to each of your children. Children, write one for your parents. Give them to one another now, or keep them and leave them to be discovered during the week.

 ## READING THE BIBLE TOGETHER

Read 1 John 4:7-11.

 ## FAMILY LITANY

One family member reads the litany and the family repeats the response together afterward.

Reader: Since God loves us, let us love one another.
All: **Let us think loving thoughts.**
Reader: Since God loves us, let us love one another.

All: **Let us speak loving words.**
Reader: Since God loves us, let us love one another.
All: **Let us do loving deeds.**
Reader: Since God loves us, let us love one another.
All: **Let us live a life of love. Amen.**

 # OPTIONAL ACTIVITY

See page 271.

 # February 18

A STORY

All family members help to read this story. Assign someone to say the lines of the people, the four men, Jesus, the scribes, and a narrator. Double up on parts if necessary.

Narrator: Word spreads quickly throughout Capernaum. Everyone is very excited!
People: Listen, have you heard? Jesus is here. He has come back to his home at Capernaum.
Narrator: A great crowd gathers at the place where Jesus is. So many people want to see and hear Jesus.
People: We can hardly move. Look, there isn't even room for anyone else in front of the door!
Narrator: Four men arrive, carrying their paralyzed friend on a mat. They come so that Jesus can help their friend.
The four men: There is no way to get through this crowd! We need a plan! Let's lower our friend through the roof and place him at the feet of Jesus.

Narrator: The four men climb onto the roof, dig a big hole, and gently let down the mat on which their paralytic friend lies.

Jesus: I see the faith of your friends. Son, your sins are forgiven.

Narrator: Some scribes are among the crowd. They do not like the words they hear.

Scribes: How can this man Jesus speak in this way? Only God can forgive sins.

Narrator: Jesus is aware of the scribes' feelings. He knows what they are talking about. Jesus wants to show the scribes that the Son of Man has authority on earth to forgive sins.

Jesus: Stand up, take your mat, and go home.

Narrator: The man does what Jesus tells him to do. The crowd is astonished!

People: What we have seen is amazing. Praise and glory to God!

SHARING TOGETHER

Share your reactions to the story. What does it say about the love of friends? Each family member can tell about a good friend he or she has and how the friend has shown love and care for him or her.

READING THE BIBLE TOGETHER

Listen to the story again as it is told in Mark 2:1-12.

PRAYING TOGETHER

Praise and thanks to you, Lord, for your love. Praise and thanks to you, Lord, for the love of friends. Thank you for…(each family member verbally or silently names their friends). Amen.

February 19

SOMETHING TO CONSIDER

Have you ever stood by the edge of a pond, picked up a pebble, and then tossed it into the water? If you have, you know that ripples are set in motion from the spot where the pebble hits the water. If you continue to watch, you will see the ripples reach the edge of the pond, bounce off the bank, and gently come back toward you. It has been said that love is like that. When we show love, our love goes out from us like the ripples in a stream to touch other people. Sometimes the love we give comes back to us, and we are blessed.

TELL US MORE

There is a special ministry of caring in many churches called the Stephen Ministry. This ministry is named after Stephen, the first Christian martyr. You can read the story of Stephen in your Bible in Acts 7:54-60. The primary purpose of this ministry is to reach out in love to those in a congregation or the immediate area who are facing serious problems such as illness. The people who commit to such a ministry devote much time to learning, praying, sharing with one another, and giving care in many ways to those in need. Above all, Stephen Ministers are trained to listen to others in a caring way. Stephen Ministers want to return the love that they have received during difficult times. They know how much love means, and they want to send those ripples of love back.

SHARING TOGETHER

Remember a time or times when your family has experienced an outpouring of love from others. How did it affect you? What feelings did you have? What happened as a result of that love?

READING THE BIBLE TOGETHER

Read John 15:12-17.

PRAYING TOGETHER

Lord, help us love one another as you have loved us. Amen.

OPTIONAL ACTIVITY

See page 271.

See page 271.

February 20

A STORY

The time on the clock reads 3 A.M., but Jim cannot sleep. He is wide awake and very excited about the fishing trip he is going to take in just a few hours. Jim loves to fish!

Jim's friend Tom, who also loves to fish, is going along this time.

To get ready for the trip, Jim has made all kinds of preparations. The boat is clean, filled with gas, and in good working order. Fishing poles have been checked and fitted with the proper fishing line. Jim has thoroughly gone through each one of his tackle boxes to make sure it contains just the right amount and types of lures to attract the fish. He has listened to the weather forecast to know what clothes he needs to wear and if it is safe to be on the water. He has studied a map of the lake and determined what he feels are the best fishing spots. A cooler filled with food and soft drinks is ready to go.

At last it is time for Jim to leave. As he steps outside, the sun is just rising, and it feels like it's going to be a beautiful day. For a moment he lovingly gives thanks for his father who taught him to fish and who was never too busy to take him on fishing trips. What wonderful memories he has of those times! Then Jim's thoughts turn toward the present and that five-pound bass he just knows he will catch today!

READING THE BIBLE TOGETHER

Read Mark 1:16-20.

IMAGINE THIS

Imagine that Jesus is calling you to go on a fishing trip with him. But instead of fishing for fish, Jesus wants you to help him fish for people, to help them know about God's love. What preparations would you need to make? What would you take with you? What types of things could you do to help others come to believe?

SINGING TOGETHER

Say the words below or sing them to the tune of "Holy, Holy, Holy."

Follow, follow, follow,
Go where Christ leads you.
Spreading the love of God wherever
  you might be.
Follow, follow, follow,
Go where Christ leads you.
Trust him to guide you and let love
  show the way.

PRAYING TOGETHER

Lord, help us to follow and go where you lead us. Help us to spread your love wherever we might be. Amen.

February 21

READING THE BIBLE TOGETHER

Read Mark 1:16-20.

IMAGINE THIS

Close your eyes. Clear your mind. Create this imaginary story. You are in a place you know well, a place where you often spend time. Picture this place in your mind. You are doing something you enjoy here. It is an activity you do often and one you feel comfortable doing. Maybe there are other people with you, or maybe you are alone.

You are interrupted from your activity by the sound of footsteps approaching. You turn and raise your eyes to see a kind-looking man standing before you. The man says, "I am Jesus." Then he holds out his hand, calls you by name and says, "Come, follow me. I want you to be my disciple." Why do you think Jesus is calling you? What do you say to Jesus?

Discuss what you have imagined and the questions from the story with one another.

SINGING TOGETHER

Say the words below or sing them to the tune of "Kum Ba Yah."

Jesus calls you to follow him. (Sing 3 times.)
Will you go and follow him?
Jesus calls you to spread God's love. (Sing 3 times.)
Will you go and follow him?
Jesus calls you to answer him. (Sing 3 times.)
Here I am, Lord. I will go!

PRAYING TOGETHER

Say this prayer echo style:

Lord, help me to listen.
Lord, help me to hear.
Lord, help me to follow.
Lord, help me to love.
Lord, help me to be your disciple. Amen.

February 22

READING THE BIBLE TOGETHER

Read Mark 4:30-32 and Luke 13:20-21.

A STORY

Every Christmas Amy looks forward to a special family tradition. She continues this tradition out of love for her family. It is the day she bakes stollen. Stollen is a German bread that Amy's grandmother and mother made every year at Christmas time. Baking stollen always brings to mind wonderful family memories. The bread takes all day to prepare and contains many different ingredients. One of the most important ingredients is the yeast. The yeast, when combined with the flour, causes the dough to multiply greatly in size. It always amazes Amy how a very small amount of yeast can make her dough grow to fill a large roasting pan to the brim!

Amy then divides the dough, places it in five loaf pans, and bakes the bread to a golden brown. Everyone in her family enjoys the wonderful bread over the Christmas holidays.

CONSIDER THIS

In our scripture readings, Jesus gives illustrations of two very small things—a mustard seed and yeast—which have the potential of growing and becoming something much greater. Perhaps Jesus is telling us that if we begin with just the smallest amount of faith, God's abundant love for us will help that faith to grow and grow and be multiplied many times over! Then, in turn, our faith will be living examples to others and help them learn about God and how God wants us to live. What a wonderful promise of God!

SHARING TOGETHER

It has been said that "The best gifts come in small packages." It is often the seemingly small, everyday acts of love—a prayer, a kind word, a hug—that can mean the most to someone and help God's love to grow.

Think about the tiny mustard seed from our Bible passage. Think about the many small ways you can express your faith in God and plant tiny seeds of love to spread the good news of Jesus Christ. Share these with one another. Tell about a time when an act of love was a special blessing to you. Who has helped you grow in your faith?

PRAYING TOGETHER

Read Psalm 92:1-4 as a closing prayer.

February 23

READING THE BIBLE TOGETHER

Read Matthew 28:16-20, known as the Great Commission, and talk about what Jesus was asking his disciples to do.

SHARING TOGETHER

Jesus' disciples were very effective in traveling about and spreading God's word. As Jesus' disciples today, how can we spread God's word? One way might be to set up a web site that people all over the world could access and find out what it means to be a disciple of Jesus Christ and how to become one. What a way to spread God's word! Whether or not you own a computer, think and talk about how your family could create a web site to help people become disciples of Jesus. Here are some questions that will help you decide what to include:

- What name or web address would you have to interest people?
- How would you explain what a disciple is?
- Who are some well-known disciples in our time?
- Who may become a disciple?
- How do you become one?
- What does a disciple do?
- Where do you get help for being a disciple?

PRAYING TOGETHER

Pray this prayer echo style:

Lord, come into my heart,
so that I may go where you lead me.
Lord, come into my heart,
so that I may go and make disciples. Amen.

LOOKING AHEAD

Have a flashlight ready for tomorrow.

February 24

A STORY

It is summertime and Elizabeth and her parents are spending a week at a cabin on the lake. Elizabeth is very excited because her dad has told her that she is finally old enough to go night fishing with him. For years, Elizabeth has heard her dad and her older brother, Jake, talk about how much fun night fishing is. Tonight just Elizabeth and her dad are going.

When it is almost dark, they set out on their adventure. Though it's several hours past her usual bedtime, Elizabeth isn't the least bit sleepy as the boat glides across the water. They find a good spot a long way from the shore and catch several fish.

Finally, Elizabeth and Dad decide it's time to head back to the cabin. But as Dad starts the engine, they are surprised to see that a thick blanket of fog has covered the entire area. Even the boat lights can't cut through the dense fog. How will they get back? It's too dangerous to drive the boat through the dark.

Elizabeth feels a little scared, but Dad has an idea. He eases the boat over to the shoreline and slowly follows it back to their cabin.

It seems like hours since they left their fishing spot. Elizabeth is tired and hungry; she wonders if they will ever make it back to the cabin. Dad doesn't say so, but Elizabeth has the feeling that he is worried too.

Suddenly, up ahead, a light shines brightly through the fog. "Look, Liz! It's the light from our cabin!" shouts Dad excitedly. "What a wonderful sight!"

READING THE BIBLE TOGETHER

Read Matthew 5:13-16.

CONSIDER THIS

Think about today's story. What might have happened if there hadn't been a light on at the cabin? Think about our scripture. Name some persons who have been lights for you and helped you to know Jesus and God's love. In the Bible reading, Christ says that we all can become lights to others. Why is it so important for each of us to let our lights shine?

SHARING TOGETHER

Make it as dark as possible in the area where your family is gathered. Pass the flashlight to each person. When each family member has the flashlight, he or she should turn it on and tell a way that he or she can be a light to others.

PRAYING TOGETHER

Repeat together:

Lord, help me to let my light shine and to glorify you! Amen.

LOOKING AHEAD

You will need a cream pitcher for tomorrow's devotion.

February 25

READING THE BIBLE TOGETHER

Read Deuteronomy 26:1-11.

SOMETHING TO CONSIDER

A long time ago most families had milk delivered to their homes. The milk came in a clear glass bottle. If you looked closely, you could see where the cream from the milk had risen to the top of the bottle. Of course, the cream is the richest and best part of the milk.

In today's scripture, Moses is telling the Israelites that they need to offer God the first of their fruits, not the second or last fruits of their harvest. Moses is saying, "Give God the cream of what you possess." Like the Israelites, we need to offer God the best of what we have, in response to God's great love for us.

SHARING TOGETHER

What loving gifts do we have to offer God? We can give God the gift of our time, our talents or abilities, and our possessions.

Think about the things you can do for God. Share these things with one another. Then write them on a slip of paper and place it in the cream pitcher as a commitment and reminder to give God the best you have!

FAMILY LITANY

One person reads the litany and signals to the family to join in with the response, "Help us to give you our best."

Reader: Dear God,
All: **Help us to give you our best.**
Reader: Let love guide us.
All: **Help us to give you our best.**
Reader: Each and every day.
All: **Help us to give you our best.**
Reader: And place you first in our lives.
All: **Help us to give you our best.**

Reader:	Let us serve you with gladness.
All:	**Help us to give you our best.**
Reader:	Help us to give of our time, talents, and treasure.
All:	**Help us to give you our best. Amen.**

OPTIONAL ACTIVITY

See page 271.

February 26

READING THE BIBLE TOGETHER

Read Exodus 3:1-12.

CONSIDER THIS

Have you ever been to the circus or watched one on television? Many of the circus acts involve risk and require a great deal of courage to perform. The flying trapeze is an example. The trapeze artist stands on a ledge high above the floor. As the trapeze swings toward the performer, he or she

leaps from the security of the ledge to grasp the flying trapeze and swing to a second ledge on the other side. When the performer leaps, there is a split second when he or she is suspended in midair. This person has jumped off the ledge, trusting that the trapeze will be there.

Sometimes our faith is like that. When God called Moses to leave the security of his home and lead the Israelites out of Egypt, Moses had to have the courage to trust in God. Moses had to believe that God would be with him and show him what he must do to free God's people from their bondage.

Not only was God there for Moses, but God is present for you and me too. Maybe God is calling you to help a friend in need, to teach Sunday school, to forgive someone who has hurt you, to speak out for a cause, to make a move, or to fulfill some commitment.

Whatever God calls us to do, we must take that leap of faith and know in our hearts that God will be there to guide us and show us the way.*

SHARING TOGETHER

Talk about a time when you felt God was calling you to do something that took courage. How difficult was it to trust that God would be there for you? Share your experience. What is God calling your family or members of your family to do at this time?

PRAYING TOGETHER

Someone prays and signals for all to repeat "Here I am, Lord."

Reader:	Help me to have the courage to reach out to you in faith.
All:	**Here I am, Lord.**

Reader: Help me to know in my heart that you are there to help me, guide me, and show me the way.

All: Here I am, Lord.

Reader: Help me to realize your great love for me.

All: Here I am, Lord.

Reader: I am here for you.

All: Amen.

*The central idea contained in today's reflection comes from a sermon by the Reverend Jerry Anderson, a United Methodist minister.

February 27

IMAGINE THIS

Picture in your mind a new video game. This is a special game called Follow Me! The object of the game is to overcome obstacles that appear on your imaginary screen as you try to follow Jesus and be a true disciple. As different obstacles come into view, you must choose how to eliminate them. To help decide, ask yourself how you think Jesus might deal with each situation. Play this game as a family team working together to solve each problem as it presents itself.

Are you ready to play? Remember to stay alert, and prepare to face the obstacles that will block your path. Press your start button, and have faith in Jesus to guide you. Your journey begins!

Obstacle 1 – Someone is making fun of you and hurts your feelings.

Obstacle 2 – You find yourself in a group of people that you like and where you want to be accepted as a member of the group. But they are going to try to shoplift from a store, and they want you to join in too.

Obstacle 3 – You have told a lie to keep from getting yourself in trouble.

Obstacle 4 – A family of a different nationality and race has moved into your neighborhood. Another neighbor who strongly feels that this family doesn't belong starts talking about the new people and criticizing the way they live.

Obstacle 5 – You have been asked to join a new ministry of your church, but it is something you have never done before and you don't feel confident about doing it.

You are nearing the ending of the game. You see the words *Follow Me!* flash on the screen.

READING THE BIBLE TOGETHER

Family members can take turns reading Psalm 37:3; Psalm 84:11-12; and Proverbs 3:5

PRAYING TOGETHER

The LORD bless you and keep you;
the LORD make his face to shine upon you,
and be gracious to you;
the LORD lift up his countenance upon you,
and give you peace (Num. 6:24-26).

February 28

READING THE BIBLE TOGETHER

Family members can take turns reading Ephesians 1:1-2; 1 Corinthians 1:1-3; and Colossians 1:1-2.

February 29

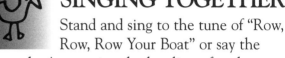

READING THE BIBLE TOGETHER

Read 2 Samuel 22:30-34.

TELL US MORE

The Apostle Paul wrote many letters because of his great love for Jesus and his desire to spread the word of God. Paul loved the people to whom he wrote. He sent letters to churches in many cities and also to individuals to guide, encourage, and help them as they tried to grow in their faith and draw others into the fellowship of believers.

The letters of Paul are found in the New Testament. Sometimes Paul wrote them personally and other times Paul dictated them to someone else. Ancient letters all began with a greeting. The scripture verses you read today are greetings from three of Paul's letters.

IMAGINE THIS

Let each family member imagine this scene: You are the Apostle Paul living in present times. You plan to dictate a letter to send to your church. What might your greeting be? What positive thoughts do you have to share? What ideas do you have to teach others about Jesus? Share with one another your thoughts.

PRAYING TOGETHER

Hold hands as someone reads the closing blessing in Ephesians 6:23-24.

SINGING TOGETHER

Stand and sing to the tune of "Row, Row, Row Your Boat" or say the words. As you sing the last line of each verse, take a leap forward.

Take, take, take a leap.
Take a leap of faith.
Trust in God to show the way.
Take a leap of faith!

Take, take, take a leap.
Take a leap of faith.
Always pray before you do.
Take a leap of faith!

Take, take, take a leap.
Take a leap of faith.
Don't let chances pass you by.
Take a leap of faith!

Take, take, take a leap.
Do not be afraid.
Know that God is by your side.
Take a leap of faith!

SHARING TOGETHER

If your family is using this particular devotion, it is a leap year. Leap years are unique because they occur only once every four years! In a leap year, the month of February has an extra day.

On this special day in leap year, think about your faith and what it means to take a leap of faith instead of a leap in days. Share with one another. What are some challenges or hurdles facing you or your family right now? Is there something you feel God is calling you to do, but you are afraid to try? Are there people who need your love and forgiveness, but for some reason you have been unable to respond? Is your family facing an illness, a move, or some other change? How does your faith help you in situations like these? What does today's scripture have to say about faith?

PRAYING TOGETHER

Invite family members to lift up challenges they are facing. One family member can close the prayer time by praying this prayer:

> We give these challenges to you, God.
> Give us the love and the will
> to take a leap of faith
> and put our trust in you. Amen.

MARCH

READING THE BIBLE TOGETHER

Read Mark 1:12-13.

CONSIDER THIS

Every year many churches observe a season leading up to Easter called Lent. Lent is 40 days, not counting Sundays. In the Bible, 40 is a special number. It is often used to speak about a time of preparation, waiting, praying, or struggle in which God is present in a special way. In today's reading, Mark tells us that Jesus was in the wilderness, for 40 days. This happened just after Jesus was baptized and just before he began his ministry of teaching and healing people. It was an important time of preparation for Jesus, a time to make room for God before beginning his work with people.

The season of Lent always begins on a Wednesday called Ash Wednesday. On that day many people attend services in which ash is placed on their foreheads in the sign of a cross as a reminder that all things come from the earth and that Jesus died on a cross as a sign of love for us. Has your family been to an Ash Wednesday service?

Good Friday, two days before Easter, marks the day Jesus died on a cross. It is called Good Friday rather than Bad Friday because Jesus' love for people—even those who put him to death—was so strong and good.

Easter is like the word east, which reminds us that just as the sun rises in the east to warm the earth, so God raises Jesus from the dead, and God will raise up Jesus' followers too. For Christians, Easter is the biggest day of joy and celebration of the whole year.

SHARING TOGETHER

Think of an Easter memory. Does it include the joy of new life, new discovery, or a new promise? How could your family prepare for such an Easter festival? How can you make room for God in your life and in your family's life during the season of Lent? You may want to have less TV, radio, and online activities and more time for prayer, Bible study, and helping others. You can give money to a special project and attend worship and Sunday school regularly.

On the calendar, find the date for Easter this year. Then begin counting backward 40 days, beginning with the day before Easter (Holy Saturday) and skipping Sundays. You should arrive on a Wednesday, the day we call Ash Wednesday. Imagine Jesus spending all that time in the desert, and with wild beasts!

PRAYING TOGETHER

The prayer below is a paraphrase of Psalm 16:5. It is suggested for use each time your family gathers for devotions during the season of Lent. Take time to discuss what you will do as you pray this prayer. You may want to light a candle or hold hands in a circle before reading it each day. Today, if possible, let two family members read the prayer, either in unison or alternating phrases.

> You, Lord, are all we have.
> You give us all we need.
> Our lives are in your hands. Amen.

OPTIONAL ACTIVITIES

See special Lenten and Easter activities on pages 271–272.

LOOKING AHEAD

Collect baptismal photos for tomorrow's devotional time if you have them.

March 2

PRAYING TOGETHER

You, Lord, are all we have.
You give us all we need.
Our lives are in your hands. Amen.

READING THE BIBLE TOGETHER

Read Mark 1:9-11 together.

CONSIDER THIS

When Jesus was about thirty, he came to be baptized by John. Mark tells us that when Jesus came up out of the water, he heard a voice from heaven. What did that voice say?

Do you remember a time when someone who means a lot to you said, "I love you," or "I'm proud of you"? Imagine how Jesus felt when he heard his Father in heaven say these things to him!

If you have been baptized, are there pictures of that event? If so, who else is in the pictures with you? Are they people who love you the way God loves Jesus?

TELL US MORE

If you read the next few verses in your Bible (Mark 1:12-13), you will see what happens next—Jesus is sent out into the wilderness for 40 days to get ready for his ministry. For 40 days he will be in a dry, out-of-the-way place! But he has just been baptized, and he has just heard those special words from God. These things will help sustain him through the hard experiences of the desert.

SHARING TOGETHER

Discuss with one another times in your life that were really hard. What helped you through that time? The encouragement of certain people? A memory of something or someone? Looking forward to something coming later? A prayer or Bible verse or story?

PRAYING TOGETHER

Let a parent place his or her hands on each child and say, "(name), you are

God's beloved son/daughter. With you God is well pleased, and so am I." Then have children place their hands on the parent and offer the same blessing.

OPTIONAL ACTIVITIES

See page 272.

March 3

PRAYING TOGETHER

You, Lord, are all we have.
You give us all we need.
Our lives are in your hands. Amen.

READING THE BIBLE TOGETHER

Read Luke 4:1-13.

CONSIDER THIS

Luke tells us that Jesus was tempted in the wilderness by the devil. Each time the devil offered him something really attractive but wrong, Jesus said no, remembering a verse from scripture.

See if you can find the three things the devil offered Jesus, and the three scripture verses Jesus recalled to turn the devil down.

SHARING TOGETHER

Many times temptation is about wanting something that doesn't belong to us or being offered something we really shouldn't

have. Sometimes standing up to temptation is just a matter of saying no at the right times. "No, I won't do that—it's wrong." "No, I won't say that—it's not the truth."

Can you think of some examples of temptations that are most easily answered by saying no? Is saying no sometimes hard? What verse or story from the Bible might help you in making a choice or deciding on a direction?

A STORY

Act out this story of temptation without using any words. One person can be the tempter, trying to lead the second person to do something that is wrong (taking something that is not his or hers, talking back to a teacher, playing instead of cleaning up, cheating on a test, making fun of someone, etc.) The second person refuses to do the wrong thing. Take turns playing the two roles.

PRAYING TOGETHER

Let members of the family, one by one, add words to complete the sentence. They can use examples of temptations they may face in their lives. After each person speaks, the whole family responds with the words, *Give us the courage to say no.*

Individuals: God, I am tempted when . . . (describe the temptation).

All: Give us the courage to say no.

March 4

PRAYING TOGETHER

You, Lord, are all we have.
You give us all we need.
Our lives are in your hands. Amen.

READING THE BIBLE TOGETHER

Read Mark 1:12-13 together.

IMAGINE THIS

Mark doesn't say as much as Matthew and Luke about the time Jesus spent in the wilderness, but he gives us some other things to think about. Let's imagine what it was like for Jesus from the description Mark gives us. Choose one person (probably a grown-up) to read the following imaginative experience. All others should find a comfortable spot, close their eyes, and take a few deep breaths as the reader begins.

Imagine you have just had the most wonderful experience of your life. You have been baptized, and everyone you know and love was there—family, friends, your favorite teachers and Sunday school teachers, other people you know from church, your favorite neighbors, maybe a favorite coach. It was a wonderful, wonderful day, and you have felt the love and closeness of God ever since.

Now imagine that a difficult challenge is ahead for you. You must go into the wilderness to be alone with God in prayer. You say your good-byes and begin your journey. You walk for what seems like miles, until there is no one in

sight—only cliffs, jagged rocks, sand, and the broiling sun. You are there to pray, but your eyes are studying the surroundings for signs of danger. Sure enough, you see a snake slither from under a rock. Moments later, a lion leaps from one hidden crevice to another. It seems to have its eye on you. Your heart is pounding now. You wonder what kind of place this is. The sun beats down. Sweat is forming on your brow. Your knees are weak from hunger and fear.

Suddenly you feel a warm presence nearby. It is not unlike the feeling you had days before when so many dear people surrounded you at your baptism. You know they are not out here, but someone certainly is. You can feel a presence like a ring of protection and safety. It must be angels! Angels have come to watch over you and guard you from danger—God is taking care of you! Your heart begins to quiet; your knees are strong again. The fear is gone. You are in God's hands, and everything is going to be okay.

Now take a deep breath or two, and when you are ready, open your eyes.

SHARING TOGETHER

What was it like imagining yourself in a lonely place, surrounded by snakes and wild creatures? Mark tells us that angels helped take care of Jesus in the desert. Did you feel them surrounding you there? Could you see them too or were they invisible?

Sometimes we talk about angels watching

over us. Can you think of a time when you were taken care of or protected from some harm, and later it seemed there must have been someone looking out for you?

SINGING TOGETHER

As your closing prayer, sing or read this spiritual together:

Refrain:
All night, all day, angels watching over me, my Lord.
All night, all day, angels watching over me.

Verse:
Now I lay me down to sleep.
Angels watching over me, my Lord.
Pray the Lord my soul will keep.
Angels watching over me.

Refrain:
All night, all day, angels watching over me, my Lord.
All night, all day, angels watching over me.

OPTIONAL ACTIVITIES

See page 272.

March 5

PRAYING TOGETHER

You, Lord, are all we have.
You give us all we need.
Our lives are in your hands. Amen.

READING THE BIBLE TOGETHER

Together look at Mark 1:14-34. Make a list of everything Jesus does in these verses. Now have one person read Mark 1:35. Then read the verse again, phrase by phrase, with the rest of the group echoing each phrase.

CONSIDER THIS

After he returns from the wilderness, Jesus' life becomes very busy. People want to see him. He encounters many different situations, and he is eager to teach and heal as well. Jesus seems to keep a very fast pace in his work and teaching. Yet even with a busy life, he chooses to make time to be alone with God.

SHARING TOGETHER

Sometimes we say that prayer is talking to God and listening to God. It's that simple! And yet, sometimes talking about certain things can be hard for us, and listening for a reply or direction can be even harder. What things are easy to talk with God about? What things are hard? How do you listen for what God may be saying to you?

Sometimes praying alone is easier for us than praying with others, at least at first. Have each family member go off alone for four or five minutes to pray.

If you have a hard time getting started, pretend God is sitting with you. Tell God something about your day or week that is a good thing and something that is difficult. Some families call this "Highs and Lows."

Jesus would also have been listening to God during his prayer time. What might God say back to you to complete the conversation? If at first your mind wanders, try writing a letter to God, then writing a reply from God.

After your time away, come back together for a closing prayer or to share what your time alone with God was like.

LOOKING AHEAD

Buy or bake some pretzels with crossed loops for tomorrow's devotional.

March 6

PRAYING TOGETHER

You, Lord, are all we have.
You give us all we need.
Our lives are in your hands. Amen.

READING THE BIBLE TOGETHER

Read together 1 Thessalonians 5:17.

CONSIDER THIS

One of the shortest verses in the Bible, this phrase gives big directions: *pray without ceasing!* Sometimes praying is all we do at a given time, such as in worship or in personal quiet time. But we can also pray while we do other things, such as washing dishes, taking a walk, or getting ready for school. Lent is a good time to practice praying at a specific time and also to learn how to pray at other times through the day.

A STORY

A long time ago, in the seventh century, members of a German monastery were preparing for the season of Lent. A monastery is a place where people choose to live their whole lives focusing on prayer and knowing God. In those days, just as in ours, Lent was a season in which people observed certain simpler ways of eating and living—less fancy food, fewer extra activities, more time for prayer and serving.

In this monastery, a monk was cooking some simple food for the season when he decided to make a kind of salted bread in the shape of praying arms. It was common during that time to pray with arms crossed over the chest, while hands were placed on the shoulders. The monk took a rope of dough and shaped it into these praying arms. The Latin word for arms is *brachia*, from which came the German word *pretzel*. The monk hoped that having pretzels at mealtime would be just one more reminder that Lent is a special season of prayer and that a person can pray, as today's Bible verse says, at all times—even when eating a pretzel!

PRAYING TOGETHER

Cross your arms over your chest in the shape of a pretzel. Now pray this prayer echo style:

Dear God,
Teach us to pray at school and at home,
at work and at rest,
with friends and alone,

in chores and in fun,
in sadness and joy,
at church and away.
Teach us to pray.
Amen.

OPTIONAL ACTIVITY
See page 273.

March 7

PRAYING TOGETHER
You, Lord, are all we have.
You give us all we need.
Our lives are in your hands. Amen.

READING THE BIBLE TOGETHER

Read together Psalm 33:20-22.

CONSIDER THIS

Sometimes we want to pray for one another in the family, and yet it is hard to know how to express our deepest prayers for another person. One way to pray is to let the Bible guide our words as we pray.

PRAYING TOGETHER
Have one person at a time sit in the middle of a circle or within arm's reach of everyone else. Others can place a hand on that person's head or shoulders, as one leads the rest in prayer for this person. Borrow from the psalm you've just read to shape your prayer. For example: *Dear God, may Sarah's soul wait for you. May she know that you are her help and shield. May Sarah's heart be glad in you, and may she trust in your holy name. May your steadfast love be upon her, Lord, even as she hopes in you. Amen.*

Repeat the prayer for each person present. If someone you care about is ill or in need you may want to repeat the prayer using that person's name too.

March 8

PRAYING TOGETHER
You, Lord, are all we have.
You give us all we need.
Our lives are in your hands. Amen.

CONSIDER THIS
We will spend the next seven days reading and telling stories from the Book of Exodus about the people of Israel, Moses, and God.

READING THE BIBLE TOGETHER

Read Exodus 1:1-14; 2:23-25.

TELL US MORE

Things were going from bad to worse for the people of Israel. They had come to Egypt many years earlier to find food and live in safety. Now they were not being treated well at all by the Egyptian rulers. Things were so bad that the Israelites groaned and cried out in their misery. We can imagine their cries: *How long can this go on? God, help us! Rescue us! Save us!* They must have felt as though God had forgotten them and was a million miles away.

But God was not far away and had not forgotten the people. God heard their cry, saw their great suffering, and began to act.

SHARING TOGETHER

Can you imagine what it must have been like to be a slave? Everything you did would be decided by somebody else—your work, your free time, where you lived, what you had to eat. Do you know of groups or a whole country where people live in hardship because of their rulers? Even if they are not slaves, perhaps they have very little freedom or lack the basic things they need to be healthy and strong.

Look at Exodus 2:24-25; find the different verbs used to describe the ways God responded to the cry of the people. Make plans to collect an offering during Lent from whatever money or allowance you have to help people in trouble. Set it aside in a simple offering container for this purpose. At the end of Lent, donate the money to an agency that helps suffering people.

PRAYING TOGETHER

Sometimes the writers of the psalms and the prophets express their weariness with suffering in their prayers. They often use two phrases to cry out to God: "How long, O Lord?" and "Hear us in your mercy." Together name some needs you always seem to have as a family or needs you often see in the world. As each need is expressed, let a parent paraphrase it and fold it into a prayer such as this: *How long, O Lord, will we have to wait for Jonas to be healthy again? Hear us in your mercy.*

LOOKING AHEAD

You will need crayons and paper for tomorrow's devotion.

March 9

PRAYING TOGETHER

You, Lord, are all we have.
You give us all we need.
Our lives are in your hands. Amen.

READING THE BIBLE TOGETHER

Read together Exodus 3:1-12.

CONSIDER THIS

The flaming bush that Moses saw burned on and on. In a way, God's love is like that—going on and on and never ending. God said from the flame, "I am the

God of your father, the God of Abraham, the God of Isaac, and the God of Jacob." God goes back a long, long way, even to the beginning of time! And God was there for the people in Egypt who were in trouble, and God wanted to help them. Like a flame that never stops giving light and warmth, God's love is always near. Moses was curious about the burning bush at first. How could it continue to burn without burning up? When he found out that God was speaking from the bush, Moses was no longer curious—he was afraid!

SHARING TOGETHER

Have you ever seen or heard about something that seemed too amazing to be real? Some speak of Niagara Falls that way, or the Grand Canyon, or Mount Everest, or the great Amazon River basin. Imagine what it would be like to hear God's voice come from one of these places. What would it sound like? Do you think that if you heard such a voice you would be scared as Moses was?

Look at the ways the Bible says God responded to the cries of the people in trouble in Egypt. See if you can name them all, after reading verses 7-10. Is there any doubt that God was going to act?

Draw a picture of a small bush with branches and green leaves. Then, with other crayon colors, draw fire over it. Place your picture on the refrigerator or in your room, and let it remind you this week that God's love for us is like a flame that will never go out.

PRAYING TOGETHER

Dear God, thank you that you hear the cries of those in need and that you always hear us when we cry or are hurting. You are like a steady flame that will never go out, warming us and lighting our way. Amen.

March 10

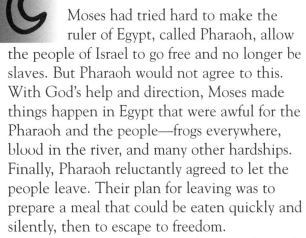

PRAYING TOGETHER

You, Lord, are all we have.
You give us all we need.
Our lives are in your hands. Amen.

CONSIDER THIS

Moses had tried hard to make the ruler of Egypt, called Pharaoh, allow the people of Israel to go free and no longer be slaves. But Pharaoh would not agree to this. With God's help and direction, Moses made things happen in Egypt that were awful for the Pharaoh and the people—frogs everywhere, blood in the river, and many other hardships. Finally, Pharaoh reluctantly agreed to let the people leave. Their plan for leaving was to prepare a meal that could be eaten quickly and silently, then to escape to freedom.

The Passover meal was to be eaten by each family in a hurry, so they could be ready to leave at a moment's notice. They were to be fully dressed, with sandals on their feet and a walking stick in their hands. Can you imagine eating a meal with a walking stick in one hand? At the Passover meal, leaving was just as important as eating.

READING THE BIBLE TOGETHER

Read Exodus 12:1-13.

SINGING TOGETHER

Either sing or say the words to this traditional spiritual, "Oh, Freedom":

Oh, freedom! Oh, freedom!
Oh, freedom over me!
An' befo' I'd be a slave,
I'll be buried in my grave,
An' go home to my Lord an' be free.

PRAYING TOGETHER

God of freedom, Lord of love, we remember now those who are in need and who wait for your deliverance. Some may be nearby, even in our own home, and others far away. Give all of these who wait to be free what they need in their waiting and come quickly to bring them out to freedom. Amen.

OPTIONAL ACTIVITY

See page 273.

LOOKING AHEAD

Bring dolls, toy figures, or puppets and a beige sheet or cloth and two blue sheets or cloths for tomorrow's devotion.

March 11

PRAYING TOGETHER

You, Lord, are all we have.
You give us all we need.
Our lives are in your hands. Amen.

A STORY

The time had finally come for the people of Israel to escape from Egypt, where they had been living as slaves for over four hundred years. But Pharaoh, the ruler, chased after them with his powerful army. The Israelites were hurrying as fast as they could, but when they came to the Red Sea, with nowhere to turn, they felt sure they were going to be captured again, or worse!

They cried out to God in fear. And just as God had heard their cry when they were slaves in Egypt, God heard them again. God told Moses to hold out his staff over the water, and the sea was divided, forming a path with a great wall of water on the left and on the right. The Israelites walked through and safely reached the other side.

Pharaoh and the Egyptian army decided to chase them through the dried-up sea as well. But just as the Egyptian army had filled the floor of the sea, the waters came crashing down on them, and they were drowned.

When the Israelites had reached the other side, caught their breath, and looked around, they realized something marvelous—they were free!

READING THE BIBLE TOGETHER

Read this story from the Bible now. Part of it is found in Exodus 14:10-16, 21-29.

CONSIDER THIS

Can you remember a time when you had to do something really scary and even though you were scared, you went ahead and did it? How was that like the Israelites' escaping Egypt and passing through the Red Sea? When you finally did that difficult thing, were you less afraid afterward? Can you picture your fear and nervousness chasing you from behind and your fear being swallowed up by the water?

SHARING TOGETHER

Set up a scene of the Exodus. You could use dolls, toy figures, puppets, etc. Lay out a beige piece of cloth or sheet for the desert and two blue pieces for the Red Sea. Act out the story you read and discussed.

SINGING TOGETHER

If your family knows this song, called "Wade in the Water," sing it together. If you don't know the song, let someone read the words.

Refrain:
Wade in the water, wade in the water, children,
Wade in the water, God's a'gonna trouble the water.

Verse 1:
See that band all dressed in white—
God's a'gonna trouble the water.
The leader looks like an Israelite—
God's a'gonna trouble the water.
Refrain: (as above)

Verse2:
See that band all dressed in red—
God's a'gonna trouble the water.
It looks like the band that Moses led.
God's a'gonna trouble the water.
Refrain: (as above)

PRAYING TOGETHER

Share this prayer responsively:

One: God, you heard the cry of your people.
All: **Alleluia!**
One: You opened up the sea.
All: **Alleluia!**
One: You led the people through.
All: **Alleluia!**
One: You brought them safely to the dry land.
All: **Alleluia!**
One: God, you brought your people to freedom; and we have never been the same.
All: **Alleluia!**

LOOKING AHEAD

Prepare musical instruments for tomorrow's activity in Sharing Together.

March 12

PRAYING TOGETHER

You, Lord, are all we have.
You give us all we need.
Our lives are in your hands. Amen.

READING THE BIBLE TOGETHER

When the Israelites arrived on the other side of the Red Sea, they realized they were free from slavery. They wanted a way to celebrate.

And so they sang, danced, and played music. We still have some of their songs. They are found in the Bible in the Book of Exodus.

Read together Exodus 15:1-2, 20-21.

Praise God, praise God,
   praise God in the morning,
   praise God in the noontime!
Praise God, praise God,
   praise God when the sun goes down!

SHARING TOGETHER

Imagine how the people of Israel felt after they realized they were finally safe from the Egyptian army—they had made it to freedom!
Have you ever been in trouble or in a frightening situation? How did you feel when it was finally over?

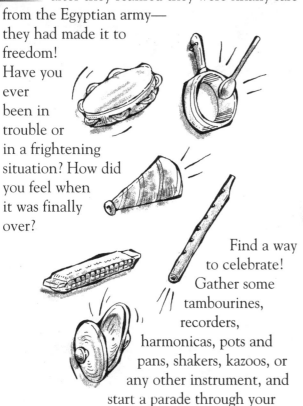

Find a way to celebrate! Gather some tambourines, recorders, harmonicas, pots and pans, shakers, kazoos, or any other instrument, and start a parade through your house or in your yard or a parking lot. Older children may enjoy setting up a percussion section of rhythm instruments as you sing around the table. Others may prefer to make up a dance to the words in the song below. If you know the song, sing it as you parade.

SINGING TOGETHER

Sing or chant this song as you parade, dance, or play your instruments.

PRAYING TOGETHER

You, Lord, are all we have.
You give us all we need.
Our lives are in your hands. Amen.

CONSIDER THIS

The people of Israel were finally free! They had endured slavery for so long, but now they were out from under that heavy burden. Now no one would tell them what to do, where to go, or how to live. They had freedom, but they still needed to eat! And in the desert, finding food was a problem. The scripture reading for today talks about how God provided for this need for food to eat, which we sometimes call daily bread.

READING THE BIBLE TOGETHER

Exodus 16:2-4, 13-18.

A STORY

Minerva was nervous the whole way to camp. She had never been away from home for a whole week before, and she didn't know anybody else who was going to this church camp.

Minerva and her family had just moved from another state two weeks earlier, so she didn't even know the other children from the church in her neighborhood that had arranged for her to go to camp. Would she like those kids? Would they like her? What about the counselors? And the food? Would there be any fun at all, or just work and lessons and stuff? It was all a big, scary question mark!

She and her mother pulled into the parking lot, unloaded her things, and signed her in. After a kiss and a hug, her mother drove back down the long driveway toward home.

Minerva wanted so much to be in the car with her, heading back home herself. Even though she didn't have any friends at home, at least she had her family. She felt a tear roll down her cheek and wiped it away with her shoulder. Then she remembered something her dad always told her when he knew she was afraid or worried about something. He would kiss her on the top of her head and say, "God will provide, little Mimi."

Just then a counselor approached her and introduced herself. "Come on down to the cabin," she said. "I want you to meet the rest of our cabin group. I'll help you get your stuff."

Soon Minerva was being swept into activities and meeting new people. And she liked it all—introductions, finding common interests, learning and playing and eating together, Bible study, discussion, games, campfire, sharing time. Some of the new friends she was making were even from her new church.

By the middle of the week, Minerva was wondering why church camp couldn't go for two weeks instead of just one. She remembered again her dad's words, "God will provide," and smiled to herself. "Thank you, God, for providing," she whispered.

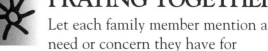

PRAYING TOGETHER

Let each family member mention a need or concern they have for themselves or someone else. As a response, all can say, "God will provide." Go around a second time, with each person naming a prayer answered or offering a thanksgiving, and the family responding, "Thank you, God, for providing."

March 14

PRAYING TOGETHER

You, Lord, are all we have.
You give us all we need.
Our lives are in your hands. Amen.

READING THE BIBLE TOGETHER

Read Exodus 17:1-7.

IMAGINE THIS

Imagine that you are with the people of Israel traveling through the desert. You have a whole world of memories from the last several weeks—fleeing Egypt, the place where you and your family had been slaves; crossing through the Red Sea as though it were dry land; dancing and singing with all the people in a celebration bigger and happier than any you had ever seen; seeing food appear as if from nowhere to feed your family and the others who traveled with you.

Now you face another challenge, maybe the most serious of all—thirst. In the desert, water has become more precious than gold, and over the last few days it has been hard to find water anywhere nearby. You are growing very thirsty, thirsty in a way you have never been before. Your mouth is sticky and dry. Every time you swallow there is a rough feeling in your throat, as if you are trying to swallow sand.

Meanwhile, the sun is bearing down on you, and sand is blowing in your face. Your family's tent provides the only protection.

Because you haven't had enough water, you are growing tired and weak. You don't feel like doing anything but sitting or lying down in the tent. All you think about is water. When will the leaders find water for all to drink? When will this long wait be over? You know that no one can live for long without water. How long is that, you wonder—another day? a week?

Your imagination begins to wander, and you picture yourself walking with your friends toward a cool, clear stream. You all wade in, cupping your hands and drinking your fill of water, spilling it all over your faces and clothes. Once you have had all you can drink, you splash and play and laugh together until you are all soaked from head to toe. Then you lie down in the stream and let the cool, refreshing water rush around you as you gaze up at the blue sky.

Suddenly you are interrupted from your faraway thoughts. Your father has just come back to the tent, excited with some news: Moses has found water nearby, among some rocks. The place is just a short walk from where you are! Everyone springs to life and follows the crowd in the direction of the water. Once again, God has provided!

CONSIDER THIS

Even though the people of Israel had learned that God would provide for their every need, they soon forgot again. When they were thirsty, they began to grumble and complain to Moses. Sometimes when we are angry or impatient, we become sarcastic— saying things we know aren't true. That's just what happened with the people of Israel. In their anger they said to Moses, "Why did you bring us out of Egypt, to kill us?"

Once again, God provided for the people— this time, water from a rock! Once again, God heard the cries of the people and reminded them that they would be provided for. This time God directed Moses to strike a rock and find water.

SINGING TOGETHER

If you are familiar with the song "Deep and Wide," sing it together using hand motions.

> Deep and wide, deep and wide,
> there's a fountain flowing deep and
>   wide.
> Deep and wide, deep and wide,
> there's a fountain flowing deep and
>   wide.

PRAYING TOGETHER

We thank you, God, for the simple things: food to eat, shelter from weather, clothes to wear, clean air to breathe, love to share, and water to drink. Give us one thing more, we ask: hearts to trust in you. Amen.

LOOKING AHEAD

Have a basket or container ready for each person tomorrow.

March 15

PRAYING TOGETHER

You, Lord, are all we have.
You give us all we need.
Our lives are in your hands. Amen.

CONSIDER THIS

Sometimes Jesus told stories called parables. Parables were a way of talking about God and God's world without explaining everything. They are more awesome and mysterious than explanations—they are like a story we can learn from. The parable of the pearl of great value is one good example.

READING THE BIBLE TOGETHER

Read Matthew 13:45-46.

IMAGINE THIS

Imagine what it would be like to be a merchant who buys only the finest pearls in the world. You would have eyes trained for the proper look and luster of a pearl, hands trained for the proper feel and weight of a pearl, and a business sense to know the worth of one pearl over another.

Imagine your excitement when one day you come across the most beautiful pearl in the world. Maybe you would know right away that in order to purchase that pearl, you would have to sell every other pearl you had and all your other possessions as well. Jesus seems to be saying that finding God and God's ways is like finding that special pearl.

Pretend you are a pearl merchant, and you have just found the most beautiful pearl you have ever seen. Make a list of the things you have that mean the very most to you. Imagine yourself giving these up in order to buy the one great pearl. You can even act this out: Set up a shop with an imaginary pearl on the shelf; then let each person take a container or basket and go throughout the house to fill it with some of their favorite things. One at a time, put them on the counter to trade for the pearl, until they are all given away.

PRAYING TOGETHER

God, you are our pearl of great price, more awesome, more beautiful, more to be treasured than any other thing in life. All that we have—our home, our clothes, our toys, all our favorite things—mean so much less than knowing you. Amen.

LOOKING AHEAD

Tomorrow you will need crayons and paper for each person.

March 16

PRAYING TOGETHER

You, Lord, are all we have.
You give us all we need.
Our lives are in your hands. Amen.

READING THE BIBLE TOGETHER

Read Matthew 18:21-22.

A STORY

Patrick was a young boy living happily with his family in Britain long ago. He had a normal childhood—school, playing with friends, weekend adventures, helping around the house. But when Patrick was sixteen, he was kidnapped from home by pirates on the sea. They took him away from his country and sold him as a slave to some people in Ireland, a country north of Britain. For six years, Patrick tended herds of sheep in a place that became very cold in the winter and was far from home. There he had no school, no friends, and no weekend adventures, only work.

Finally, at the age of twenty-two, he escaped and was reunited with his family in Britain. Imagine how Patrick must have felt toward the pirates and the people in Ireland who had made him a slave! The best years of his youth had been taken away from him.

Shortly after his return home, Patrick was praying one day when he heard God speak to him. God was calling him to go back to Ireland, not to get even with the people there, but to love them. God wanted Patrick to share the Christian faith with the people there.

So Patrick went back to Ireland, this time without being forced to go by pirates. He spent the rest of his life loving the people there and sharing the stories of the Bible. He started many churches too—about 300 in all! He died on March 17, 461 C.E. Ever since, many people have remembered Patrick's courage, forgiveness, and love for God and people, especially on March 17, Saint Patrick's Day!

SHARING TOGETHER

The blessing below is often used on Saint Patrick's Day. Let each person pick out a phrase or two from the blessing and describe what it brings to mind.

PRAYING TOGETHER

Say together or say in echo style this blessing:

May the road rise to meet you,
may the wind be always at your back,
may the sun shine warm on your face,
the rain fall softly on your fields;
and until we meet again,
may God hold you in the palm of
his hand.

LOOKING AHEAD

You will need a clover leaf or a picture of one for tomorrow.

March 17

PRAYING TOGETHER

You, Lord, are all we want.
You give us all we need.
Our lives are in your hands. Amen.

READING THE BIBLE TOGETHER

Read together Mark 16:15.

A STORY

While he was a missionary in Ireland, Saint Patrick started many churches and baptized many, many people. He taught them about God's love and care in their lives. One time he wanted to explain a very confusing idea— the Trinity. He plucked a three-leaf clover from the ground and said the Trinity was like a leaf of clover—three in one: God the Father, God the Son (Jesus), and God the Holy Spirit.

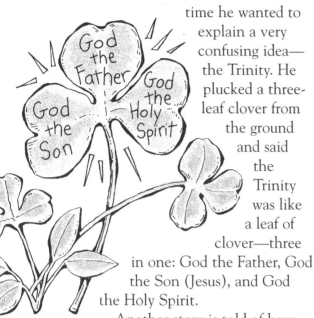

Another story is told of how, when snakes were causing many problems for the Irish farmers and sheepherders, Patrick led all the snakes out to the sea, and they were never to be seen again!

When asked by some people to tell them about God, Patrick did not explain God with ideas and theories. Instead, he sang a song, a great prayer celebrating the work of God in the whole universe. It is printed as the prayer to end today's devotional time.

SHARING TOGETHER

Patrick spent most of his life teaching people who had never heard of God or Jesus or the Bible. Imagine that you wanted to teach these things to someone who knew nothing about them. What would you say about God? about Jesus? about the Bible? How would you explain the Trinity or Jesus' calming a storm?

PRAYING TOGETHER

The prayer Saint Patrick shared with the people who were asking about God went something like this:

I buckle to my heart
This day,
The love of God
To show the way,
His eye to watch,
His ear to hear,
His hand to lead
Me on the way.*

*J. Janda, *The Story of St. Patrick* (New York: Paulist Press, 1995).

March 18

PRAYING TOGETHER

You, Lord, are all we have.
You give us all we need.
Our lives are in your hands. Amen.

CONSIDER THIS

Jesus told stories and used examples from common life to explain who God is and what it means to live as God's people in the world. The saying about the mustard seed is an example of how he taught in parables.

READING THE BIBLE TOGETHER

Read together Matthew 13:31-32.

MORE TO CONSIDER

The mustard shrub in Jesus' parable would be an important source of income for the person who sowed it in the field. What Jesus emphasized, however, was not that it produced a lot of mustard, but that it became a great nesting place for the birds of the air! Sometimes God's ways in the world are not the same as our expectations. Can you think of a time when what you started to do was changed, and it became something even better than you had planned?

SHARING TOGETHER

Go outdoors or open a window and listen for the sounds of birds. (If it's rainy or not a good time for bird-spotting, recall birds you've seen or heard in the past.) How many different birds do you hear? Can you see some? Describe them. Can you figure out which song is from which bird? Remember that every bird you hear or see has a home somewhere. Have you ever found a bird's nest in a tree or in the brush?

Do you think God's kingdom has a home for every person? For you?

PRAYING TOGETHER

Naming each person in your family, have a reader lead the prayer below until all members of the family have been named. Then you may wish to add others.

Thank you, God, that (name) has a place with you. Amen.

LOOKING AHEAD

You will need small beanbags in addition to paper and pencils tomorrow.

March 19

PRAYING TOGETHER

You, Lord, are all we have.
You give us all we need.
Our lives are in your hands. Amen.

READING THE BIBLE TOGETHER

Read Philippians 4:10-13.

TELL US MORE

When Paul wrote this letter to the people in the church of Philippi, he was in prison! Can you imagine writing about being content while you were in prison? Paul must have really known a special secret, just as he says—the secret of being content with little or a lot. He tells us that secret in verse 13: It is the secret of finding strength in God.

A STORY

It was a late Saturday afternoon like most others. Everybody was just coming in from soccer and the library and running errands. There was dinner to fix, then the older children were planning to watch a video in the den while their little sister played with her computer painting program in the playroom. Mrs. Rosset had some e-mails to send and other work to do at the computer.

Suddenly, without any warning, the lights flickered, then went out. "Oh, cool," Luke said. "The power went out." But he didn't realize what that was going to mean for his plans.

Everyone carried on with what they were doing, until they happened to remember that there was no power—picking up the cordless phone to call a friend ("oh, yeah, there's no power") or turning on the microwave to start dinner ("oh, that's right, the electricity's out"). Again and again they were brought up short as they began to do something by the force of habit. At first everybody was a little upset, realizing what they were giving up—movies, video games, the computer.

But as the evening went on, the lack of power in their house became something like an adventure. They went from one simplifying decision to another: simple dinner, simple cleanup, simple plans for the evening. The family went outside and stood studying the stars and the half-moon. Then they saw some neighbors down the street with a flashlight, so they walked down to say hello to them— neighbors they really didn't know well at all.

No one seemed in a hurry to leave; but eventually the Rossets went indoors, lit some candles, and sat around the living room. They started telling stories, first remembering other times the power had gone out, then snow days, then a time Mr. Rosset's car had broken down on the highway. They laughed and teased and filled in one another's stories. They sat silent for stretches, and then someone would start up again with another story. Before they knew it, it was bedtime—which was one thing they did not need electricity for!

As they went to sleep, the whole family realized something: It really doesn't take much at all to be content—certainly not television or computers. What had promised to be a boring night had turned out to be kind of fun for the Rosset family.

At three in the morning, as everyone slept, power was restored, and lights came on all over the house, including the bedrooms!

PRAISING GOD TOGETHER

Memorize Philippians 4:13 as a family. Here are two simple methods for memorizing Bible verses:

1. Let one person read a phrase while the others repeat it. Lengthen the phrase until the whole verse is being recited. Then have the group recite the verse without any prompting.

2. Print each word of the verse on a different piece of paper, scramble them, and have the group unscramble them. Place them in order and read the verse. Now gradually remove a few of the words and say the verse, filling in the missing words. Repeat until there are no pieces of paper and everyone is reciting the verse.

PRAYING TOGETHER

Pray an ABC prayer, where each person takes a turn naming something he or she is thankful for, beginning with A, then B, then C, and on through the alphabet.

LOOKING AHEAD

You will need crayons or markers in addition to paper for tomorrow's devotion.

March 20

PRAYING TOGETHER

You, Lord, are all we have.
You give us all we need.
Our lives are in your hands. Amen.

READING THE BIBLE TOGETHER

Read Matthew 6:25-33.

SHARING TOGETHER

Have you ever heard the phrase, *Take time to stop and smell the roses?* What are some ways each of you or your family as a whole can stop and smell the roses more often?

Are there signs of spring where you live? Color pictures of some birds of the air or flowers of the field. Then draw yourself or your family in the picture. Under your picture write Matthew 6 as a reminder of God's care for creatures great and small—including you!

Matthew 6:33 is a good verse to memorize. You can review the verse you worked on yesterday, Philippians 4:13, to see if your family is ready to memorize another verse.

March 21

PRAYING TOGETHER

You, Lord, are all we have.
You give us all we need.
Our lives are in your hands. Amen.

READING THE BIBLE TOGETHER

Read together Psalm 36:5-10.

CONSIDER THIS

Some things that matter most in life cannot be seen. The writers of the Bible knew this, and we can learn about it from the way the Bible talks about happiness and fulfillment. In the psalm you have just read, the words come from a person who has found deep joy in God's love and care. These words are a good reminder of what the season of Lent is about—doing away with excessive material things, such as fancy foods, special treats, entertainment, and possessions we don't really need in order to make more room for God in our lives. During Lent, we focus more on unseen things that make us rich on the inside. These things include caring for others, praying, reading the Bible, and delighting in God's love.

SHARING TOGETHER

Sometimes the church has called Lent "the springtime of the soul." Can you think of some reasons why this might be so? In what ways has this season of Lent been such a springtime in your life? in your family? What practices make this so? Your family can plan an outing to see wildflowers, visit an arboretum, or do some gardening of your own.

PRAYING TOGETHER

Dear God, there are things in our lives that fill our time, but don't always fill our hearts, or that keep us busy, but don't always keep us close to you. Lead us to choose the best things for our lives and to let the lesser things fall away, so that our hearts will be filled and we will always be near you. Amen.

OPTIONAL ACTIVITIES

See page 273.

March 22

PRAYING TOGETHER

You, Lord, are all we have.
You give us all we need.
Our lives are in your hands.
Amen.

READING THE BIBLE TOGETHER

Read Matthew 19:23-26.

CONSIDER THIS

What we do with our money is an important part of our spiritual lives. When we choose to be generous with money, sharing it with others in need, our hearts are more open to God's kingdom, that is, God's love in the world. When we are afraid to share and always keep our money for ourselves, our hearts become closed to God's kingdom. Jesus says being rich makes it hard to be open to God's kingdom, maybe because being selfish with our money can get in the way of loving God and other people.

A STORY

Rudy was so excited that the day of the trip had finally arrived. He had been looking forward to going with his Scout pack to spend three days at the beach. His grandmother had given him twenty dollars to take with him. His uncle must not have known that because he gave Rudy ten dollars more to spend! The other boys in his group didn't bring more than a few dollars for spending money. Their families couldn't afford more.

At first Rudy spent his money all on himself. He bought an ice cream cone at their lunch stop on the way. None of the other boys did, so he ate it alone. He bought a key chain later when they stopped for gas, but he kept it in his pocket because he knew the other boys hadn't bought anything. There was a video arcade at their dinner stop, and he went to play by himself while the other boys played

199

outside. He was glad to have his special money to spend, but something about spending it was not much fun. He wasn't enjoying having special treats when no one else in the group did.

The next day Rudy had an idea. At lunchtime he decided to buy ice cream for everyone in the group. The boys enjoyed that special treat and thanked Rudy for sharing. The next day, on the beach, a woman was renting small rafts. Rudy had an idea—he had enough money left to rent two rafts, and two would be enough for all the boys to share for the day. The other boys pitched in as well with their own spending money. As they played with the rafts through the day, Rudy had a warm feeling deep inside. He had learned a wonderful lesson—sharing his special gifts from his grandmother and uncle was much more fun than keeping them all to himself.

SHARING TOGETHER

Is there something you want to share or give up in your life? In what ways could you be more giving with your money or possessions? Who would you share these things with—the church? a friend? a neighbor?

Did you start putting aside money for a special Lenten offering on March 8? If so, are you adding to the offering every day? If not, you can always begin now.

If the idea of giving up or sharing some of your money or things sounds difficult, remember Jesus' words to his disciples: *For God all things are possible.* God can help us undertake difficult things, and do them!

March 23

PRAYING TOGETHER

You, Lord, are all we have.
You give us all we need.
Our lives are in your hands. Amen.

CONSIDER THIS

In Jesus' time, Pharisees were people who were careful to follow God's teachings and to obey all the rules. They were thought of as good people, but sometimes Pharisees began to feel proud of themselves for behaving so well. A tax collector gathered taxes for the Roman government, never a popular occupation. Sometimes tax collectors became rich by cheating people. They were often thought of as bad people. In this story, there is a *good* person (Pharisee) and a *bad* person (tax collector); then they get switched around in a funny way.

READING THE BIBLE TOGETHER

Read Luke 18:9-14.

SHARING TOGETHER

Words like "I'm sorry" or "I was wrong" are some of the bravest words we can say. In the story Jesus told, the person who willingly admitted his sin was justified, which means forgiven.

Think of a time you have had to say "I'm sorry" or "I was wrong." Was it hard to do?

Can you remember a time when someone wasn't willing to say those words and acted as though nothing was wrong when it really was?

PRACTICING WHAT JESUS TAUGHT

Act out the story of the Pharisee and the tax collector. One person can be the Pharisee, all puffed up and proud of himself or herself. The Pharisee thinks that he or she is perfect and never does anything wrong. The Pharisee feels better than everyone else and believes that he or she has no sins.

The tax collector is kind of a trickster whom no one likes. This person probably cheats other people out of their money and isn't very nice.

Look again now at the Bible story and act out how the Pharisee and the tax collector talk to God.

PRAYING TOGETHER

Let each person fill in this prayer:

Dear God, I'm sorry for . . .
or
Dear God, I'm sorry when . . .

LOOKING AHEAD

You will need crayons and paper for tomorrow's devotion.

March 24

PRAYING TOGETHER

You, Lord, are all we have.
You give us all we need.
Our lives are in your hands. Amen.

READING THE BIBLE TOGETHER

Read Mark 10:46-52.

A STORY

Everything in the world seemed to be going against Bartimaeus. He was not born blind, but by some illness or accident had become blind. Now he spent his days begging by the road at the edge of the city of Jericho, remembering what it was like to see and wishing he could see again as he stared into darkness. He sat by the road, day after day, while people who could see perfectly well hurried by, not even noticing him or choosing not to see him. Sometimes he felt as if he were a sore on somebody's leg, too tender to touch or even to look at. People must have wished he would just go away.

But something inside kept Bartimaeus going, gave him what it took to come back every day to the same spot, hold out a hand, and beg for money for his bread. Was it faith? Courage? Stubbornness? Force of habit? We can only guess.

One day Bartimaeus heard a bustling crowd, and he overheard someone say the name *Jesus*. Could it be Jesus of Nazareth? He had heard of this teacher who sometimes healed people. In fact, he had not stopped thinking about him since a passerby had told him weeks ago that this Jesus healed people in miraculous ways. *If he ever comes this way,* Bartimaeus had thought to himself many times, *I will be certain that he knows I am here. Maybe, just maybe, he will bring healing to me.*
The noise around him grew louder. "Jesus, Son of David, have mercy on me!" Bartimaeus shouted out from his darkness. The people nearby tried to make him hush; they thought

there was no place for a beggar near Jesus. Bartimaeus didn't care what they said. "Son of David," he cried even louder, "Have mercy on me!"

Jesus heard him and stopped in his tracks. "Call him here," he said.

The people called Bartimaeus: "Hey, get up! He's calling you!" Bartimaeus sprang up and felt his way to Jesus.

"What do you want from me?" Jesus asked.

"Teacher, let me see again," he said boldly. Jesus said, "Your faith has made you well."

Bartimaeus couldn't believe it—he could see again! For the longest time he just stood there, looking around, trying to take it all in.

From that moment, he followed Jesus. It felt as though the whole world was his once more. And the darkness, the loneliness, and the begging by the Jericho road were gone forever.

SHARING TOGETHER

What do you think Bartimaeus saw when his eyes were first opened and he could see again? Draw a picture of some of the things or people Bartimaeus might have seen at that moment.

PRAYING TOGETHER

Dear God, we thank you that nothing can keep you from us or us from you. When we need you and call on you, you always hear us and help us through. Amen.

LOOKING AHEAD

If convenient, provide a loaf of bread for tomorrow's devotion.

March 25

PRAYING TOGETHER

You, Lord, are all we have.
You give us all we need.
Our lives are in your hands. Amen.

CONSIDER THIS

Jesus had shared meals many times with his friends, the disciples. He seemed to enjoy such times together. One night, near the time of his death, Jesus told his disciples this would be the last meal they would share together. It was Passover, the meal people shared once a year to remember the time their ancestors escaped from Egypt. Today churches remember this last supper of Jesus with a meal called Communion, or the Lord's Supper, or Eucharist. We call this meal a sacrament because it is a sign of God's love for us.

READING THE BIBLE TOGETHER

Read together Luke 22:14-22.

SHARING TOGETHER

Have you ever had a meal with someone who was about to go away for a long time? Do you remember your feelings then?

What are your experiences of Communion or the Lord's Supper? In your congregation, do children receive the bread and cup? Share some of your memories of the Lord's Supper. Do you have questions about why the church celebrates Communion?

Share a common loaf of bread at a meal today or in the next few days. As you break the loaf, remember Jesus' last supper with his disciples and God's love for us.

SINGING TOGETHER

If you know this song, sing it together as your closing prayer:

Let us break bread together on our knees.
  (Sing 2 times.)
When I fall on my knees with my face to the rising sun,
O Lord, have mercy on me.

Let us praise God together on our knees.
  (Sing 2 times.)
When I fall on my knees with my face to the rising sun,
O Lord, have mercy on me.

PRAYING TOGETHER

Loving God, thank you for your son Jesus, whom we remember when we eat and drink together. Amen.

LOOKING AHEAD

You will need a basin or large bowl and a towel for tomorrow's devotion.

March 26

PRAYING TOGETHER

You, Lord, are all we have.
You give us all we need.
  Our lives are in your hands. Amen.

READING THE BIBLE TOGETHER

Read John 13:1-11.

CONSIDER THIS

While Jesus was with his friends sharing their last meal together before his death, he did something quite unusual. He knelt down and began washing their feet— something a servant in the house would normally do. Since most people wore open sandals and walked on dusty roads and dirt paths, we can imagine that the disciples' feet were pretty dirty, maybe even smelly! Jesus told his disciples to do what he had done for them. Since we don't have occasion to actually wash others' feet very often, what are some other ways of helping or serving other people?

SHARING TOGETHER

Think of a time when you have taken care of another person in a way that was unpleasant—changing a diaper, dressing a wound, giving a bath, etc. Why did helping that person seem important at that time?

Share a simple foot-washing ritual in your family. All you need is a big basin of warm water (or bathtub), a towel, and a place to sit. Wash one another's feet in whatever way seems natural. You might end with a family hug.

READING THE BIBLE TOGETHER

Read together John 13:12-15.

PRAYING TOGETHER

Jesus, we thank you for your love for those who follow you. Give us such love for one another that we may learn to serve others as you have served us. Amen.

March 27

PRAYING TOGETHER

You, Lord, are all we have.
You give us all we need.
Our lives are in your hands. Amen.

READING THE BIBLE TOGETHER

Mark 14:26-31, 66-72.

TELL US MORE

Jesus' last days before he died were, in some ways, really tense. There were signs all around that he was in trouble. Even though the disciples may have sensed this, they would not speak about it. Sometimes when Jesus talked about how near his death was, they changed the subject.

On the night before he died, he told his disciples what they surely did not want to hear—that they were going to desert him. Peter objected strongly to that statement. But later we read that he denied knowing Jesus.

When the rooster or cock crowed the first time (see Mark 14:68), it might have reminded Peter of what Jesus had told him: "Before the cock crows twice, you will deny me three times" (see Mark 14:30). But Peter didn't want to hear Jesus then, and he didn't seem to hear the rooster crowing the first time.

Only after he had denied knowing Jesus three times did he hear the cock crow the second time and remember Jesus' words. When Peter realized what he had done, he was very sad and wept.

SHARING TOGETHER

Sometimes it's easy to do the right thing when we're alone. But when we're with other people we may do something wrong because we don't want to be embarrassed or we're afraid of looking foolish in front of others.

When we do something that we know is wrong, it's like telling Jesus, "I don't know you." Do you think this is what happened to Peter?

SOMETHING TO CONSIDER

Find a picture of a rooster or a rooster figurine in your home and place it where it can be seen for the remaining days of Lent as a reminder of this story.

PRAYING TOGETHER

Let each person fill in this prayer:

Dear God, I'm sorry for . . .
or
Dear God, I'm sorry when . . ."

LOOKING AHEAD

You will need some sticks and string or wire for tomorrow's devotion.

March 28

PRAYING TOGETHER

You, Lord, are all we have.
You give us all we need.
Our lives are in your hands. Amen.

READING THE BIBLE TOGETHER

Read John 19:16-18, 26-30.
Perhaps the saddest day described in the Bible is the day Jesus died.

TELL US MORE

Part of the reason Jesus was put to death was because he loved people. How strange that is! But sometimes his love for other people scared the leaders who were in power. In a selfish way, they were nervous that Jesus would take people away from them and they would lose their power. But despite the frequent threatens, Jesus continued to love.

Even when he was on the cross, Jesus was showing concern. To his mother, who was close by, he said, "Woman, here is your son." He was referring to John, who was standing near her. Then he said to John, "Here is your mother." Jesus wanted his mother and the beloved disciple, John, to take care of each other. In his own suffering, Jesus was loving others. Ever since, the cross has been a reminder of Jesus' love for us.

Sometimes we think of the cross as representing God's open arms, demonstrating God's eternal love for the world.

SHARING TOGETHER

Make simple crosses with two sticks and string on thin wire. Older children may elaborate by using a fancier knot to tie the sticks. Those old enough to use a pocketknife can whittle the bark off. When everyone has finished, place all the crosses where they can be seen each day until after Easter.

PRAYING TOGETHER

Dear God, we thank you for the love Jesus showed us in his life of service and in his death. When we see the cross may we remember your open arms of love toward us and toward the world. Amen.

March 29

PRAYING TOGETHER

You, Lord, are all we have.
You give us all we need.
Our lives are in your hands. Amen.

READING THE BIBLE TOGETHER

Read Luke 15:11-24.

205

CONSIDER THIS

In the Bible, people don't run often. So when we are told that someone runs, we know something very important or exciting is happening. Who runs in the story you have just read? Why do you suppose he does?

SHARING TOGETHER

Can you imagine what it would be like to leave your whole family and go to a strange town or city? If you were far from home for a long time, what would you miss the most?

The younger son had really messed up his life by the time he started for home. He didn't know if he would be forgiven or turned away when he arrived. Imagine his surprise when he saw his father running toward him with joy!

Have you ever felt really bad after doing something wrong? How did it feel to face people and ask forgiveness? Does it often seem easier to avoid a problem rather than face it?

If you were throwing a party for someone in your family who had left home, made some mistakes, and was coming back home to ask forgiveness, what would you have at the party? Let each one take a turn being the runaway who has come home, and let the others guess what that person would like to have at his or her party.

PRAYING TOGETHER

Have one person read this prayer. Another person can guide the group in the suggested motions.

Dear God,
We do not always love you with our whole hearts
    (push out and away with one hand),
or love one another as ourselves
    (push out and away with the other hand).
Please forgive us

(bow head, fold hands together),
and renew our hearts for love
    (place hands over heart).
We thank you that no matter what mistakes we make or wrong turns we take, your arms are always open to us
    (open out arms),
to forgive us and welcome us home
    (hug self).
Amen.

OPTIONAL ACTIVITY

See page 273.

LOOKING AHEAD

You will need a candle for tomorrow's devotion.

March 30

PRAYING TOGETHER

You, Lord, are all we have.
You give us all we need.
Our lives are in your hands. Amen.

READ THE BIBLE TOGETHER

If you haven't yet read the first part of this story in Luke 15:11-24, do so now. Then read Luke 15:25-32.

CONSIDER THIS

In this story, the older brother was angry because his younger brother was forgiven and given special treatment because he had made it home safely. It can be hard to ask forgiveness from someone else when we have hurt him or her, but sometimes it can be even harder to offer forgiveness to someone who has hurt us.

SHARING TOGETHER

What makes it hard to forgive someone when he or she has done something wrong? What can we do with angry feelings inside of us when we continue to be mad at someone who has hurt us?

PRAYING TOGETHER

Ask the group to identify anyone they might be angry with or jealous toward. Light a candle and pray, with each one naming the person they've thought of:

Dear God, I remember _____ before you now. May she (he) know the light and warmth of your love for her (him). In your strength, I forgive her (him) for hurting me. Help me to find within me a love for her (him). Amen.

March 31

PRAYING TOGETHER

You, Lord, are all we have.
You give us all we need.
Our lives are in your hands. Amen.

READING THE BIBLE TOGETHER

Read John 21:1-14.

CONSIDER THIS

In many of the stories told about Jesus after he has been raised from the dead, he is eating with his friends. In this story from the Gospel of John, the risen Christ fixes breakfast for everybody!

Why do you suppose eating together is such an important part of the Easter stories? When Easter comes, does your family have a special meal together?

IMAGINE THIS

Act out the story of Jesus and the disciples on the beach. Find an area and pretend it is the beach and an object to be the boat. A blue bedspread or sheet could be the water in between (although imagination doesn't require it!). Young children especially enjoy toiling with the big haul of fish, recognizing Jesus, and jumping out of the boat to pretend-swim to shore.

PRAYING TOGETHER

Dear God, you raised Jesus from the dead and gave him power to fill our lives with good and beautiful things. Even though we cannot see Jesus, open our eyes to see his hand in our lives. Open our hearts to share with him and others the great feast of Easter. Amen.

April 1

READING THE BIBLE TOGETHER

Have someone read John 20:1-18 to see how John (who calls himself "the other disciple" in this story) tells about the first Easter morning.

SHARING TOGETHER

Take time to look at this story more carefully. Answer the following questions together:

- Who first went to the tomb where Jesus had been buried?
- What was her response when she saw that the stone was gone?
- What happened when Peter and the other disciple came to the tomb?
- What did the two disciples do after seeing the empty tomb?
- When she saw him outside the tomb, who did Mary Magdalene think Jesus was?
- How did she recognize him?
- How does she respond to Jesus' words to her in verse 17?

SOMETHING TO CONSIDER

The Easter story in Matthew, Mark, and Luke is slightly different from the one we read in John. This is because any four people who saw or heard about the same event would each tell about it in his or her own way. As John tells the story, the disciples ran to the tomb, saw that Jesus was not there, and then "returned to their homes." Mary Magdalene, on the other hand, "went and announced to the disciples, 'I have seen the Lord.'"

We can't know what was in the minds of Peter, John, or Mary Magdalene, but we do know ourselves. Are we today more like Mary Magdalene or the two disciples? Is it easy for us to tell our friends about Jesus' gift of new life, or are we shy about telling the Resurrection news?

SINGING TOGETHER

Say or sing these words to the tune of "Mary Had a Little Lamb."

God gave us the only son, only son, only son.
God gave us the only son so we might have
    new life.
That's news to tell to everyone, everyone,
    everyone,
That's news to tell to everyone, in Jesus is new
    life!

PRAYING TOGETHER

Gracious God, you know us and understand us. You love us when we are fearful and you love us when we're brave. You also want us to spread the good news of how Jesus came to bring us everlasting life. So we ask that you give us the courage to tell the

Easter story. Thank you for sending your only son to give us new life. What a gift! In his name, we pray. Amen.

OPTIONAL ACTIVITY

See page 273.

LOOKING AHEAD

You will need paper, markers or pens, and tape for tomorrow's devotion.

April 2

PRAISING GOD TOGETHER

Repeat these praise statements with one person saying the words for Part A, and the others saying Part B. Start with a whisper, getting louder and louder each time until both lines are shouted.

One: Jesus is alive!
All: God is with us yet!

A STORY

Take turns telling a story. One person reads the first lines of the story below, then the next person continues for a sentence or two, stopping so the next person to pick up at that point until every person has had a turn and the story feels complete.

The day after Easter, Joshua's friend, Matty, asked, "So what's the big deal about Jesus? He rose from the dead a long time ago; so what?"

Joshua searched his mind for the right answer. "So what? Jesus' rising from the dead means that . . ."

READING THE BIBLE TOGETHER

Paul wrote to the church in Rome, reminding them that Jesus brought us new life. Have someone read Romans 8:35, 37-39.

A FAMILY LITANY

Make a list of the hard times in life that may keep you from God and fill in the blanks of the verses below. When the blanks are filled, ask each family member to share what he or she has written, pausing after each question mark. Others should be ready to shout NO! after each question.

Who will separate us from the love of Christ?
Will _____ ? (NO!)
Or _____? (NO!)
Or_____? (NO!)
What about _____ or _____?
(NO!)
Or _____, or _____?
(NO!)
Is there anything that can keep us from God's love? (NO!)
There is nothing in all creation that can ever separate us from the love God showed us in Jesus.

SHARING TOGETHER

Let each person decide where to post reminders of God's love so that anyone who sees them will remember new life in Jesus. Some possibilities are the front door, the refrigerator, and next to each person's bed. Using the markers or pens, write *Can anything separate us from God's love? NO!* on each paper. Help younger family members make their own signs; then tape the papers to your chosen places.

PRAYING TOGETHER

We are so thankful that you are always with us, loving God. Whatever happens to us, help us remember that nothing in all creation can separate us from your love! In confidence, we pray. Amen.

LOOKING AHEAD

You will need a long sheet of newsprint or several pieces of paper taped together, and markers or paints for tomorrow.

April 3

READING THE BIBLE TOGETHER

Read Isaiah 40:6-8.

What do these words mean to you?
Does it seem odd to compare human beings to grass or flowers?
These words seem to point out that although people live only a short life span on earth, God and God's Word are forever.

Now look at 1 Peter 1:23-25.
See how Peter slightly changes the meaning of Isaiah's words by adding verse 23? He tells us that if we believe in Jesus Christ (the seed that lasts forever), then things are changed even though people will pass a short time on earth. Aren't you glad that Jesus came to bring eternal life?

SHARING TOGETHER

Using paper and markers or paints, draw a time line of world history. At one end, write *The beginning of the world*. At the other end, write *Forever*. Put *today* somewhere in the middle. In between, add whatever other events you want (dinosaurs, certain wars or inventions, dates from your own family's lives, depending on how much time you have). Don't worry about exact dates—this is not a history lesson! When you have a number of events on your time line, look at each one and ask, "Was God around when this happened?" If the answer is yes (and it should be!) color around that event with bright sun rays, rainbows, or some other symbol of God's love. When you finish, look at what you have created and ask, "Who was there at the beginning? Who will be there at the end? Who is with us always? God!"

SINGING TOGETHER

Do the "Hokey-Pokey" song together but change the words of the chorus to:

God is with us always.
God is with us now.
That's what it's all about.

Try these movements:
   —right foot in   —left foot in
   —right arm in   —left arm in
   —head in   —whole self in

April 4

SHARING TOGETHER

Take time to think of any deaths your family has experienced—family members, pets, or acquaintances. Give time for each person to share:

- How did you feel when this death happened?
- How did you express your sadness?
- When did it become real to you that this person/ pet was not coming back?
- Do you still think of this loved one?

CONSIDER THIS

Like all human beings, Jesus died. Yet, because God raised Jesus from the dead, his story—and ours—has a different ending. There is life after life! Death does not have the last word.

Remember how sad Jesus' friends were when they went to the tomb? When Jesus saw Mary Magdalene outside his tomb, he asked, "Woman, why are you weeping?"

And two of Jesus' disciples left the empty tomb and went home because "as yet they did not understand the scripture, that he must rise from the dead" (John 20:9).

READING THE BIBLE TOGETHER

Even those people who actually walked and talked with Jesus didn't understand that because of him, death would no longer be the same.
Read Paul's words in 1 Corinthians 15:51-55.

Then, have one reader say verse 55 one line at a time, with the others repeating those words.

A STORY

Joaquin and Lourdes were sad. Their dog, Pancho, had died. Their eyes filled with tears as they helped dig the hole for Pancho's grave in their backyard.

"Will Pancho be okay?" Lourdes asked.

"Pancho is with God," Mamá replied.

When the hole was ready, Mamá and Papá carefully laid the collie in the grave. The children added a dog biscuit and one of Pancho's favorite toys. They took turns talking about how much they had loved Pancho.

"He didn't bark—much," Joaquin remembered.

"He's lived with us all of my life," Lourdes added.

"And we are thankful to you, O God, for many long years of this good pet's life," Mamá said, wiping her eyes.

Each of them threw in a handful of dirt, then they worked together to fill in the hole. Papá began singing the last verse of "Amazing Grace." Mamá placed the wooden sign they had made on the grave. Pancho, Beloved Friend, it said.

They stood together, singing, happy that God had let Pancho live with them.

PRAYING TOGETHER

Thank you for being with us in life and in death, Loving God. Amen.

OPTIONAL ACTIVITY

See page 273.

April 5

A STORY

Three-year-old Jeremy yanked a truck out of Mario's hand. Mario slapped Jeremy's face. Jeremy banged the truck on Mario's knee. Mario shoved Jeremy to the ground, and the boys began to fight. The truck lay on the floor beside them, forgotten.

SHARING TOGETHER

Jeremy and Mario forgot to use their words. Hopefully, everyone in your family knows not to slap, hit, or fight when he or she is angry. Have you ever been angry when someone hurt your feelings? How did you respond? Has anyone ever stolen something that belonged to you? Were there other times when you felt wronged by someone?

CONSIDER THIS

Over 1750 years before Jesus, an old set of laws called the Code of Hammurabi directed that if someone did something bad to you, you should do something bad back to them. This tit-for-tat law is mentioned in our Old Testament as well.

When Jesus came, he brought a new way of dealing with those persons who don't treat us well.

READING THE BIBLE TOGETHER

Read Matthew 5:38-42.
Then take turns filling in the following sentences:
If someone hits you on one cheek . . .
If someone takes your coat . . .
If someone begs or wants to borrow from you . . .

TELL US MORE

In Jesus' day, anyone could be pressed into service to help carry heavy things or do other jobs for a Roman soldier. Many people were unhappy to walk a mile carrying someone else's luggage. So Jesus said to them, "If anyone forces you to go one mile, go also the second mile." He meant: Be happy to be of service to others; give cheerfully of yourself instead of complaining. We call this "going the extra mile."

PRACTICING WHAT JESUS TAUGHT

We won't be asked to carry someone's baggage a mile, but there will be times when we are asked to help out others in ways that may not sound like much fun for us. How could you go the extra mile in these situations?

- Your parents ask you to sweep the house.
- Your friend asks for help on a math problem.
- Your brother or sister needs help working out a conflict with a friend.
- A neighbor is not physically able to put out his garbage.

PRAYING TOGETHER

God, help us always to be willing to go the extra mile. Amen.

April 6

READING THE BIBLE TOGETHER

Read Matthew 5:43-46.

CONSIDER THIS

Throughout history, many groups of people have called each other "enemy." Can you name any pairs of enemies? (Some examples: Union and Confederate armies in the Civil War, Protestants and Catholics in Ireland, Israelis and Palestinians in the Holy Land.) What do the words from Matthew 5:43-46 say about how we treat people we may consider enemies? What two things are we supposed to do to our enemies?

Most of us don't have enemies who are soldiers in an opposing army. So what might Jesus' words mean for us? Do we need to work out conflicts with anyone?

SHARING TOGETHER

Act out what it might mean to love your enemies and pray for those who persecute you in the following situations:

- A boy in your class has been spreading rumors about you.
- A new neighbor seems unfriendly and never returns your greetings.
- The school bully frightens you on the playground.
- A group of popular students make fun of your clothing.
- A former friend always gives you angry looks.
- A grocery store clerk seems to suspect that you might be shoplifting.

- A colleague at work undermines your authority and wants your job.

A FAMILY LITANY

One person leads the following litany. The others will respond with *We will love and pray for them*.

One: Even when someone is mean to us,
All: We will love and pray for them,
One: Even when someone considers us an enemy,
All: We will love and pray for them.
One: Even when we feel only negativity from another person,
All: We will love and pray for them.
One: Even when someone says means things about us,
All: We will love and pray for them.
One: For if you love only those who love you, what reward do you have? As Jesus taught us, whether people are nice to us or not,
All: We will love and pray for them.

PRAYING TOGETHER

God, it is not easy to follow Jesus. It is much easier to love those who love us than to love and pray for people who make our lives miserable. Yet we know in our hearts that love is stronger than hate and that being a friend is more important than being an enemy. Thank you for the new way to live that you showed us in Jesus. Help us to follow him and live in love. Amen.

OPTIONAL ACTIVITY

See page 274.

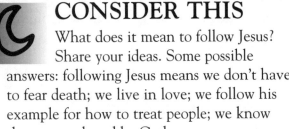
April 7

CONSIDER THIS

What does it mean to follow Jesus? Share your ideas. Some possible answers: following Jesus means we don't have to fear death; we live in love; we follow his example for how to treat people; we know that we are loved by God.

Now, another big question: What difference does it make if we follow Jesus?

READING THE BIBLE TOGETHER

Read Colossians 3:16-17.

A STORY

Jaime had a terrible day at school. Nick the bully made some nasty remarks that made Jaime want to punch him. But Jaime remembered that his Sunday school teacher had said, "In everything you do, follow Jesus," so Jaime tried to be calm and nice to Nick. It wasn't easy.

Then, when it was time for his math test, Jaime's mind went blank. He knew he could copy from Annabelle's paper. She was really smart in math. But as he started to glance over at her test paper, he thought, *Is this what a follower of Jesus would do?* He sang a chorus of "Jesus Loves Me" in his mind and was surprised to find a few of the answers coming to him from his studies. It seemed like stories he had learned in church and Sunday school kept popping into his head at the oddest times. And somehow, when he thought of Jesus, he knew what to do.

Jaime had forgotten his lunch so he stood around with a group of boys who liked to use swear words. "You man enough to talk like this?" one kid asked him. "I can say what I want to without using those words," he said and went to play handball.

As Jaime lay his head on his pillow at bedtime, he couldn't help but smile as he thought of how following Jesus had made his day easier. The bully, the test, the boys trying to act tough—with Jesus' help, Jaime had done the good thing in all those situations. *Jesus was with me. Thank you, Jesus. Be with me tomorrow, Jesus,* he thought, as he fell peacefully to sleep.

PRAYING TOGETHER

Jesus, you are always with us. Let your words be part of us. Help us to share what we know of you, and let songs about you ring in our hearts. In everything we do, in word or deed, we want to give you thanks and praise. Amen.

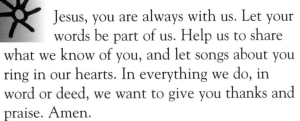
April 8

A STORY

Mariko ran to her grandmother. "I'm so angry, I could spit!" Grandmother hugged her close and listened to Mariko. "Kio makes me so mad. He dug up Mother's tulip bulbs, even though I told him not to, and I got blamed. I wish he weren't my brother!"

Grandmother sat quietly, holding Mariko, murmuring soothing words.

"I never want to see him again!" Mariko said.

"That will be hard since you live in the same house."

"Well, maybe I just won't talk to him then. It's not my fault he's my brother. Who asked for him to be born?"

"You have good reason to be angry. But what will you do with that anger?" Grandmother asked.

"What do you mean?"

"Like it or not, Kio is your brother. And anger is a bitter acid that eats up the one who is angry more than the one you're angry at. Do you control your anger? Or does it control you?"

Mariko was puzzled.

"We all have moments of anger. But by the time we go to bed each night, we must let go of that anger so that we can start the new day without the heavy burden of anger. Now go take a walk," Grandmother suggested. "And figure out how you will make peace with your brother."

SHARING TOGETHER

Do you understand Mariko's anger? How might she make peace with Kio? Can you think of a time in your family's life when two people were angry but they worked things out?

READING THE BIBLE TOGETHER

Read Ephesians 4:26 and James 1:19.

PRACTICING WHAT JESUS TAUGHT

Even the most loving families will have times of anger. What advice is there in the two scripture lessons that would help your family deal lovingly with anger?

Work together to form your family's list of

ways you want to deal with anger. You might include things like:

- Share your honest feelings.
- Be a good listener.
- Understand that others have a right to their anger.
- Assume that things will work out.
- Pray together.
- Ask yourself how Jesus would work in this situation.

SINGING TOGETHER

Make up your own words to this song and sing it to the tune of "If You're Happy and You Know It." The first line will be:

If you're angry and you know it. . .

Some examples of the second line might be **say a prayer** or **stomp your feet**.

PRAYING TOGETHER

Close with a family hug, and ask one family member to say a prayer.

April 9

IMAGINE THIS

All family members but the one who reads can close their eyes and imagine themselves in this story:

You were a simple fisherman until the day Jesus came to you by the Sea of Galilee and called to you and your brother, "Come, follow me."

From that day on, you followed Jesus. Up hill and down, over dusty paths, through towns and cities, you stayed close to him, listening to his every word. You didn't understand everything he said or like it when he talked about dying, but you were faithful to him.

When others were unsure of who Jesus was, you said, "You are the Messiah, the Son of the living God." Jesus replied, "Blessed are you, Simon, son of Jonah!...You are Peter, and on this rock I will build my church." You have always been close by Jesus' side.

And now you are heartsick. Was it only last night that you and the disciples ate together in the upper room? So much has happened since then. You remember the horror of Jesus' arrest in Gethsemane, how the soldiers marched him off. You watched from a distance as Jesus went before the council that tried to find a reason to kill him. You were afraid and kept your mouth shut. Otherwise, they might have arrested you too!

And then came that horrible moment when, just at dawn, you heard the rooster crow. Just last night you had promised, "Even though I must die with you, I will not deny you." Yet moments before you heard the cock crow, you had three times denied knowing the man whom you loved most in the world—Jesus.

You were afraid and confused, only wanting to live. So you said—three times!—"I do not know the man!" Your head aches but the pain in your heart is worse, and it will not go away. You are heartbroken by your own betrayal.

SHARING TOGETHER

Why did Peter deny Jesus? How did that make him feel?

How have we denied Jesus? Do our words or actions ever say, "I don't know the man"?

READING THE BIBLE TOGETHER

Read Matthew 26:69-75.

PRAYING TOGETHER

Jesus, we know you and love you. Help us always to claim the love and new life you offer us as we seek to live by your example. Amen.

LOOKING AHEAD

You will need some bread or crackers to share for tomorrow's devotion.

April 10

CONSIDER THIS

Remember how afraid Peter was when Jesus was arrested and put on trial? He was so fearful that he denied knowing his best friend. All of the other disciples were afraid too. They kept themselves locked in a room where they hoped no one could find them. After a while, however, they had to return to their ordinary lives. They did not yet understand how their lives had been changed forever.

READING THE BIBLE TOGETHER

Read John 21:1-14.

SHARING TOGETHER

See if you can answer these questions about today's scripture:

- Why didn't the disciples recognize Jesus?
- What did he call the disciples when he saw them?
- When was it that they recognized Jesus?
- What happened when the disciples followed his instructions about fishing?
- What does eating bread and fish together remind you of?

IMAGINE THIS

Sit on the floor together in a circle and pass around the bread or crackers. Set a timer for two minutes. Invite everyone to sit quietly in the silence, holding a piece of bread or cracker in hand while, with eyes closed, each person tries to imagine what it would have been like to sit with Jesus on the beach, eating bread and fish. When the

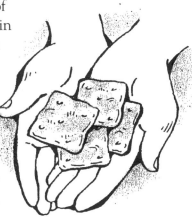

timer goes off, gives persons a chance to share what they imagined during the silence.

PRAYING TOGETHER

Jesus, you come to us, offering so much more than bread and fish. Just as you knew your disciples as close friends, you know us. You love us. You come to us when we least expect it, and you offer us new life. Give us eyes and faith to recognize you however you come to us, and help us have the courage to follow you. In your sweet name we pray. Amen.

LOOKING AHEAD

Ask a child to make three separate signs that say: ONE, TWO, THREE.

April 11

SHARING TOGETHER

Was there ever a time when you did something hurtful to another person and wanted to make it up to that person? Have you ever found it hard to say, "I'm sorry"? Tell about your experiences. In baseball, what does "Three strikes, you're out!" mean? How does it feel to strike out?

Remember when Peter denied that he knew Jesus? Even though Jesus had predicted that Peter would deny him, how might Jesus have felt when he knew that Peter had said, "I do not know the man!"? If you had been Jesus, would you have wanted to punish Peter? What would you expect Jesus to do the next time he saw his old friend?

READING THE BIBLE TOGETHER

Read John 21:15-17.

IMAGINE THIS

Act out the story you just read in John 21. One person can be Jesus and another Peter. An adult can serve as narrator, giving Jesus and Peter their lines, as needed. One person will hold up signs saying ONE, TWO, THREE each time Jesus asks Peter, "Do you love me?"

MORE SHARING

Why did Jesus ask Peter the same question three times? (It gave Peter three chances to make up for the three times he denied Jesus.) The good news is that, just as Jesus forgave Peter his denials, God forgives all our mistakes. All we have to do is tell God we're sorry and ask for forgiveness. With God, there is no *three strikes and you're out!* policy but everlasting love and forgiveness.

SINGING TOGETHER

Try these words to the tune of "Take Me Out to the Ballgame." You may want to sing the song several times so everyone can get the words.

> Jesus came to bring new life.
> Jesus calls us his friends.
> Even when Peter denied his Lord,
> Jesus gave him a second chance,
> For it's love, love, love—that's the new way.
> Jesus forgives all our sins.
> It's not One! Two! Three strikes you're out!
> But a second chance.

LOOKING AHEAD

For tomorrow, you will need paper, scissors, glue, and markers to make the sheep mural. Cotton balls are optional.

April 12

READING THE BIBLE TOGETHER

Either read again the story in John 21:15-17 when Jesus asked Peter, "Do you love me?" or tell the story in your own words.

SHARING TOGETHER

Draw or cut out at least one sheep per person, using the sheep outline on this page as a pattern. You can also glue cotton balls on each sheep so that it looks wooly.

PRACTICING WHAT JESUS TAUGHT

What did Jesus mean when he said, "Feed my sheep"? On each sheep, write out one of the ways we can love Jesus by loving his people. For instance, *Help at a soup kitchen* or *Help an older neighbor with yard work*. (If you do cover the sheep with cotton balls, you can write your idea on the back of the sheep.) Find a place in your home to display the sheep as reminders of how we can follow Jesus.

MORE SHARING TOGETHER

Vertically write out the words FEED MY SHEEP. Then work together to think of one sentence for each of the eleven letters in that phrase that describes what it means to show love for Jesus' people in our day and age. Read each sentence aloud, one at a time, pausing between each to say together, "Jesus says to feed his sheep."

OPTIONAL ACTIVITY
See page 274.

LOOKING AHEAD
You will need paper, pencils, a metal bowl, and matches for tomorrow.

April 13

A STORY

Mrs. Santiago told her Sunday school class, "Jesus wants us to forgive everyone. No matter what."

"Even," Marisa challenged, "if somebody punches you in the arm?"

"Tell them you don't like their action," Mrs. Santiago responded. "Then forgive them."

"If that same person trips you, shouldn't you trip them back to get even?"

"I know you'd be upset, and you need ask them not to trip you again. You might try to stay out of that person's way. But, forgive, still."

Marisa sank lower in her chair. "You're telling me I have to forgive over and over, even if the same dumb person keeps bugging me?"

"It does sound incredible, I know," replied Mrs. Santiago. "If problems continue, you might need an adult to help you with the situation. But Jesus asks that you have forgiveness in your heart."

Marisa said, amazed. "Wow! Jesus sure asks a lot!"

READING THE BIBLE TOGETHER

Read Matthew 18:21-35.

SHARING TOGETHER
Answer these questions together:
Do you think Peter was surprised at the answer to his question?
How many times did Jesus say we must forgive?
Why did Jesus tell the story of the unforgiving servant?
Whom does the king represent?
Which character are you more like: the forgiving king or the unforgiving servant?

PRACTICING WHAT JESUS TAUGHT
Most of us could be more forgiving. We hold petty grudges and keep track of wrongs against us. On a small piece of paper, write any grudge or wrong against you that you have not yet forgiven. When you have finished writing, fold the paper up.

Have an adult put the metal bowl in the kitchen sink and add the papers before lighting a match to set a small fire. (Alternative: use a fireplace or barbecue.) As the fire is burning, say the prayer below.

PRAYING TOGETHER
Loving God, we give you our inability to forgive and ask that you help us plant seeds of peace where now grudges and grumbles grow. In the name of Jesus, who taught us to forgive. Amen.

LOOKING AHEAD

Save the ashes for tomorrow's activity. You will also need a planter and potting soil or an outside garden location, a trowel, and some flower seeds.

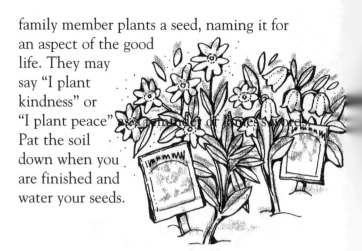

family member plants a seed, naming it for an aspect of the good life. They may say "I plant kindness" or "I plant peace" as a reminder of James's words. Pat the soil down when you are finished and water your seeds.

April 14

SHARING TOGETHER

Have everyone tell what their favorite flower is and why. What makes a beautiful garden? Does anyone in your area have an especially lovely garden?

READING THE BIBLE TOGETHER

Read James 3:13-18.

MORE SHARING

List positive aspects of a good life that come from above. Then answer these questions together:

- What characteristics (like envy) are not parts of the good life?
- How would you summarize James's message?
- For those who make peace, what is the harvest?

In the planter or a place outside, prepare the soil by mixing yesterday's forgiveness ashes with either soil for the planter or earth in the ground. Give everyone a chance to stir the soil.

Next, take turns planting the flower seeds according to directions on the package. Each

PRAYING TOGETHER

God, creator of every living thing, help us to plant in our own lives the seeds of peace that we may bloom forth your love to all creation. Amen.

OPTIONAL ACTIVITY

See page 274.

April 15

READING THE BIBLE TOGETHER

Read Romans 12:9-18 and 14:19.

SHARING TOGETHER

Paul wrote to the people in the church at Rome, giving them practical ideas for how to get along together and live in a way that showed the true spirit of Jesus. Do you agree with the actions he mentions as being ways to *live peaceably with all*? Can you think of anything he left out?

CONSIDER THIS

Over sixty years ago, the National Council of Jews and Christians published "Ten Commandments of Good Will." Among those commandments were:

- I will honor all men and women regardless of their race or religion.
- I will exemplify in my own life the spirit of good will and understanding.
- I will do more than live and let live; I will live and help live.*

PRACTICING WHAT JESUS TAUGHT

Work together to come up with your own set of rules or commandments for peace. You can use the ideas above that Paul wrote to the Romans and add your own.

SINGING TOGETHER

Sing a song such as "Let There Be Peace on Earth" or "Peace Is the World Smiling."

PRAYING TOGETHER

God of peace, sometimes it is hard for us to live in peace. Help us to remember to treat one another with caring and respect and to live peaceably with all people. Amen.

*As quoted in Blanche Wieson Cook, *Eleanor Roosevelt* (New York: Viking, 1999), 2:491.

LOOKING AHEAD

You'll need some markers and paper for tomorrow's devotion.

April 16

SHARING TOGETHER

Draw several pictures in sequence to show how a seed in the ground grows to be a flower above ground. Work together to make a colorful reminder of how a tiny seed planted in the earth can become a beautiful plant that lives above ground. As you draw together, talk about the process, answering these questions:

- Why does the seed need to be covered by earth?
- How does the seed look when it is put into the earth?
- What does the seed need in order to grow?
- Who makes the seed grow?

READING THE BIBLE TOGETHER

Read John 12:24.
Then talk about how Jesus is like the seed or grain of wheat that, when put in the ground, comes alive again.

CONSIDER THIS

Have an adult read these words slowly and with feeling:

Now the green blade riseth, from the buried grain,
Wheat that in the dark earth many days has lain;
Love lives again, that with the dead has been:

221

Love is come again, like wheat that springeth
	green.

In the grave they laid him, Love who had been
	slain,
Thinking that he never would awake again,
Laid in the earth like grain that sleeps unseen:
Love is come again, like wheat that springeth
	green.

Forth he came at Easter, like the risen grain,
Jesus who for three days in the grave had lain;
Quick from the dead my risen Lord is seen:
Love is come again, like wheat that springeth
	green.

When our hearts are wintry, grieving, or in pain,
Jesus' touch can call us back to life again,
Fields of our hearts that dead and bare have been:
Love is come again, like wheat that springeth
	green.*

A FAMILY LITANY

Divide the last three lines of the previous poem so that everyone has a part:

**Jesus' touch can call us back to life again,
Fields of our hearts that dead and bare have been:
Love is come again, like wheat that springeth
	green.**
Two people could each take one line, then
share the last line. Three people could take
one line each. More readers could share parts
of a line. Say these words three times in
thanksgiving for God's gift of new life.

PRAYING TOGETHER

Loving God, thank you for the promise
of new life in Jesus. Amen.

*J. M. C. Crum, "Now the Green Blade Riseth," from
The United Methodist Hymnal (Nashville, Tennessee: The
United Methodist Publishing House, 1989), 311.

April 17

A STORY

*Close your eyes while one reader tells the
story of Zacchaeus:*

It's not my fault I'm short. And who
wouldn't have been curious to see this man,
Jesus. He had the whole town buzzing—a
miracle man! I wanted to see for myself so I
shinnied up a sycamore tree for a better view.
Imagine how stunned I was when Jesus looked
up through the branches right at me. He even
knew my name! And he invited himself over
to my house!

Well, I hurried down
that tree and proudly took
him to my not-so-
humble home, offer-
ing him the best of
my hospitality. I
tried not to let it
bother me when
other people
grumbled in the
background; they
didn't think I was good
enough to host Jesus. Just
because I was a tax collector!
Okay, so it may not be the most
honest profession, but I was good
at what I did and proud of it.

Believe me, I wanted to show those
grumblers that I wasn't some lousy
moneygrubber. And somehow, looking into
Jesus' eyes, I wanted to be like him too. "Hey,
Jesus," I said in front of everyone, "I'm going to
give half of all I own to the poor." There was a
gasp from the crowd in my house. "And if I
have cheated anyone, I'll pay it back four times
over."

I don't know exactly why I was ready to

change my life but when I heard Jesus respond to me, I knew I had made the right decision.

"Salvation has come to this house today," he told the crowd and I bowed my head in humility. Not only had Jesus come to my house but he had brought me new life!

READING THE BIBLE TOGETHER

Read the story of Jesus and Zacchaeus in Luke 19:1-10.

SHARING TOGETHER

Share your answers to the following question: If you had been in the crowd at the tax collector's house, what might you have thought when you heard Zacchaeus and Jesus speak?

A FAMILY LITANY

Say these lines as you did yesterday, thinking of Zacchaeus and his gift of new life:

Jesus' touch can call us back to life again,
Fields of our hearts that dead and bare have been:
Love is come again, like wheat that springeth
green.

A STORY

Close your eyes while one reader tells this story:

For twelve long years I suffered from an illness so horrible that people avoided me when I walked down the street. "What did she do to deserve that?" they asked, and I asked the same question as I went to doctors and healers, seeking a remedy for the bleeding that sapped my energy and shamed me.

Nothing helped, not special diets or medicine or herbs. After twelve years, I was accustomed to being lonely, but people pretended I didn't even exist. I craved human touch, the love of another person.

Can you blame me that I risked everything in hopes that Jesus could cure me? According to Jewish law, a woman mustn't touch or talk to a man in public. And I was diseased, worthless, and loved by no one. So when Jesus passed me in the street, I thought it couldn't hurt to try to get some of the power that was so clearly in him. After all, the crowd was thick; he couldn't feel my light touch on the hem of his robe with so many crowding around him. I summoned my courage and reached out my hand.

As I touched the hem of his robe, my bleeding stopped and I was cured. Just like that! But somehow, Jesus had felt his power go out. And when he turned around to ask, "Who touched my clothes?" I thought I would die of shame. Fearful of what might happen to me, I fell on my knees before him.

There was no anger in his eyes, only love. "Daughter, your faith has made you well; go in

223

peace, and be healed of your disease." My eyes filled with tears of joy, of gratitude, of understanding that from this day on, nothing would ever be the same for me. Jesus brought me new life!

READING THE BIBLE TOGETHER

Read Mark 5:25-34.

SHARING TOGETHER

How long had the woman been sick? What was the woman's life like when she suffered from the bleeding? What could her life have been like after Jesus healed her?

A FAMILY LITANY

Say these lines again, thinking of how Jesus healed the woman and gave her new life:

Jesus' touch can call us back to life again,
Fields of our hearts that dead and bare have
  been:
Love is come again, like wheat that springeth
  green.

OPTIONAL ACTIVITIES

See page 274.

A STORY

Close your eyes while one person reads this story:

One day Jesus came to our village, and I saw a group of lepers cautiously approach him. They were careful to keep their distance, of course, being lepers and despised people, but they called out to him, "Jesus, Master, have mercy on us!"

How could lepers have the nerve to talk to Jesus? He didn't get angry, though, but just looked at them with his clear, kind eyes. He told them to go show themselves to the priests. They never questioned him but left at once to do as he said.

Not fifteen minutes later, the village gossips were already telling how all ten lepers were instantly cured of their horrible disease when they followed Jesus' advice. I was still wondering how this could be when to my amazement, I saw one of the healed lepers, a Samaritan, return to Jesus. The man threw himself at Jesus' feet and thanked him for the healing. I have to admit I was touched.

Jesus looked serious. "Weren't ten of you healed? Where are the others?" Then he looked out over the crowd and said, "Do you notice that only this one man, a foreigner, came back to give his thanks?" Pulling the man to his feet, Jesus said in a soft voice, "Get up and go on your way; your faith has made you whole."

I watched the scene with a vague sense of guilt for I knew I often forget to give thanks for the good things in my life. And my eyes followed the one who had been a leper as he joyfully walked out of our village toward his new life.

READING THE BIBLE TOGETHER

Read Luke 17:11-19.

SHARING TOGETHER

Why was Jesus so struck by the gratitude of the one leper? Why do you think the other nine lepers did not return to give thanks? When have you failed to thank God for blessings?

A FAMILY LITANY

Say these lines again, thinking of how Jesus healed the lepers and gave them new life:

Jesus' touch can call us back to life again,
Fields of our hearts that dead and bare have
  been:
Love is come again, like wheat that springeth
  green.

April 20

A STORY

Close your eyes while a reader tells the story of Nicodemus.

I am a learned man, a Pharisee and Jewish leader. I don't know what it was about Jesus that caught my fancy, but I knew I had to speak with him. He said and did things as if filled with God's power; yet it was hard for me, the learned Nicodemus, to admit that I didn't understand. Curious, I sneaked out in night's darkness to find Jesus. As we sat together, I was relieved that Jesus did not make fun of me, though I thought he was joking when he told me "no one can see the kingdom of God without being born from above."

How can anyone be born after having grown old? What on earth did he mean? He spoke of being "born of water and Spirit." Jesus meant we must be ready to change our lives. When he told me, "God so loved the world that he gave his only Son, so that everyone who believes in him may not perish but may have eternal life," I listened carefully.

That meeting with Jesus changed me. Oh, I left him in the darkness, carefully hiding my movements so no one would know where I had gone. But he didn't leave me. His words kept ringing in my ears, interrupting my discussions of the Law, haunting my dreams.

When the Jewish authorities planned to arrest him, I spoke on his behalf. And when they killed Jesus, I brought spices to his tomb, that he might be blessed in death, as I never blessed him in life.

Did I wait too long? Is eternal life for me too? I do believe in him, but though it is easy to grasp the gift of new life now, it is hard to trust the gift of eternal life in the future. Trust. Isn't that what faith is all about?

READING THE BIBLE TOGETHER

Read John 3:1-6, 16-17.

SHARING TOGETHER

Why didn't Nicodemus go to Jesus in the daytime? What did he want from Jesus? How did new life come to Nicodemus?

A FAMILY LITANY

Say these lines again, thinking of how Nicodemus received new life from Jesus:

**Jesus' touch can call us back to life again,
Fields of our hearts that dead and bare have
been:
Love is come again, like wheat that springeth
green.**

April 21

READING THE BIBLE TOGETHER

Read Acts 8:1-3; 9:1-18.

SHARING TOGETHER

Act out the story of Paul in the following scenes. You'll need a Saul/Paul, the voices of Jesus and Ananias, and someone to read the scripture verses. You may also have some persecuted followers of Jesus. (You can double up on the parts.) Remember: This is a very dramatic story!

Scene One: Saul persecutes those who follow Jesus. Acts 8:1-3; 9:1-2

Scene Two: Saul's conversion on the road to Damascus. Acts 9:3-9

Scene Three: Ananias places his hands on Paul, and Paul receives his sight. Acts 9:10-18

MORE SHARING

What kind of person was Saul? What happened on the road to Damascus? How do you think Saul felt when he was struck blind? What role did Ananias play? Can you understand why Saul would have changed his life to become Paul, the one who told so many people about Jesus' power? Do you know of anyone else who has had a dramatic experience of Jesus as Paul did?

SINGING TOGETHER

Use these words from Galatians 2:20 to the tune of "Pop Goes the Weasel":

It is no longer I who live,
But Jesus who lives in me.
And the life that I now live,
I live by faith in Jesus.

A FAMILY LITANY

Say these lines again, thinking of how Paul's encounter with Jesus on the road to Damascus changed his life:

**Jesus' touch can call us back to life again,
Fields of our hearts that dead and bare have
been:
Love is come again, like wheat that springeth
green.**

OPTIONAL ACTIVITY

See page 274.

April 22

SHARING TOGETHER

In the following situations, what would it mean to be saved?

- You are trapped in a burning house.
- You hit a fly ball to left field and wonder if you will be out.
- Your house sits on a river whose waters are rising, threatening flood.

- It's almost time for class to end when your teacher calls on you, asking a question to which you don't know the answer.
- You find out about Jesus Christ and hear his offer of new life.

READING THE BIBLE TOGETHER

Read Acts 16:25-34.

MORE SHARING

Who was in jail? What happened to let the prisoners go free? How did the jailer's react to the prison doors' opening? Why did the jailer ask how he could be saved? How long did the jailer take to get himself and his family baptized? Why was the jailer so happy at the end of the story? In what ways does Jesus save us every day as well as for all time?

PRAISING GOD TOGETHER

Tell stories of people you know whose lives have been changed since they knew Jesus. For instance, someone who had abused alcohol in the past might now be able to stay sober. How do you feel when you hear about people who know themselves saved by God?

PRAYING TOGETHER

Ever-loving, always-saving God, we are so thankful that you offer us safety and salvation. When we are fearful, you give us strength. When we think about making wrong decisions, you guide us in the right path. When we are in trouble, you stay close by us. Help us to live with the enthusiasm of the jailer who saw your power and instantly wanted new life for himself and his family. Let us never forget your constant love that reaches out to us even when we take you for granted. In the name of Jesus who came to save us. Amen.

April 23

SHARING TOGETHER

Let different members of the family see if they can come up with commercials for the following new products in a given amount of time:

- dental floss that also works as fishing line,
- a television that fits on your bicycle handle bars,
- a book that reads itself out loud to you,
- a kitchen robot.

Share the commercials. Then ask, do you think anyone would buy these new products? Why or why not?

Why are human beings attracted to anything that says *new* or *improved*? What new thing have you tried that you later realized was not so important to your life? When do you prefer to stick to what is tried and true rather than try something new?

READING THE BIBLE TOGETHER

Read Mark 2:21-22.

TELL US MORE

 Jesus used everyday items and situations when he tried to explain the new message he was bringing to the world. When he spoke of sewing new cloth onto an old garment, Jesus knew that his audience understood that new cloth is unshrunk, and a new patch would shrink if it got wet and probably tear the old cloth, thus needing yet another patch.

In the same way, he spoke about wineskins, which were soft and pliable when new, but hard and unbending when old. New wine is still fermenting and gives off gases that cause pressure. New skin will yield to the pressure, but old, dry skin will just explode from the pressure of the wine's gases. Those who first heard Jesus' words knew these things from their daily lives and understood his words in this passage.

MORE SHARING

Take turns sharing what has been the biggest or hardest change in your life so far. This could be a move, death, divorce, new school, or other change. At the time of the change, did you remember that Jesus was with you? What might his words about old and new patches and wineskins mean to you in times of such change?

PRAISING GOD TOGETHER

 Say this short poem in echo style:

What is old
Once was new.
Changes came—
That's how we grew.
Jesus offers
New life to all.
No old patches
If we hear his call.

OPTIONAL ACTIVITY

See page 274.

April 24

READING THE BIBLE TOGETHER

Read John 11:38-44.

A STORY

 Lazarus had been dead four days. For four days, the stone had been heavy against the cave where his body lay. His family and friends still gathered outside the tomb to mourn him, sharing memories of his life and crying together.

Then Jesus came, tears in his eyes, for Lazarus had been a good friend. Jesus drew himself up and said with authority, "Take away the stone." Martha, one of the dead man's sisters, protested. "Are you kidding? Can you imagine how bad the smell will be? After all, he's been dead four days."

Jesus looked at her with a steady gaze and asked, "Did I not tell you that if you believed, you would see the glory of God?" So Martha stepped back and let the stone be moved. Jesus stood in all his power and talked with God. "Thanks for all the times you have heard me, O God. I know you've always heard me, but I say this now so that everyone here will also believe that you sent me here." The people in the crowd looked at one another, puzzled.

Then Jesus took a step forward and pulled himself up to his full height as he stood in front of the open tomb. "Lazarus!" His voice echoed through the hills. "Come out!"

The people who had gathered to mourn the dead man watched in amazement as Lazarus walked out of the cave. He was still wrapped in the grave clothes and looked more dead than alive but there he was in front of them, no longer a corpse.

"Unbind him," said Jesus, "and let him go." No one there that day ever forgot how their friend, four days past death, began his new life at the sound of Jesus' voice.

READING THE BIBLE TOGETHER

Read John 11:25-26.

These verses contain words said by Jesus to Martha before he raised Lazarus from the dead. Work together to memorize what Jesus said. Take turns saying the verses aloud.

PRAYING TOGETHER

Loving God, we are thankful that you offer us new life in Jesus whose power we see in the raising of Lazarus. We know in our own lives how Jesus can make all things new. Help us each day as we try to live new life in the spirit of our Savior. Amen.

April 25

CONSIDER THIS

Two words sound similar but have very different meanings. *Transform* means to make a big change. A caterpillar transforms to a butterfly. An old house could be transformed by being remodeled. An unhappy person could be transformed into a content person.

Conform means to go along with rules and customs already in place. A new member of a sports team conforms to its uniform code. A teenager might conform to the accepted way of speaking among local teens.

READING THE BIBLE TOGETHER

Read Romans 12:1-2.

Paul's words to the people in the Roman church are words for us. He is urging us to give our whole selves to God. This means standing true to what God calls us to be instead of changing ourselves to fit the situation. Those who follow Jesus are not chameleons!

SHARING TOGETHER

How might someone be faithful to Jesus (transformed, not conformed) in these situations? Be specific about what actions would show a transformed life.

- In a school classroom
- A place of business
- At a social party
- On the school playground
- In Sunday school

SINGING TOGETHER

Sing this song to the tune of "My Bonnie Lies over the Ocean."

Be not conformed to this world.
Don't let others change you
Instead, be transformed by Jesus
To him always try to be true.
Jesus, Jesus, to him always try to be true, be true.
Jesus, Jesus, Jesus, the one who loves you.

LOOKING AHEAD

You will need aluminum foil, scissors, and cardboard or heavy paper for tomorrow's devotion.

April 26

READING THE BIBLE TOGETHER

Read Philippians 2:12-15.

SHARING TOGETHER

Play a game where each person chooses between two options in the situations below. Designate one side of the room for the first option, another for the second. One person reads the choices; everyone goes to the place they feel they would choose.

1. You are not prepared for an important test but take it giving your honest and probably incorrect answers,

OR

You copy answers from a better student.

2. When you see others making fun of someone, you stand up for that person,

OR

You remain silent even though you don't like what is happening.

3. You buy a group's latest CD even though the words to their songs contain bad language,

OR

You find an alternate group that is more positive and free of bad language.

4. You make do with the clothes you have and give some money to the local clothes closet,

OR

You spend all your money on great clothes in the latest style.

Think about Paul's words to the church at Philippi above and let volunteers tell why they made their decision. Respectfully listen to why each person made the choice he or she did.

PRACTICING WHAT JESUS TAUGHT

As you cut out star shapes from cardboard or paper, discuss whether or not others know you as followers of Jesus? In what ways do we *shine like stars*? Cover the stars with foil and place them in various locations around your house as reminders that you are called to show the light of Jesus.

PRAYING TOGETHER

God, help us to live in your light, shining for all the world. Amen.

April 27

READING THE BIBLE TOGETHER

Read Matthew 5:23-24.

IMAGINE THIS

Close your eyes while one person reads:

I have always followed the many laws of my Jewish faith. So Jesus' words caught me off guard. I was a good and generous employer, a pillar of the community, a leader in my town.

And then, as I was walking to Sabbath services at the Temple, I overheard Jesus talking to a crowd. Why did I stop? He really wasn't my kind of prophet or teacher. Yet his words grabbed hold of me and wouldn't let me go. "When you are offering your gift at the altar," he said, "if you remember that your brother or sister has something against you, leave your gift there before the altar and go; first be reconciled to your brother or sister, and then come and offer your gift." *What did he mean by that?* I wondered. I felt in harmony with God and was at that moment carrying a pair of turtledoves to leave at the altar to show my love for God.

So why did I stop in my tracks and cover my face with my hands? My cousin, Nathaniel, that's why. Oh, Jesus said, "brother or sister" but I knew he meant that if I had an unsettled problem with any person, I wasn't really ready to go to the altar and be at one with God. Nathaniel and I had not spoken since a terrible argument five years earlier, even though we lived within a stone's throw of each other.

I left my doves and ran to my cousin's home, where I threw my arms around him and apologized. Was he surprised! And when I returned with my doves to the Temple, I felt the difference. For the first time in five years, my gift was given with my whole heart, not just with my hands.

CONSIDER THIS

Some people say that Jesus' cross is a reminder of our responsibility to be reconciled to God and to other people. The upright beam of the cross represents our relationship with God, and the crossbeam, our relationship with others. The more we love God's people, the more God feels our love.

PRAYING TOGETHER

God, help us to settle our differences with others and be ready to come to you with an open, loving heart as Jesus taught. Amen.

LOOKING AHEAD

An option for tomorrow is to make a pair of glasses out of pipe cleaners or have an old pair of glasses ready to use as Jesus glasses.

April 28

READING THE BIBLE TOGETHER

Read 2 Corinthians 5:16-17.

Remember that these verses were written by Paul who, in his earlier life, was Saul, the persecutor of those who followed Jesus. Look at verse 16 and reread it with that in mind. Since he has known Jesus, Paul's standards have changed.

CONSIDER THIS

Most situations can be seen from more than one point of view. Usually what we see on the surface is not all there is to be seen. If we put on our *Jesus glasses*, we see beyond the surface of a person's life and look deeper into who they are and why they do what they do.

SHARING TOGETHER

Let each family member make a pair of glasses from pipe cleaners and wear them as the family considers the following situations. Share how one could look at them, first from a human standpoint, and then from the standpoint of one who follows Jesus, as a new creation.

- Barry is a troublemaker with few friends. His parents are dead, and he lives in a foster home.
- Mrs. Carlile lives alone. She is a crotchety widow who yells at kids who walk in her beloved vegetable garden.
- Andre just moved to your town. You don't know much about him except that he has a funny accent and walks home alone from school.
- Mr. and Mrs. Stephens go to your church. You don't know them well, but they are always friendly—too friendly, almost pushy.
- Patti is always bragging about how much money she has and how many famous people she knows.

PRAYING TOGETHER

God, in Jesus, you made us new creations. Help us to live that new life and see beyond our human standards. We want to see with Jesus' eyes, but sometimes we forget that everything old has passed away and everything has become new. In the name of Jesus who came that we might live in love, we pray. Amen.

LOOKING AHEAD

You will need markers and paper for tomorrow's devotion.

April 29

SHARING TOGETHER

How many different instances can each person remember of Jesus relating to other people. How did he show love to those who followed him? Make a list of some of the words that describe how Jesus showed love.

READING THE BIBLE TOGETHER

Read John 13:34-35.

MORE SHARING

Using paper and markers, draw pictures of the many people in your family's life. You can divide the people into groups for individuals to illustrate: extended family, church family, school friends and teachers, neighbors, etc. Let each family member draw one person for each group.

PRACTICING WHAT JESUS TAUGHT

Jesus loved not only his family and friends, but everyone with whom he came into contact. List people in the world who need your love whom you may not have a chance to meet personally. How can you show love to them?

FAMILY LITANY

Form into two groups to say the words below. Have each group stand while they are saying their line and sit when they are silent. You can increase speed as you say the words over and over.

Group 1: Love one another, love one another,
Group 2: As Jesus said.
Group 1: Love one another, love one another,
Group 2: As Jesus said.
Group 1: As Jesus said, as Jesus said,
Group 2: Love one another.
Group 1: As Jesus said, as Jesus said,
Group 2: Love one another.
All: **As Jesus said, love one another.**

What was Jesus' new commandment? Look at the list you made above of words describing how Jesus showed love to others. Then look at the pictures you drew of the people in your family's life. How can each of you show Jesus' love to those people?

PRAYING TOGETHER

God of love, help us to love one another as you love us. Amen.

OPTIONAL ACTIVITY

See page 274.

April 30

- Will human lives be different? How?
- What do you like about this image of the future?

SHARING TOGETHER

Name the things in your family's life that have changed since the children were born (a new house, someone changed jobs, others started school, new pets, etc.). Then ask, does anyone ever miss the way it used to be? Discuss what was good about the way it used to be. What do you like about how it is now?

CONSIDER THIS

Newness comes in many ways. Situations can change, as in jobs or schools. Things like a computer or car or pet can bring about change. People face changes like a move or divorce. Just getting older brings changes. All of us will undergo many changes in our lives—some big, some little—but our attitude determines whether these changes are good or bad for us.

READING THE BIBLE TOGETHER

Read Revelation 21:1-5.

Share your ideas from the scripture about the following:

- What will be different when God brings a new heaven and new earth?
- Where will God live?

CONSIDER THIS

Take two or three minutes of silence for each family member to think about how he or she would like to be new in their lives. Encourage everyone not to focus on material things but on other ways of being new.

A FAMILY LITANY

Take turns sharing what each person has just decided about being new in his or her life. After each sharing, everyone says together:

God is making all things new.

This is not a time for discussion but for listening. When everyone has finished sharing, all say together one last time:

God is making all things new!

PRAYING TOGETHER

God of all newness, thank you for the opportunities you give us. In sorrow, you offer hope. When we have doubts, we can move to faith. Our anger can turn to acceptance, our resentments to love, our fears to courage. Help us to remember to lean on you, to give you the chance to make all things new in our lives this day and always. Amen.

MAY

May 1

READING THE BIBLE TOGETHER

Each verse in Psalm 136 includes the phrase: *for his steadfast love endures forever.* Practice this response together. Let someone read Psalm 136:1-9, with the family saying the response together at the end of each verse.

SHARING TOGETHER

This morning the sun rose, painting the clouds pink. Did you see it?
The dew sparkled on the grass.
   Did you see it?
The moon lingered for a while in the sky.
   Did you see it?
The light painted valleys and houses, steeples, and skyscrapers.
   Did you see it?
Your shadow grew smaller and at noon disappeared.
   Did you see it?

   Sometimes we forget to open our eyes and see the wondrous things around us, those amazing gifts that God gives us.
   An old Irish festival on May 1 is called *Bealtaine* (Be-all-ta-na). Bushes are decorated and bonfires are lit to welcome the beginning of the summer season.

This is a season when God's earth is beautiful. Name all the things you can that are God's gifts of nature. Think again and name some more. What a beautiful world we have if only we stop to notice its wonders!
   As you go to and from school or work today, look around you and pretend that everything you see in nature has a bow on it because it is a gift from God. Silently, say *thank you* for each thing.
   Tomorrow take turns sharing some of the things you saw.

PRAYING TOGETHER

Let each person thank God for living in our beautiful world. Then pray together:

Dear God, we thank you that your steadfast love endures forever. Amen.

PRAISING GOD TOGETHER

Sing (or say echo style) the chorus of "All Things Bright and Beautiful":

All things bright and beautiful,
all creatures great and small,
all things wise and wonderful,
the Lord God made them all.

OPTIONAL ACTIVITY

See page 275.

May 2

SHARING TOGETHER

If you pretended yesterday that everything you saw in nature had a bow on it as a gift from God, tell how it felt to see those things as gifts from God.

READING THE BIBLE TOGETHER

Read Psalm 148:1-4, 7-12.

Reread verse 1 and repeat together:
Praise the Lord!

CONSIDER THIS

David McManaway of Dallas, Texas, is an artist who likes to find objects and assemble them into works of art. He puts interesting and surprising things together.

People look closely at his work and think about what they are seeing.

Every day each of us receives gifts from God. It may be a beautiful sunrise or sunset, a bright moon, a flower blooming in a surprising place, a tree with gnarled limbs, a beautiful bird outside a window, a child in a swing, an older person whose limp shows courage, or a smile from a teacher or colleague. Interesting and surprising things appear all day long. God's gifts abound! We forget to look.

MORE SHARING

Today begin to watch for God's daily gifts. Make your own work of art by collecting interesting and surprising things and gluing them to a piece of paper. Take turns sharing your collection tomorrow.

PRAYING TOGETHER

Loving God,
thank you for your many gifts.
Help us to wake up and see them!
Amen.

PRAISING GOD TOGETHER

Sing (or say echo style) the chorus of "All Things Bright and Beautiful":

All things bright and beautiful,
all creatures great and small,
all things wise and wonderful,
the Lord God made them all.

May 3

READING THE BIBLE TOGETHER

Read Psalm 147:7-11, 16-18.

SHARING TOGETHER

Have you ever gone backpacking or camping or slept outdoors or sat outside and listened to the sounds at night? Beyond the sounds of the motors and people are the wonderful sounds from God's gifts of nature. Chelsea Oden, age ten, portrays these gifts in a poem, "Wilderness":

Listen to the chirps of the crickets,
listen to how they sing.
Their wondrous little voices,
speaking mysterious things.

Or listen to the sound of deer hooves,
prancing around your tent.
Carrying curious bodies,
with deer necks that are bent.

Or listen to the way the wind hums,
gliding between giant trees.
Making them dance so gracefully,
dressed in pine needles and leaves.

Listen to the cry of the wolf,
howling with all his might.
To let the world know he is there,
in the dark of the northern night.

Just take a breath of fresh air,
and listen to all of these sounds.
They are the sounds of wilderness,
where nature's heart is found.*

Listening is something we have a hard time doing. Sometimes we don't listen because we are impatient for our turn to talk. Or we put on earphones to shut out everything except our choice of music. Sometimes we forget to open our ears and hear the wondrous things around us, the amazing gifts that God has given us. What are your favorite sounds? Which of these are gifts from God?

PRAYING TOGETHER

Take turns thanking God for your ears and the many gifts of sound.

PRAISING GOD TOGETHER

Sing (or say echo style) the chorus of "All Things Bright and Beautiful":

All things bright and beautiful,
all creatures great and small,
all things wise and wonderful,
the Lord God made them all.

*Oden, Chelsea, "Wilderness." Poem used by permission of the author.

May 4

READING THE BIBLE TOGETHER

Read 1 Timothy 3:14-16.

CONSIDER THIS

As human beings, we cannot be fully aware of God's mystery. It is too large. Our own view of the way things are, the opinions we are quick to offer, and what we know are all too small to understand that mystery. Even the view of our own congregation or denomination cannot grasp all of God's mystery, for it is still too large.

IMAGINE THIS

Imagine a wall-to-wall chalkboard in your classroom (or remember one from your childhood). Pretend that you make a tiny chalk dot in the center. Now imagine that you stand back and look at it. The entire chalkboard represents God's mystery. The tiny dot represents what you know about that mystery, the mystery of faith.

SHARING TOGETHER

Do you ever think you have the one and only right answer about faith or some issue in the church? Does thinking about the dot on the chalkboard make you wonder if we know too little to be sure that we are right and someone else is wrong?

A STORY

Brother Roger of Taizé was highly influenced by his great-grandmother's faith. When she became ill and was near death, there was still so much he wanted to learn from her. He sat beside her bed and asked her to teach him about her faith.

She said, "I don't have anything to say about faith. All I know is that what I see is very beautiful."

Yes! We can be sure that God's mystery of faith is very beautiful!

PRAYING TOGETHER

Thank you, God, for your beautiful mystery of faith. Help us to remember that when we think mean thoughts, say mean things, or treat another in a mean way we are stepping away from faith—even when we think we are defending it. Amen.

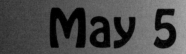

May 5

READING THE BIBLE TOGETHER

Read Psalm 150.

A STORY

Three children in stair-step sizes waited at the airport. They laughed excitedly, and, though they tried to be patient, they could hardly wait for the plane to land. Finally it arrived. As passengers began passing through the doorway, the children watched carefully for the right face. They held high a poster so large it took all three

of them to lift it. They had drawn pictures on it and written words in many colors: *Welcome home! Happy birthday, Daddy! We love you!*

How surprised and pleased their father was! His face beamed with love when he saw them and their gift.

OPTIONAL ACTIVITY
See page 275.

CONSIDER THIS

It is so easy to give each other gifts of love. This takes time but not necessarily money. It takes time to think of a gift of love. It takes time to really think about the person who will receive the gift and what would be meaningful to him or her. It may also take time to prepare the gift. But money is not important in a gift of love. Common things become sacred because of the love they represent.

What gift of love could you give to a family member? to a friend? to someone else who is important to you?

May 6

READING THE BIBLE TOGETHER

Read and repeat 1 John 4:10.

A STORY

God's love is like the ocean. God's love is big enough to hold all the fish and hold up all the ships. It is big enough to hold each person in our family, our neighborhood, school and workplace, our town and state, our whole country, and all the people around the globe. God's love is so big that it can hold everyone who has ever lived and everyone who will live in the future.

The ocean waves flow onto the sand and out again. As the tides ebb and flow, it is as though God is breathing in and breathing out. This great Creator of the universe is also the One who loves each of us and is as close to us as our own breathing.

SHARING TOGETHER

Prepare gifts of love for each member of your family who lives with you. A gift could be a copy of a poem, a picture made from items gathered outside, a picture you have drawn, or anything that says *I love you.*

PRAYING TOGETHER

Loving God, may each breath we take remind us to praise you. Help us to show our praise for you by being more thoughtful in our gifts for others. Amen.

LOOKING AHEAD

You will need a map of the world or a picture of an ocean, or paper and pencils/crayons to draw one.

SHARING TOGETHER

If you have a globe or a map of the world, look at how big the oceans are. Or find a picture of an ocean. Think about how much of the earth's surface is covered by water and remember that God's love is even bigger.

Share a recent time when you most felt God's love. When recently did you have a hard time feeling God's love?

Think about a recent time when you showed God's love to another. When recently did you not show God's love?

PRAYING TOGETHER

Dear God, thank you for your love, a love bigger than we could ever imagine. We pray for the people in our community who do not know about your love for them. Help us to show others your love today by the way we treat them. Amen.

PRAISING GOD TOGETHER

Say or sing the refrain to "Jesus Loves Me."

May 7

READING THE BIBLE TOGETHER

Let a child, if possible, read 1 John 4:10. Read and repeat 1 John 3:1.

CONSIDER THIS

God loves us so much that each one of us is called God's child—no matter how young or old we are. Since God claims us, we are God's children. Every one of us! To God, each of us is beloved.

A FAMILY LITANY

Have one person to read a line and all to repeat it.

Reader:	I am beloved by God.
All:	**I am beloved by God.**
Reader:	I am a precious child of God.
All:	**I am a precious child of God.**
Reader:	I am God's special creation.
All:	**I am God's special creation.**
Reader:	Everyone at school, at the workplace, and the volunteer place is beloved by God. Yes! Everyone!
All:	**Yes! Everyone!**
Reader:	Even…

(Each person names someone he or she has trouble getting along with.)

Reader:	Each one is a precious child of God.
All:	**Each one is God's special creation.**

SHARING TOGETHER

How do we treat something precious? How then do we want to treat ourselves, since each of us is beloved and precious to God? How do we want to treat people we work with and go to school with, since each of them is beloved and precious to God?

Are there persons or groups that you have a hard time thinking of as God's children and, therefore, as your brothers and sisters? Who are they? You may want to share these thoughts.

PRAYING TOGETHER

Thank you, Loving God, for creating each person in our family. Today help us to treat others as your precious children. We pray for people near and far away who don't know they are special in your eyes. Amen.

PRAISING GOD TOGETHER

Say or sing the refrain to "Jesus Loves Me," changing "loves me" to "loves them."

LOOKING AHEAD

Tomorrow you will need squares of paper to make a family quilt, markers or crayons, and tape or glue.

May 8

READING THE BIBLE TOGETHER

Read and repeat 1 John 3:1.
You may want to try to say 1 John 4:10 from memory.

CONSIDER THIS

All of us feel alone at times. Perhaps sometimes we feel that we are loved less than another person in our family. Maybe we feel left out at school or work. Perhaps we make mistakes and feel embarrassed, or we get behind in our work. Maybe classmates or co-workers, teachers or bosses, friends or family members criticize us or say mean things to us.

When we have these feelings, we can remember that God's love is like a warm quilt. We can imagine curling up in that quilt and being held in God's arms as God rocks us and hums a comforting song. It doesn't matter whether we are children or grown-ups, God's love is always there, ready to enfold us.

IMAGINE THIS

Take turns sharing a time when you felt alone or sad. Pretend that you tell God about these times, and imagine that God wraps you in a quilt of love. (Give time to imagine this.) How does that feel?

SHARING TOGETHER

Cut out squares of paper to make a family quilt. On some of the squares write acts you did that you feel sad about (one act per square per person). On others write acts you did that you feel glad about (again, one act per square per person). Use as many squares as you wish. Tape or glue them together like a quilt.

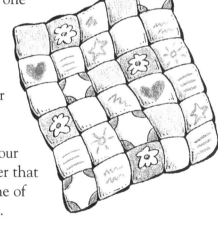

When you are finished, look at your quilt and remember that God loves each one of you just as you are.

PRACTICING WHAT JESUS TAUGHT

Name someone you know whom you would like God to wrap in a quilt of love. As a family, choose one of these people. If possible, contact that person today (in person, by phone, letter, or e-mail), and tell the person that you are praying for him or her.

PRAYING TOGETHER

Thank you, Loving God,
for making a beautiful quilt
from the scraps of our lives.
Thank you for your love
that comforts us
when we cry out to you.
Please put your arms around . . .
  (name the person chosen above).
Help us to comfort others today.
Amen.

PRAISING GOD TOGETHER

Say or sing the closing praise to the tune of "Jesus Loves Me" without the refrain.

Praise God! Praise God! We praise God!
Praise the Loving Holy One!
Praise God! Praise God! We praise God!
Praise the Loving Holy One!

LOOKING AHEAD

Tomorrow you will need an umbrella for the Sharing Together segment.

May 9

READING THE BIBLE TOGETHER

Try to say 1 John 3:1 from memory. Then read and repeat 1 John 4:16a.

CONSIDER THIS

Sometimes things happen that we don't want to happen. It feels as if rain is pouring down on us. Maybe we are worried or afraid. Maybe we feel upset about something that happened at school or work. Maybe a job was lost, or there was a car accident.

God's love for us is like an umbrella in these storms. It does not keep the storms from coming into our lives. But, like an umbrella, God's love shields us as we walk through the storm because we know that God is with us. We are not alone.

Under God's umbrella of love, we don't have to hide until the storm goes away. We know that God will help us make it through the day, each day. We can trust that God's love is with us and that someday the storm will end and the sun will shine again.

SHARING TOGETHER

You may want to go outside for this activity. Take your umbrella, raise it, and pass it from one family member to another. As members hold the open umbrella, they can share a time when they felt God's umbrella of love during a stormy time of life.

PRACTICING WHAT JESUS TAUGHT

Think of someone with whom you can share the umbrella of God's love today. Mention that person's name during the prayer below.

PRAYING TOGETHER

Let one person read each phrase below and all others repeat it.

Thank you, Loving God,
for your umbrella of love
on stormy days.
Help me today
to share that umbrella
with others who need it.
We pray for . . .
   (each family member names
   the person identified earlier)
Amen.

May 10

READING THE BIBLE TOGETHER

Read and repeat 1 John 4:16a.

CONSIDER THIS

Sometimes family members become angry. Sisters and brothers get mad at one another. Parents get mad at each other. They get angry with children, and children get angry with them.

When people in a family are upset with one another, they handle it in different ways. Maybe an angry silence fills the room. Or maybe they begin to shout. One person may even hit another. We often feel scared or sad at these times.

God knows our feelings. God's love for us is like a tall pine tree. The pine tree rises toward the sky, reminding us that God's love reaches above and beyond people's anger. We can huddle in its shade, and it will shield our hearts when hot tempers explode around us. The pine tree is always green—both summer and winter—just as God's love is always with us.

Always. No matter where we are. No matter what is happening.

When we see a pine tree or picture one in our minds, we can think of it as being like a message from God, saying: "My love is with you, my child."

SHARING TOGETHER

Share a time when you felt scared or sad because someone was angry.

IMAGINE THIS

Pretend you are sitting beside a pine tree. Imagine giving your fear or sadness to God. Just let go of it, like letting go of a balloon. Now imagine that God receives your fear and sadness and fills that sad place inside you with love, healing the hurt in your heart.

Draw and color a picture of a pine tree and think about God's love for you. You may want to hang the picture in a special place.

PRAYING TOGETHER

Loving God, thank you that we can be secure and safe in your love no matter what is going on around us. Help us not to do anything today that causes anyone to be scared or sad. Amen.

PRAISING GOD TOGETHER

Say or sing the closing praise to the tune of "Jesus Loves Me" without the refrain.

Praise God! Praise God! We praise God!
Praise the Loving Holy One!
Praise God! Praise God! We praise God!
Praise the Loving Holy One!

May 11

READING THE BIBLE TOGETHER

Let anyone who knows either 1 John 4:10, 16a or 1 John 3:1 by memory share it. Then read both passages slowly.

CONSIDER THIS

These scripture verses tell us three things about God's love: (1) that God loved us so much God gave us Jesus, (2) that we are children of God, and (3) that we can know God's love for us and trust it. When, yesterday or today, did you feel God's love?

Recently we have read about God's love being like the ocean or a quilt or an umbrella or a pine tree. Think of something else that reminds you of what God's love is like.

SHARING TOGETHER

Individually or as a family, do something that shows what you think God's love is like. Color a picture about God's love, or make up a song about it, or write a poem. Take turns talking about the image or song or words you are creating. You may want to keep what you do in a special place.

A FAMILY LITANY

Reader: We praise you, O God, for . . . (Each family member names one thing to praise God for).
All: We praise you, O God.

PRAYING TOGETHER

(A parent prays):
Loving God, thank you for our family time when together we think about you and your gift of Jesus. Thank you for your many blessings. Help us as a family to remember your love for each of us all through the day. Amen.

PRAISING GOD TOGETHER

Say or sing the closing praise to the tune of "Jesus Loves Me" without the refrain.

Praise God! Praise God! We praise God!
Praise the Loving Holy One!
Praise God! Praise God! We praise God!
Praise the Loving Holy One!

LOOKING AHEAD

You will need paper and pencil or paints tomorrow.

May 12

READING THE BIBLE TOGETHER

Read and repeat Mark 12:30. This scripture verse is called The Greatest Commandment. It is also found in Matthew 22:36-38 and Luke 10:27.

CONSIDER THIS

How do we love God? It is not easy to think about that. God is beyond our grasp. Yet God is present with us—like the sun we cannot touch but can count on to warm us.

God is the creator of the whole universe, from the tiniest flowers to the distant planets. Yet God is close to each of us—like the unseen air we breathe.

Even though God is hard for our minds to understand, our hearts know we can trust God's love, a love without limit. In our thankfulness for the love God gives us, our love wells up for God.

We cannot put our arms around God and give God a hug. But we can pray to God and speak of our love. We can also love God by loving others.

May 13

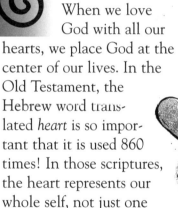

READING THE BIBLE TOGETHER

Read and repeat the first part of Mark 12:30:

You shall love the Lord your God with all your heart.

SHARING TOGETHER

Take turns sharing a recent time when you strongly felt your love for God. Then talk about how you showed that love. Let each person write a letter or e-mail to God expressing their love. Plan to read the messages tomorrow.

TELL US MORE

When we love God with all our hearts, we place God at the center of our lives. In the Old Testament, the Hebrew word translated *heart* is so important that it is used 860 times! In those scriptures, the heart represents our whole self, not just one small part of our body.

PRAYING TOGETHER

Thank you, God, for Christ, who showed us how much you love us. Help us to show our love for you today. Amen.

PRAISING GOD TOGETHER

Say or sing the closing praise to the tune of "Jesus Loves Me," without the refrain.

We love you, God! We love you!
Praise God! Praise God! We praise you.
We love you, God! We love you!
Praise God! Praise God! We praise you.

CONSIDER THIS

We too use the word *heart* a lot.

Heart. Candy hearts.
Heartthrob. Heartstrings.
Love God with all your heart.

Heart. Heartbeats.
Heart of my heart. Heart to heart.
Love God with all your heart.

Heart. Coldhearted? Heavyhearted?
Lighthearted? Lionhearted?
Love God with all your heart.

Heart. Heart failure. Heartless.
Lose heart? Broken heart?
Love God with all your heart.

Heart. Heartsick.
Pure hearted? Heart of gold?
Love God with all your heart.

To love God with all our hearts is to love God no matter how we feel. To love God with all our hearts is to think of God when we first wake up in the morning and before we drop off to sleep at night. To love God with all our hearts is to try to keep our love for God at the center of our lives, wherever we go and whatever we do all day long.

SHARING TOGETHER

Take turns sharing what it means to you to love God with all your heart. If you wrote messages to God expressing your love for God yesterday, share them now.

PRAYING TOGETHER

Thank you, Loving God, for giving us life and love. Help us to love you with all our hearts today. Amen.

PRAISING GOD TOGETHER

Say or sing the closing praise to the tune of "Jesus Loves Me," without the refrain.

We love you, God! We love you!
Praise God! Praise God! We praise you.
We love you, God! We love you!
Praise God! Praise God! We praise you.

May 14

READING THE BIBLE TOGETHER

Read and repeat the first part of Mark 12:30:

**You shall love the Lord your God
with all your heart,
and with all your soul.**

A STORY

A boy about six years old was playing in a grassy park in Annecy, France. He wore sneakers and jeans, a red T-shirt, and a Mickey Mouse cap with the bill facing backwards.

He pulled his cap down over his eyes and stretched out his arms like wings. Though he couldn't see anything, he began turning around and around blindly, singing, "Alleluia! Alleluia! Alleluia!"

We cannot see what is ahead of us in life. Yet, like that boy, we can dance in trust and sing in praise. That is how we love God with all our soul.

CONSIDER THIS

When we want to do something better—like playing a sport or a musical instrument, we practice. When we want to do a better job of loving God with all our soul, we practice that through our spiritual habits.

This time together as a family is part of our practice. Together we read the Bible, pray, talk about our faith, think about Jesus' teachings, and practice them with our family.

We can also practice spiritual habits by

ourselves. We can read the Bible or Bible story-books or look at Bible picture books. We can pray alone too, making time to talk with God and to listen for what God may be saying to us. We can pray at any time throughout the day.

When we try to love God with all our souls, our lives themselves become prayers. Even when we are troubled and feel unsure of the way, we can still trust God. In this trust—in loving God with all our soul—we can dance round and round, even blindly, singing alleluia!

Do you take this time for practicing spiritual growth together as a family as seriously as you take, say, getting to soccer practice? If this time together is important to you but you do not always share it, remember that God's grace abounds. Burying ourselves in guilt does not help us grow spiritually!

 ## PRAYING TOGETHER

Pray this prayer as an echo prayer:

Thank you, Loving God,
for your Holy Spirit
that can live in each of us.
Help me today and everyday
to love you with all my soul.
Amen.

PRAISING GOD TOGETHER

Say or sing the closing praise to the tune of "Jesus Loves Me," without the refrain.

We love you, God! We love you!
Praise God! Praise God! We praise you.
We love you, God! We love you!
Praise God! Praise God! We praise you.

May 15

 ## READING THE BIBLE TOGETHER

Read and repeat the first part of Mark 12:30:

**You shall love the Lord your God
with all your heart,
and with all your soul.
and with all your mind.**

CONSIDER THIS

God has given us marvelous minds, and God has given us the freedom to use those minds or to waste them. We can allow others to influence us to do things we know are not right. We can let commercials and ads influence us to buy things we know we don't need.

In some ways, our minds are like computers: *garbage in, garbage out.* Part of what it means to love God with all our minds is to feed our minds with good things, to read good books and watch good programs on TV. It is to sort out the trash and not waste our brainpower on it. Even when we don't use our minds well, God loves us anyway. But, oh, what we miss! At home and school and the workplace, we settle for less than our wonderful minds are capable of. To love God with all our minds is to use our minds—to think.

To love God with all our minds invites us to read and listen to stories about Jesus, about other people from the Bible, and about people who have lived since then and tried to follow Jesus' teachings. It invites us to figure out how to follow those teachings in our daily lives, even in difficult situations. When we try to love God with all our minds, God is close to our thoughts and can influence our decisions.

SHARING TOGETHER

Act out a TV commercial. One person can be on TV doing the commercial. Another can tell whether what is said is really true. Another (if possible) can get hooked and beg to buy it.

Then talk about times when you did not use your mind with regard to choices. When did you use your mind well? Share what it means to you to love God with all your mind.

PRACTICING WHAT JESUS TAUGHT

Today try to love God with all your mind, using your mind well, feeding it well, and being mindful (mind-full) of God.

PRAYING TOGETHER

Thank you, Loving God, for our amazing minds. Help us to use them in ways that show our gratitude. Help us today to love you with all our minds. Amen.

PRAISING GOD TOGETHER

Say or sing the closing praise to the tune of "Jesus Loves Me," without the refrain.

We love you, God! We love you!
Praise God! Praise God! We praise you.
We love you, God! We love you!
Praise God! Praise God! We praise you.

May 16

READING THE BIBLE TOGETHER

Read and repeat Mark 12:30:

**You shall love the Lord your God
with all your heart,
and with all your soul.
and with all your mind.
and with all your strength.**

IMAGINE THIS

One person reads, allowing time between each sentence to imagine. Pretend you are building a church.

. . . .

Imagine how strong you would build it.

. . . .

Imagine what kinds of materials you would use.

. . . .

Now pretend that it is finished. Can you see it in your mind?

. . . .

Imagine what you put inside your church.

. . . .

Imagine what you will do to take good care of it.

CONSIDER THIS

God created our bodies to be temples of God—each of us beautiful to behold in God's eyes.

One way to love God with all our strength is to help our bodies be strong temples. We do this by forming healthy habits and respecting the holiness of our gift of sexuality.

Just as we wouldn't take a faulty piece of lumber into the church we imagined building,

we want to be careful about what we take into our body-temples. Just as we would take good care of our church, we care for our body-temples when we eat right and get enough sleep and exercise. Many of us sit a lot at work or school. If we come home and spend the rest of the day in front of the TV or at the computer, our body-temples can begin to weaken. Just as we need strong walls for the church we imagined, we also need strong bones and muscles for our bodies.

SHARING TOGETHER

What are some things you do to take care of your body-temple? What things could you do differently to take better care of your body-temple? Make a list of everything you do to love God with all your strength.

PRAYING TOGETHER

Thank you, Loving God, for our wonderful bodies. Today help us to treat them like your temple. Amen.

PRAISING GOD TOGETHER

Say or sing the closing praise to the tune of "Jesus Loves Me," without the refrain.

We love you, God! We love you!
Praise God! Praise God! We praise you.
We love you, God! We love you!
Praise God! Praise God! We praise you.

LOOKING AHEAD

You will need a blank spiral notebook for tomorrow's devotion.

May 17

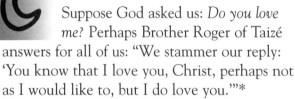

READING THE BIBLE TOGETHER

Read 1 John 2:3-6.

CONSIDER THIS

Suppose God asked us: *Do you love me?* Perhaps Brother Roger of Taizé answers for all of us: "We stammer our reply: 'You know that I love you, Christ, perhaps not as I would like to, but I do love you.'"*

We do love God. Yet we are not perfect. We try to love God with all our heart, soul, mind, and strength. We intend to. But we fall short. We mess up. We would like to do a better job of loving God.

We do this when we try to follow God's way as we walk through the day. We do this when we try to show care for others. We do not ever love God as much as we would like to, but we do love God the best that we can.

IMAGINE THIS

Pretend that your life is a book, your name is the title, and each day is a page. Imagine that when you awake and rise from bed, you have a blank sheet of paper before you. Pretend that as you go through the day, the page is filled with the sentences you write by the words you speak and with the pictures you paint by your actions. Imagine that when night comes, God lovingly looks at the page before it is turned. God forgives you for the times you fell short. God knows you tried that day to follow God's way and care for others, and God is pleased with you.

You may want to share your feelings, both about writing a page in your life book and about God's reading the page you wrote.

*Brother Roger, *Peace of Heart in All Things: Meditations for Each Day of the Year* (London: HarperCollins, 1996), 53.

SHARING TOGETHER

Share specific ways you can love God today. Now is a good time to begin a family journal (perhaps in a spiral notebook) about your life with God—how each person experiences God's love and how you show your love for God. Keep the journal in your family worship center so that individual family members can write or draw in it as they like or the family can make entries together. Your entries may be prayers, poems, songs, praises, questions, or whatever you feel like writing.

MORE TO CONSIDER

This is the God we love—the Ever-Loving, Ever-Living Holy One who loves us, forgives us, and never ever, ever gives up on us.

PRAYING TOGETHER

Join hands and take turns praying aloud, expressing in your own words your love for God and your gratitude for God's love for you.

PRAISING GOD TOGETHER

Say or sing the closing praise to the tune of "Jesus Loves Me," without the refrain.

We love you, God! We love you!
Praise God! Praise God! We praise you.
We love you, God! We love you!
Praise God! Praise God! We praise you.

May 18

READING THE BIBLE TOGETHER

Let different family members (if possible) read Matthew 22:37-39; Mark 12:30-31; and Luke 10:27.

TELL US MORE

After stating the first and greatest commandment (Mark 12:30), Jesus went on to the second: "The second is this, 'You shall love your neighbor as yourself.' There is no other commandment greater than these" (Mark 12:31).

Luke puts these two together in Luke 10:27: "You shall love the Lord your God with all your heart, and with all your soul, and with all your strength, and with all your mind; and your neighbor as yourself."

Matthew states that all the law and the prophets hang on these two commandments (Matt. 22:40). *Depend, based,* and *stem from* are used instead of *hang* in some translations. One Bible version suggests that if you keep only these two commandments, you will find that you are obeying all the others.

It is important to remember that when Jesus used the word *neighbor*, he meant more than the people who live in our neighborhood.

A STORY

Elizabeth was a princess of Hungary, born in 1207. Her husband died when she was twenty, and her brother-in-law took over the family's castle (a common tradition then). He made Elizabeth and her three children leave. She arranged for her children's care and then set up a home for the poor and needy.

She worked so hard that she was careless about her own health and died four years later. Though she died young, she has continued to live in Christian memory for nearly 800 years because of her love for Christ and her desire to show it by caring for the poor. After her death, she was named Saint Elizabeth by the Catholic Church.

SHARING TOGETHER

Most of us do not show our love for Christ by doing something dramatic like Saint Elizabeth. But we do have opportunities to show our love for Christ in our daily routine at school and work. Take turns sharing ways you can love your neighbor.

PRACTICING WHAT JESUS TAUGHT

Do one of the things you talked about!

PRAYING TOGETHER

Thank you, Loving God, for people who remind us to love our neighbor. Thank you for those who came before us and those who surround us now. Help us to love our neighbor today. Amen.

PRAISING GOD TOGETHER

Think of someone you know who shows love for others and take turns thanking God for them:

We praise you, O God, for….

LOOKING AHEAD

Tomorrow you will need paper or construction paper, crayons, and scissors. If you want to plant seeds, you will need a flowerpot, seeds, and potting soil.

May 19

READING THE BIBLE TOGETHER

Read 1 John 3:16-18.
Repeat together verse 18:
**Little children, let us love,
not in word or speech,
but in truth and action.**

A STORY

If you did not gather for this devotion time yesterday, you may want to read A Story from that date, which is also about Elizabeth.

Saint Elizabeth turned her sadness into service. We can get to know her through the stories told about her since her death. Some of these stories are told with paintings rather than words. Paintings often show her carrying a basket of food to symbolize her care for others.

One story about Saint Elizabeth is told in a beautiful stained glass window in the Church of Saint Mary in Somerset, England. The window shows Elizabeth's gentle caring by including a little dog at her feet, gazing up at her. Her bowed head shows humility. She wears a bluish-purple cape and maroon skirt, and the top of her dress has small yellow hearts surrounded by tears. She holds more than two dozen colorful roses, which symbolize her desire to bring the fragrance of God's love into the lives of others.

Saint Elizabeth is not remembered for her words about God's love but for her loving presence to those who needed her.

CONSIDER THIS

What does *the fragrance of God's love* mean to you? Can you think of people you like to be around because when you are with them you feel a quiet loving presence? How can you be a fragrance of God's love?

Perhaps God created flowers to remind us to be a fragrance of God's love. Think of that when you see a flower.

SHARING TOGETHER

Let each person draw, color, and cut out a picture of a flower or draw one on construction paper. Use these flowers to make a family bouquet for your worship center to remind you to try to be a fragrance of God's love.

PRAYING TOGETHER

Take turns offering a prayer of thanks and praise to God.

May 20

SOMETHING TO CONSIDER

Do you remember the second greatest commandment (Mark 12:31)? Say it or read and repeat it together:

You shall love your neighbor as yourself.

It seems that Jesus would not have used the comparison of loving our neighbors as ourselves unless he thought that we would love ourselves.

READING THE BIBLE TOGETHER

Read Romans 7:15-25.

Sometimes it is difficult for us to love ourselves. Paul understood this. He said, "I obviously need help! I realize that I don't have what it takes. I can will it, but I can't *do* it" (from Romans 7:15, THE MESSAGE).

SHARING TOGETHER

Hate and *evil* are strong words. Most of us do not do things we actually hate or things that we consider evil. But all of us do some things we wish we wouldn't do, and we don't do some things we wish we would. We don't understand ourselves! We need help!

Take turns sharing some things you have done that you wish you hadn't done. Take turns sharing some things you didn't do that you wish you had done.

Is there one thing you do that you wish you wouldn't do? If so, what is it? (You may pass if you don't want to share it.) Is there one thing you don't do that you wish you would do? If so, what is it? (Again, you may pass if you don't want to share it.)

If you are serious about these wishes, how can you help one another in your family to make a change?

PRAYING TOGETHER

Take turns asking God to forgive you for your weaknesses as each person names one. A parent concludes by thanking God for forgiveness and the wonderful gift of grace, and asking for guidance and strength to change.

May 21

READING THE BIBLE TOGETHER

Read 1 John 3:11.

SHARING TOGETHER

We know what we should do, but it is hard for us to balance love of others and love of self. Sometimes we put ourselves first and have little regard for others' needs. Sometimes we have little regard for our own needs.

Share a time when someone else hurt you in some way in order to get what he or she wanted. Share a time when you hurt someone else in some way to get what you wanted.

CONSIDER THIS

In Paris, France, there is a beautiful park where children like to play. They run, laugh, slide, swing, and climb on the bright-colored playground equipment. You may have been to a park like this in your own city. But this park has a special name, Place Bellecour, which means *place of the beautiful heart*.

When we truly try to follow Jesus, we receive a gift—the gift of a beautiful heart. Deep inside us, this place of love begins to grow. Gradually, we begin to think and see and hear and speak from this place of love, this beautiful heart.

It is as though we swing back into that place of the beautiful heart, knowing Jesus loves us. Then we swing forward toward others, bringing with us his love. Back and forth we swing, growing in love and in our ability to give it away.

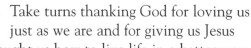

PRAYING TOGETHER

Take turns thanking God for loving us just as we are and for giving us Jesus who taught us how to live life in a better way.

OPTIONAL ACTIVITY
See page 275.

May 22

CONSIDER THIS

The end of another school year will come soon. That can be both happy and sad. Maybe we're sorry to leave a teacher we really like, or maybe a friend will be moving during the summer. Endings are sad because they separate us from people we love and change our lives. Endings can be scary because we are not sure what lies ahead.

Death brings a very sad ending. We miss the person who has died and wish that we could still see him or her. The one we love isn't present in the way we are used to. Yet we can always carry that person in our memory and in our hearts. The person can be present in a new way, within us.

Divorce brings an ending to the way things were and changes the way families live. Often after a divorce, children do not see one parent as much as they would like. Or children may have two homes that they go back and forth between. That can be hard. Divorce changes the way parents and children live, but it does not change how much each parent loves each child.

SHARING TOGETHER

Take turns talking about endings you have experienced and how you felt. If your family has experienced the death of a family member or a divorce, this would be a good opportunity to talk about it, to ask questions, or to express feelings. If you do not feel up to sharing at this time, keep it in mind for a later date and a better time.

MORE TO CONSIDER

A mountain climber on a difficult climb is always tethered (tied) to another person. Each of the climbers must climb for himself or herself. And tethered climbers cannot keep each other from stumbling or falling. But each climber can serve to break another's fall and keep that person from crashing down.

God is like the one to whom we are tethered as we climb the difficult mountain of life with its endings. We still have to do the climbing. And we still stumble. We may even fall. But as long as we stay tethered to God, God will not let us crash!

READING THE BIBLE TOGETHER

Read Romans 8:35-37.

PRAYING TOGETHER

Help us to be assured that nothing can separate us from Jesus' love. Help us to remember to stay tethered to you, O God! Amen.

PRAISING GOD TOGETHER

Sing to the tune of "London Bridge":

We praise God, O we praise God!
We praise God! We praise God!

We praise God, O we praise God, our Creator!

LOOKING AHEAD

Try to find some pictures of bridges in books or family photographs. Spread them out on your worship center for tomorrow's time together. Or have paper and crayons ready to draw pictures of bridges.

May 23

READING THE BIBLE TOGETHER

Read Psalm 69:1-3.

CONSIDER THIS

A high desert road in New Mexico goes from Tres Piedras to Taos. It is a safe, easy drive. But suddenly, without any kind of warning, the earth divides. Over the centuries, the rushing river has cut a gash 660 feet deep, separating one side of the Rio Grande Gorge from the other. It is impossible to get across without a bridge that spans from the end of one side to the beginning of the other.

Life is filled with endings, bridges, and beginnings. When an ending comes, we step on a bridge. We have to cross the bridge from where we were (before the move or school or job change or divorce or death) to a place of new beginning. We can't just be *beamed* over as on a science-fiction TV show or movie.

Each of us, even within the same family, has a separate bridge to cross. Each person's bridge is different—in how long and high it

feels, how curved or straight, how solid or swaying or slippery and icy, how narrow and creaky, or how scary.

SHARING TOGETHER

Look at the pictures of bridges (or think about bridges you have seen if you have no pictures). Which one stands out to you? Do any of the bridges remind you of one you took from an ending to a new beginning? Or the one you may be facing now?

PRAYING TOGETHER

Thank you, God, for being with us as we cross our bridges. Help us to know that you are always with us. Amen.

PRAISING GOD TOGETHER

Praise God, using the scripture verse below in echo style:

> I will praise the name of God
>   with a song;
> I will magnify him
>   with thanksgiving (Ps. 69:30).

May 24

READING THE BIBLE TOGETHER

Read Psalm 30:4-5.

A STORY

Martin and his father were playing with a truck on the sidewalk at a park. They stood far back from the truck. The father held the remote control, and the truck zigzagged down the smooth sidewalk, forward and backward, racing farther away and coming closer. The father handed the remote control to Martin, and he laughed with glee as he played with the truck from a distance.

Pavel, halfway around the world in the Czech Republic, also played with a truck. He drove it by pushing it, hands on, down on his knees. Pavel zigzagged his truck in the bumpy dirt, pushed it forward and backward. He raced it fast, revving his mouth-motor, and then slowed down and screeched to a stop.

When we face new beginnings, we can't work things out from a distance by remote control. We have to get up close to the new situation, hands on, and sometimes down on our knees. Things may not be as good as they were—or they may become better. One thing we can be sure of—if we're willing to cross the bridge, we'll find new opportunities and new possibilities that we wouldn't have had. Let's try to discover them!

SHARING TOGETHER

The word *beginnings* has several words hidden in it. See how many words you can find. Here are three:

- **Be:** In new situations we have more time just to be. We're not scheduled into a bunch of different activities yet.
- **Begin:** We can begin to think about changes we want to make, how we want to live, and how we can better follow God.
- **Innings:** Beginnings take us into new innings of our lives. If your life were divided into nine innings like a baseball game, what inning do you think you would be in now?

Take turns sharing what you like about this inning or the time you are living now. Share what you don't like about it. Take turns sharing what you liked and didn't like about earlier innings.

PRAYING TOGETHER

Thank you, God, for new opportunities and new possibilities that come with new beginnings. Amen.

PRAISING GOD TOGETHER

Praise God, using the scripture verse below in echo style:

O Lord my God,
I will give thanks to you
forever (Ps. 30:12).

May 25

READING THE BIBLE TOGETHER

Read Isaiah 55:12.

A STORY

On a train sat two children who had been traveling a good part of the day. The dark-haired girl was about ten, her fairer-haired brother about seven. The two of them were cramped in their seats amidst their luggage—a heavy school backpack, a large ice chest, and two huge, well-worn leather suitcases.

They explained to an adult nearby that they had been to their father's house for a week of summer vacation. Now they were returning to their mother and stepfather, who would be waiting for them when they got off the train. The next weekend they would return to their father and stepmother. They had been hugged good-bye, and they would be hugged hello; but they made the journey in between by themselves.

As the train slowed for their station, both children struggled to carry their heavy luggage. Expecting themselves to be self-sufficient, they were hesitant to accept any help.

Though parts of their life were hard, those children were painting a beautiful life picture, adding to it each day, changing, improving, using many colors, and doing what was required of them.

CONSIDER THIS

Have you ever seen a paint-by-number picture? Each section is clearly marked, and there is no gradual blending of one area into the next.

God did not make us with paint-by-number lines. We are unique. The lines of our lives overlap from one area to another. We unfold. We can't always determine what comes our way, but we can brush in our response, color our attitude. The canvas has limits, but we paint our own life picture on it. Every picture can be beautiful.

What do you think your life picture looks like so far? Are there some areas you want to redo by changing your attitude? Is it a joyful painting? a sad painting? Are you gradually improving it?

Remember: In God's eyes it is a beautiful painting!

PRAYING TOGETHER

Use echo style for this prayer:

Thank you, God,
for giving us a canvas
that is not paint-by-number.
Help us to paint
a joyful picture
that shows our gratitude to you.
Amen.

PRAISING GOD TOGETHER

Sing to the tune of "London Bridge":

We praise God, O we praise God!
We praise God! We praise God!
We praise God, O we praise God,
our Creator!

OPTIONAL ACTIVITIES

See page 275.

READING THE BIBLE TOGETHER

Read Psalm 122:1.

A STORY

One Sunday morning in a large church in Dallas, Texas, Susanna looked around her. A three-generation family sat in front of her, two teenagers on one side of her, an older couple on the other side of her. A metal walker stood at the end of the pew, used by the frail woman who sat beside it. A baby cried behind Susanna. A blind man sat in the front row with his guide dog. Children wiggled, eager for the Children's Moment in the service. One child held up a picture she had drawn for her father to see.

The acolytes, a boy and a girl, came forward to light the candles. The flame the boy carried blew out. But it was okay. A lit candle was hidden behind the cross just for such times. So he relit his wick and then lit the candle on the altar. (No matter how hard we try to carry the light of Christ in our daily lives, sometimes our flame goes out; but, just for such times, there is always extra light behind the cross!)

Susanna thought gratefully of the people who were there that day. There were people from all walks of life—people who lived in different-sized homes, wore different kinds of clothes, put different amounts of money in the offering, and had different joys and worries. But all of them had come to church; all were gathered together on this Sabbath morning to worship God.

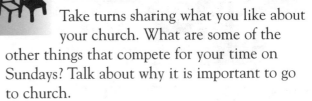

SHARING TOGETHER

Take turns sharing what you like about your church. What are some of the other things that compete for your time on Sundays? Talk about why it is important to go to church.

PRAYING TOGETHER

Take turns thanking God for your church and someone special to you whom you like to see there.

PRAISING GOD TOGETHER

Use your hands to form the church, steeple, doors, and people, saying:

Here's the church.
Here's the steeple.
Open the door,
And here are the people.
PRAISE GOD!

READING THE BIBLE TOGETHER

Read Psalm 92:1-4.

A STORY

A little boy named Michael began loving his baby sister before she was even born. Each night he would rest his head on his

258

mother's tummy and sing to his sister. He always sang the same song, "You Are My Sunshine."

When the baby was born, there were problems. She had to stay in the intensive care unit, and she continued to grow weaker. The doctor said the baby would probably live only one more day.

Michael wanted to see his baby sister. The sad parents took him to the hospital. Michael looked at his tiny sister and began to sing to her the song he had sung all those months while waiting for her to be born. And something happened! Instead of dying the next day, his little sister was better! The doctor called it a miracle. Michael's mother knew that it was a miracle of love.*

SOMETHING TO CONSIDER

Perhaps you and I cannot sing back to health someone who is dying physically. But we can *sing* to those who are dying of loneliness, grief, or sadness. And sometimes our song of love brings someone hope and joy, and that person begins to feel the stirring of new life.

PRACTICING WHAT JESUS TAUGHT

As Christians we gather for worship and then we are sent to serve. We are to feed the hungry, give drink to the thirsty, welcome the stranger, clothe the needy, care for the sick, and visit the prisoner. We are to love our neighbor and bring a song of hope and joy wherever we can.

SHARING TOGETHER

Discuss some specific ways you can serve, both as a family and individually.

Make a list of the six ways Christians are to serve (feed the hungry, etc.) and write one specific thing you can do beside each. Help one another carry out this service.

PRAYING TOGETHER

Take turns thanking God for the ways you can serve, naming each one.

PRAISING GOD TOGETHER

Use your hands to form the church, steeple, doors, and people, and say the following, noting that the last line has been changed:

> Here's the church.
> Here's the steeple.
> Open the door,
> And here are the people.
> PRAISE GOD!

*This story, as told by G. Steve Sallee, was described by Leonard Sweet, *Homiletics*, April-June 1996, and cited by James W. Moore, *The Cross Walk: A Lenten Study for Adults* (Nashville: Abingdon Press, 1999).

May 28

READING THE BIBLE TOGETHER

Read 1 Corinthians 2:9-13.

A STORY

A family on vacation was camping at the Great Sand Dunes National Monument near Alamosa, Colorado. They sat on benches at an outdoor amphitheater with other campers. The program that night was about lightning.

As the park ranger began his talk, lightning happened to appear in the distance, safely far away. The campers could see lightning bolts zigzag across the night sky, appearing to dart down from the sky to the earth. That is what most of us think happens.

But the ranger explained that this is not what actually occurs. An electric field we can't see follows along the ground below the storm clouds. As the lightning bolt starts down from the sky, a return stroke from the ground shoots up toward it, and they connect.

So lightning in the sky is made up not only of what is going on way beyond us but also what is going on right here. The two connect, and we see lightning.

CONSIDER THIS

Perhaps God's Spirit is like that—though without the storm and the danger. Perhaps the Spirit is hovering beyond us. And perhaps there is also energy required from us, energy used to follow along as we make our way through each day. Perhaps the Leader reaches for us, and perhaps when we reach up, there is a connection—there is Light in our lives, the Spirit of God.

The Spirit of God is always available to us, but we miss it when we are not putting any of our energy into facing toward God, following along, and reaching beyond ourselves.

And what about the thunder that follows lightning? Maybe it is the way God's voice sounds when God is delighted to connect with us!

SHARING TOGETHER

(Parents, remind your children that we are using the story about lightning as a symbol. A lightning storm is very dangerous and they should never be out in one—especially when the thunder sounds come about the same time as the lightning!)

How does being aware of the Spirit make a difference in your life?

PRAYING TOGETHER

Take turns sharing sentence prayers.

PRAISING GOD TOGETHER

Sing to the tune of "London Bridge":

We praise God for the Spirit!
The Spirit! The Spirit!
We praise God for the Spirit,
Holy Spirit!

May 29

READING THE BIBLE TOGETHER

Read Jeremiah 18:1-6.

Reread and repeat together echo style:
Just like the clay
in the potter's hand,
so are you in my hand.

SHARING TOGETHER

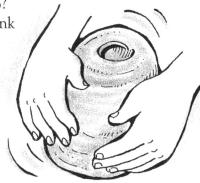

This scripture shows God as a potter. How do you think God is like a potter? How do you feel when someone holds you with love? How do you feel when someone grips you tightly by the arms and won't let you go? How do you think God holds us? Have you felt God's hands shaping you during your family devotion time together?

God does not grip us with tight fists but offers to shape us with creative hands. God lets us be free, and we decide whether to stay in those molding hands. Just as a puppy can jump from our arms or a child can climb off a parent's lap, we are free to wiggle out of God's loving hands.

IMAGINE THIS

Pretend God is the potter and you are a piece of clay. Imagine that even though you are clay, you can still slip out of the potter's hands. Pretend that you do not want to be shaped by God, and you go away. Imagine how that feels.

Pretend that you return to God to be shaped the way God would want you to be. Imagine how it feels to return to God.

Take turns talking about your feelings about these two situations.

PRAYING TOGETHER

Thank you, God, for being our potter. Help us to put ourselves in your loving hands as we go through each day. Help us to remember to reach out a loving hand to someone else today. Amen.

PRAISING GOD TOGETHER

Praise God the way a family member chooses. Be sure to thank God for shaping your family.

OPTIONAL ACTIVITY

See page 275.

May 30

READING THE BIBLE TOGETHER

Read Psalm 42:1-2.

A STORY

Jasmine called her grandmother who lived in another state a thousand miles away. "Come to my house tomorrow, Grandmom."

"I would like to, but I live too far away."

"It's okay," said Jasmine. "Just get in your car. Buckle the seatbelt. And drive down the road. And when you come to an intersection, just turn toward our house."

"I wish I could." How the grandmother longed to go!

"You can do it, Grandmom!"

PRACTICING WHAT JESUS TAUGHT

God invites us to be present. God wants us—today, tomorrow, each day. But sometimes we feel too far away. God gives us very careful directions through Jesus' teachings. What keeps us from being present to God? Remember! God remains with us, waiting patiently, encouraging us: *You can do it, my child!*

And we can—one day at a time. It can be overwhelming to think of pleasing God for our whole lives. We do better to take it one day at a time.

PRAYING TOGETHER

Pray this prayer as an echo prayer:

Dear God,
May we please you today
in our thoughts
our words
our deeds.
Amen.

May 31

SHARING TOGETHER

Take turns sharing ways you have become more aware of God's presence in your lives since beginning this family time together.

- Share ways you have become more aware of God's love for you.
- Share ways you have begun to respond to God's love.

- Are you comfortable praying together?
- Do you enjoy reading the Bible together?
- Are you comfortable talking about faith as a family?

READING THE BIBLE TOGETHER

Read Colossians 2:6-7.

MORE SHARING

To abound in thanksgiving, we first become aware of all that we are thankful for. As quickly as everyone can and altogether (like popcorn popping), name things for which you are thankful.

To abound in thanksgiving, we also say *thank you*. One by one, name again the things for which you are thankful, and after each thing mentioned, say, "Thank you, God." As you go through each day, be aware of each blessing and say a silent *thank you*.

PRAYING TOGETHER

Take turns thanking God for something you like about this family time together.

PRAISING GOD TOGETHER

Praise God each morning of the summer by abounding in thanksgiving, remembering to say a silent *Thank you, God.*

Optional Activities

The ideas for activities presented below may be used in addition to or in place of those presented for the designated days in the main portion of this book. You will find that you have more time on some days or that a family member requests some additional activity to satisfy a growing interest. As a family worships and comes to know God in everyday experiences, many opportunities for additional conversation about God will emerge. These optional activities can help satisfy that God-urging.

Throughout the year one or more members of the family may want to keep an individual notepad or journal to record *thought keepers*—brief phrases, sentences, or scripture references drawn from the daily devotion. Each thought-keeper can help in remembering the most important learning from the family's time together. Thought keeper journals may stay in the possession of the one keeping the journal or be put in the worship area with the strict understanding that they are private to the ones keeping them. It is a good idea to have several blank journals available as you begin the daily devotions.

SEPTEMBER 1

Set goals for your family devotions by talking about these questions: Why are you having these devotional times together? What do you hope will happen as a result of them?

Let a family member record the responses to these questions. Then read and discuss them together. Decide on a special place to keep these goals, such as in your Bible or near your worship area. Review them from time to time as a reminder of why your family made this special commitment, and to see if any additions or changes need to be made.

SEPTEMBER 2

Here are some suggestions for outings to help your family grow in their appreciation for God's world. Use the ones that apply to the area where you live. These outing suggestions can be taken anytime but plan to go on at least one during this week.

- Take a family walk or hike outdoors. Search for God's creatures. Pay special attention to the beauty of nature around you.
- Have a picnic in a nearby park or your own backyard. Share a special family blessing together.
- Walk on the beach. Look for shells and other ocean treasures. These treasures can be added to your worship area.

- Spread a blanket outside on a clear night and look at the night sky. Count the stars. During the day, watch the clouds. Be still and think of God's wonderful world!
- Rake fall leaves into a big pile, then jump into the middle of them.
- Wait for a windy day and fly kites together. Talk about how God is like the wind. (We cannot see God, but we can feel God's loving presence with us!)
- Visit a local zoo or aquarium.
- Set up a bird feeder. Watch and listen to birds.
- Walk in the rain. Look for a rainbow! Tell the story of Noah's Ark (Gen. 6–8). Think about God's promise of hope.
- Have your family devotional time outside.

SEPTEMBER 5

Parents, take time to write a letter to each of your children. Let them know how much you love them and how much God loves them. Share with your children the special qualities and gifts you see in them. Thank each one for the times you have spent together. Give the letters to your children to keep.

Also let your children hear you praying for them. Use the following prayer or one of your own:

Lord, we place our children into your loving arms. May they be blessed with the gift of faith. Let it be a growing faith that places you, Lord, at the very center of their lives. Impress on them the understanding that faith in you is their true foundation; for it will uphold them through all of life.

Lord, we place our children into your loving arms. We ask that you give them the precious gift of hope. Impart to them the knowledge that hope is the promise of things to come, for hope uplifts, gives purpose, and fills our lives with meaning. Hope lights our path. May our children be blessed with faith and hope.

Lord, we place our children into your loving arms. Grant them the gift of abundant love. Give them the awareness that love is the very essence of life and that without love we are nothing, for love "bears all things, believes all things, hopes all things." Let them always remember that the greatest gift we have to give is our love. May our children be blessed with faith, hope, and love.

Lord, we place our children into your loving arms. Hold them close and bless them each and every day throughout their lives. Amen.

SEPTEMBER 13

Here are two ways to enlarge your family's awareness of God at work in the world.

1. Prayer List
Keep an ongoing prayer list in your home in a prominent place. Encourage each family member to contribute to the list. Record the person's name and the reason you are praying for him or her. Set aside a regular time to pray for those named. When your family can, let people know you are praying for them. Celebrate answered prayer!

2. Memory Box
Create a family memory box as a reminder of God's love for your family. Encourage your children to decorate an empty box or purchase one. Fill it with cherished notes, cards, letters, and handmade messages of love. Include pictures or keep a list of family times together. Take time to look through the contents of this box periodically with your children and remember!

SEPTEMBER 24

Pockets is the name of a devotional magazine for children six to twelve years of age. Children can read this magazine on their own or parents can share it with them. Among its stories, poems, activities, puzzles, and games are pages devoted to helping children know about prayer and praying on their own. The Upper Room in Nashville, Tennessee (1-800-972-0433) publishes *Pockets* magazine. You may want to begin a subscription for your children as a way to encourage their personal devotional time.

OCTOBER 2

Do research on any of the people mentioned in the devotions for October 2–5 (Joan of Arc, Martin Luther King Jr., Mother Teresa, or Archbishop Oscar Romero) or about other well-known people who inspire you to be like Jesus. Try the Internet, go to your local library, or see what movies and videos are available about any of these people. Good documentaries are available on Martin Luther King Jr. and Mother Teresa. Parents should preview any visual stories first since they may contain violence, particularly those of Romero and King. As you learn more about the individual, ask yourselves how the spirit of Jesus was shown through this person's life.

And/or look up on a globe or in an atlas the countries where each of these four faithful followers of Jesus worked: France, the United States, India, El Salvador.

And/or read *Francis: The Poor Man of Assisi* (see Recommended Books for Children).

OCTOBER 6

Why not take the time to write a letter to one of the persons who inspires you to be more like Jesus? Explain what your family has been learning about followers of Jesus and why this person is an inspiration. (If you choose someone from another country, you may have to research at the library or online for their address.)

OCTOBER 15-18

Make a belovedness banner. Begin by designing a banner that represents your family. Each person can think of a symbol for himself or herself—initials, favorite activities, or a self-portrait. Brainstorm together. Once you have a design idea, you can later gather the art supplies (markers and paper, felt and fabric scraps, tempera paint on muslin—any media will do), and set aside the time to work together on this project. Make sure each family member is involved in creating the banner and that all family members are represented in the banner's design. Decide how you want to use the banner and where it will hang. Will you bring it out on baptism days? Should it be hung when one family member or another is feeling low and needs reminding that he or she is beloved? Would you want to include the word *beloved* or the phrase *You are God's beloved child?*

OCTOBER 16

Take time to mark each family member's baptism date on a calendar. (This may take some research.) Some families celebrate baptism days in addition to birthdays. Maybe the baptismal person could choose the dinner menu or a special dessert on baptism day. Each family member may choose to have a baptismal candle that is lit once a year on baptism day for a short period of time. How might your family celebrate this special day?

OCTOBER 20

Research possibilities for your family to be involved with those in need. At Thanksgiving or Christmas, there are often options to collect food for the hungry or serve turkey dinner to the homeless. Or what about finding a soup kitchen where you can help prepare and serve food any time of the year? Perhaps your church needs help with a clothing drive. Ask church and community leaders for their suggestions for ways to be of service that are appropriate to the ages of your family members. When you engage in these activities, remember that what you do for the least of these, you do for Jesus.

And/or make a Least of These prayer board where you can remember those who need your concern. Put newspaper clippings and/or the names of people and situations you want to pray about, and take time each day to pray for people in troubled situations.

OCTOBER 29

Start a gratitude journal where anyone can feel free each day to write down words of thanksgiving. You could either purchase a blank-page book with an appropriate cover, or you could decorate your own notebook with a collage for the cover. Keep the gratitude journal in a prominent place. You may want to set aside one day a week or a month to sit down as a family and read the things family members have written. Reading your blessings aloud could also be part of the yearly Thanksgiving dinner or a New Year's Day celebration.

NOVEMBER 3

This would be a good day to play Hide and Seek as a family.

NOVEMBER 8

Plan a No-TV/computer/media night or weekend and see what conversations, activities, and quiet times begin to emerge in that time.

NOVEMBER 15

Make care packages to keep in your car so you can respond when you encounter a person asking for food. The packages may include easy-to-open foods, bottled water or juice, pocket change for making phone calls, and a card with information about where to go for assistance in your area. Handmade cards with a message or Bible verse can also be included.

NOVEMBER 16

Bread and the baking of bread are an important part of the culture of Bible times. Many of the Bible's stories include images of wheat and bread. In modern culture, few of us need to bake bread for our meals, but baking can be a rewarding family activity. Children can participate in sifting and measuring the flour, mixing the dough, watching the yeast bubble, and kneading the dough. They will have fun squeezing it and forming it into a little balls. They can watch it rise and punch it down, and they can shape it into loaves or rolls to bake. It is rare to find an activity that uses all of our senses and that nurtures our body, mind, and soul. Baking bread is one of them.

Make bread together as a family. Make more than enough, and then share! Use the recipe below or a favorite of your own.

Whole Wheat Oatmeal Bread
1 $\frac{1}{3}$ c. rolled oats
2 c. boiling water
1 T. salt
2 t. yeast to $\frac{1}{2}$ c. warm water
$\frac{1}{4}$ c. honey
$\frac{1}{4}$ c. oil
5 c. whole wheat flour (or a mixture of flours)

Cook oatmeal per directions and allow to cool to room temperature.

Dissolve yeast in $\frac{1}{2}$ cup of water. Mix honey and oil in oatmeal and stir.

Pour flour in large bowl and make a well in the middle. Pour in the oatmeal mixture, followed by the yeast. Mix thoroughly.

Knead the dough for 10–20 minutes and form into a ball.

Put into a bowl that is greased or simply rinsed with warm water.

Let the dough rise to double in size. Punch down. Let rise to double in size again.

(This second rising takes about half the time.) Divide in two and shape into loaves.

Butter pans and then sprinkle the bottom with dry oats. Put in loaves seam side down.

Bake at 350° for 45 minutes.

Baste the loaf tops with butter or oil.

Allow to cool about 10 minutes, then remove from pans. Yum!

Remember: What matters most is the time you spend interacting with your children, creating something together, and working with your hands.

NOVEMBER 20

Consider ways your family can participate in gardening or planting as a means to experience good soil and growth. Some suggestions for November planting: bulbs for spring, pansies, and indoor houseplants. This is also a good time of year to mark with stakes the places where spring bulbs have been planted.

NOVEMBER 27

Do you have a tradition that helps you focus on gratitude during this time of the year? If not, consider starting one. Here are two ideas:

1. Gather nuts, such as pecans or acorns, native to your area. Place them in a bowl as a centerpiece. Have each person take two nuts from the bowl and put them back in one at a time while sharing something she or he is thankful for.

2. Make an autumn tree using brown construction paper for the trunk. Cut out fall-colored leaves, and have each person write or draw on each leaf something for which they are thankful. Then secure the leaves to the tree trunk with paste, tape, or glue. Display on the refrigerator or on a wall. You may wish to add leaves to your tree over several days.

DECEMBER 1

Advent wreaths are readily available in Christian bookstores or through catalogs, but you may want to make your own Advent wreath. Begin with a circle of evergreen for the wreath. You can buy a pre-made evergreen wreath or arrange cut branches of evergreen and use them to cover a styrofoam or wire wreath. (If you have access to greenery in your own yard, gathering greens for the wreath is a fun family activity.) Add four candles (traditionally either all purple or three purple and one pink) around the circle of the wreath, one for each of the four Sundays before Christmas. If you use a pink candle, it is lit on the third Sunday of Advent. A white candle, representing Christ and usually larger than the others, goes in the center. It is lit on Christmas Eve and Christmas Day.

Be sure to include children in the lighting of the candles. In some families, the youngest family member lights the first candle; the second youngest lights the second candle, and so forth.

Traditionally, the Advent wreath is lit only on Sundays. However, if you choose to light your Advent wreath during your daily family devotional time, you will need to use larger candles in your wreath or replace the candles as needed. (A few words of caution: if your greens become dry before the season is over, it may be necessary to replace them. Never leave burning candles unattended, and be careful that candles do not burn down close to the greenery.)

DECEMBER 14

This activity will only work if everyone in the family is old enough to understand the concept of an invisible gift. Wrap an invisible gift for each family member. For example, it might be a gift of time to do an activity together, a gift of love by offering to help with an activity, or a gift of hope for a family member's dream. You can think of other gifts that can't be seen. Put these wrapped gifts under the tree and open them Christmas Eve and tell what each gift is.

DECEMBER 23

In Hispanic families, many people celebrate Las Posadas to remember the journey of Mary and Joseph. Two people, who act as Mary and Joseph, walk from house to house asking if there is room for them. Time after time, they are turned away. Finally, at a preselected location, they are welcomed. Then there is a great celebration for all. Consider joining with some other families from your neighborhood or your church to do your own version of Las Posadas.

DECEMBER 27

You may want to expand the idea of pretending your family is a brave Christian family living in a place where Bible ownership and reading are illegal. You could pretend that someone has placed listening devices in your home. Quietly enter the bugged room, sit in a circle, and write down (or draw pictures about) all the Bible verses you can remember and pass them around to one another.

JANUARY 1

Join together in a special meal today and center the table talk on your family. Use the questions below and listen carefully to each family member's responses.
- What things do we like to do together?
- Are there other things we would like to do together?
- Can we make time to do them?
- What does attending Sunday school and worship mean to each of us?
- What realistic changes in our family life can we make to help us live closer to the way Jesus wants us to live?

Discuss changes each person can make as well as changes the whole family can make together.

JANUARY 3

Cut nine small squares of paper and write one fruit of the spirit on each piece (love, joy, peace, patience, kindness, generosity, faithfulness, gentleness, and self-control) and have each person draw one square each morning for a given period of time (perhaps a week). The fruit you draw is the one you focus on and try to practice for that day.

JANUARY 5

After Judas betrayed Jesus, the disciples wanted to choose someone to take his place—either Justus or Matthias. Both were good people. The disciples cast lots (something like drawing straws), and Matthias was chosen (Acts 1:23-26). Cut a slip of paper for each person in your family. On one slip, write *You are chosen.* Leave the others blank. Have each member draw a slip of paper. How did it feel to be the one chosen? How did it feel not to be the one chosen? All of us are chosen for things at times (teams, promotions, class helpers), and all of us are not chosen at times. Discuss some thoughtful and helpful ways we can handle our feelings about being chosen and not chosen.

JANUARY 9

Pretend that you are Paul writing a letter to the church you attend. You can do this, either individually or together as a family. Try to follow the outline of one of Paul's letters, expressing your love for the people and also noting areas where the church is being faithful or not being faithful. Your family may want to discuss ways to help your church be more like Paul wanted churches to be.

JANUARY 10

If you enjoy doing crafts together, buy some paraffin and wick string and make candles together. Milk cartons, for example, can be used for molds. Use your homemade candles on the table at a special family meal or in the place where your family gathers for devotions.

JANUARY 15

We have been singing many songs together this month. Together, make up your own family song that praises God. This might be a good thing to do while you are traveling in the car. You may want to sing this song during your family devotional time.

JANUARY 30

Let each family member cut out a pair of glasses with frames and ear loops from construction paper. Then cut a hole inside the frames where the lenses would go. When there is conflict between members of your family, have the two people give each other their glasses and look at the situation from the other person's point of view. Does this help you understand the situation better? If it does, you may want to try this (in your mind, without the paper glasses) when you are in conflict with someone at school or work.

FEBRUARY 2

Play Scripture Search. See how many Bible passages family members can find in the New Testament that use the word *love*. (This is a good way to practice using a concordance if your Bible has one.) Make a list of the verses you find. Take time every day or week during the month to read one or more and to talk about the meaning of these verses. Try to memorize those that are especially meaningful to your family. Keep this list in your family Bible. You can continue playing Scripture Search by choosing other themes to look for. Some possibilities: *prayer*, *faith*, *forgiveness*, or *children*.

FEBRUARY 6

A Prayer for Parents

Lord,
Awaken the child within me.
Let me look upon your world with a renewed sense of awe and wonder.
Give me the eyes of a child so that I can experience the miracles of creation as if for the first time.
Awaken the child within me.
Let me step out into your world and live my life with a quiet trust in things unseen.
Grant me the feet of a child so that I can walk in faith with the constant assurance that you are guiding me.
Awaken the child within me.
Let me reach out into your world and minister to each of your children freely and unconditionally.
Bestow on me the arms of a child so that I can wrap them around a troubled world and be a witness of your everlasting love for us.
Awaken the child within me.
Let me gaze upon the face of baby Jesus, your Light to the world.
Give me the heart of a child so that the promise of hope is rekindled anew.
Awaken the child within me.
Let me recapture the true essence of wonder, faith, love, and hope!
Let me discover and enter the kingdom of God.
Amen. *

*From *Prayers for the Seasons of Life*, by Sue Downing (Nashville, Tenn.: Providence House Publishers, 1997), 57–58.

FEBRUARY 9

Picture in your mind Jesus dwelling within the people you saw yesterday. Does this change how you feel about them or what you might do or say to them? Gather as a family to share your thoughts.

Family members can never say *I love you* too much! Consider creating a special way for your family to say I love you to one another.

One way is to develop a secret code. You can use the numbers 1, 2, 3 to stand for the words *I love you*. There are several ways to send this message, and it can be given just about anywhere and anytime. You can squeeze someone's hand three times, hold up three fingers, write 1, 2, 3 on a note, or say "1, 2, 3."

FEBRUARY 19

If you did not choose to prepare the prayer board suggested in Optional Activities for October 20 or if you stopped using the idea, you may want to try this. Gather as a family to look over your local newspaper, church newsletter, or a news magazine, or watch the TV news together. As you are doing this, make a list of persons and situations you want to pray for. Set aside a regular time to pray for persons and situations named. Also take time to celebrate good things in the news!

FEBRUARY 25

Place a special offering container in a prominent place in your home. Designate this as a Pennies from Heaven bank. Your family can donate the special offering to the church or to a worthy cause that your family wishes to support. Ask all family members to help to fill the container by donating leftover change, part of an allowance, or coins they may find.

When the container is full, say a prayer of thanks, celebrate, and decide together what the money should be used for.

HOLY WEEK ACTIVITIES

Holy Week, the week before Easter, sometimes occurs during the month of March. It is a time that deserves a special place in the home. In order for Easter to have the sense of the day of Resurrection, your family may choose to delay the use of any Easter or spring decorations in the home until Easter. Waiting until Easter morning to decorate the home with bright and colorful cut flowers, Easter egg trees, bunnies, and chicks can create a sense of anticipation and joy when the day arrives. Three suggestions for making Holy Week significant in your family are described below.

1. Holy Week Worship Table

Just as an Advent wreath can help the family prepare for Christmas, so a special table or shelf holding symbols of Jesus' last days can prepare the family for Easter. In preparing a Holy Week worship table, begin with a purple cloth or tissue paper to cover the table. Add a simple candle. If possible, on Palm Sunday bring home one palm branch from your congregation's celebration and lay it on the table. On each day of the week between Palm Sunday and Easter, light the candle and add items to the table that correspond with that day or the Holy Week stories in general. Here are some suggested items and the Bible story they might call to mind:

A donkey–Jesus' entry into Jerusalem
Coins—the moneychangers
Perfume—the woman who anointed Jesus
Bowl and towel—washing the disciples' feet
Bread and cup or grapes—the Last Supper
Thirty silver coins—the payment to Judas
Rooster—Peter's denial
Dice—soldiers casting lots for Jesus' clothes
Thorns—the crown of thorns
Red scarf—Jesus' blood
A cross—Jesus' cross
Rock or cluster of rocks—tomb

On Easter morning (or late Saturday night) the table can be cleared and completely rearranged. The purple cloth may be replaced with white. Typical Easter decorations may be placed on the table, such as a cross decorated with flowers, dyed Easter eggs, butterflies, and pots with blooming bulbs—perhaps the ones you planted on November 20.

Note: In relating the story of Jesus' death, parents will want to consider the age and sensitivity of each child. For example, details of the graphic way in which Jesus died may be inappropriate for younger children. Certain symbols (such as a cross or nails) can be present without being explicitly explained. Children can appreciate, as adults do, the symbols without fully exhausting their meanings.

2. Dramatizing This Month's Bible Stories

Several stories from this month's devotions lend themselves to dramatizing. Try acting out one or more of these stories:

March 2: The story of Jesus' baptism

March 4: Jesus in the wilderness

March 8: The Hebrew people as slaves in Egypt.

March 14: Finding water in the desert

March 15: The parable of the merchant and the pearl

March 24: The healing of Bartimaeus

(See page 12 for suggestions on Dramatizing a Bible Story.)

3. Turning Off the Television

Watching less television can be a good Lenten discipline for the whole family. Each spring a Washington-based group organizes a week emphasizing non-television activities for children. Information on this project can be obtained on line at www.tvturnoff.org or by writing to the following address:

TV-Turnoff Network
1601 Connecticut Ave., NW, #303
Washington, DC 20009

MARCH 1

During the season of Lent, the forty days before Easter, many congregations take on special activities or practices, such as designated offerings, mission days, study or prayer groups, or midweek services. See what your congregation has planned for the season, and decide as a family how you will participate. You may also choose to participate in a program or ministry of your congregation, such as visiting home-bound members.

MARCH 2

Baptism is a moment in our lives we may not actually remember. One way to recall that sacramental event as a family is by commemorating the day each year. Here are suggestions for your family:

Determine the actual dates of baptism for each family member, if possible. Mark these dates on your family's calendar. Set up a special candle for each family member (or use one candle for all). When the baptismal anniversary date arrives, light the candle and reflect on that person's baptism, either from memory or by reading the passage from the Bible suggested for today's devotion. Close with a prayer affirming the person's worth before God and in the family.

MARCH 4

Many children relate to angels in a special way. The whole family can enjoy making an angel to hang in a child's bedroom window. These angels also make a great gift for a newborn. The raw wool or wool fleece to make these angels can be purchased in yarn shops or in craft supply stores, sold as wool fleece hair or beard.

Woolen Angel

— Cut a piece of wool fleece about 1 inch wide and a foot long. Tie a knot in the middle of the wool to form a head. Lay the two ends beside each other and tie the neck (just under the knot) with gold thread leaving long strings hanging to tie later.

—Take a second piece of fleece about 1 inch wide and 4 inches long for the arms and wings and slide it between the first two strips under the head. Cross the gold thread both left and right across the breast and tie in back at the waist. The remaining wool hanging down can be fluffed to be the gown.

—Take the smaller horizontal piece of wool and divide about a third for the arms. Tie a small bit at the wrist on each side to make hands and fluff the remaining wool behind to make the wings.

—To hang, simply sew a gold thread up through the head with a needle, experimenting with the placement and length until it hangs well.

MARCH 6

Below are two pretzel recipes offered by Gloria Thomas, a Christian educator with a lifetime of experience making things with children.

Pretzels 1:
Purchase refrigerated breadstick dough. Form dough into pretzel shape and bake as directed on the package.

Pretzels 2:
1 package quick rising yeast
1 c. warm water
⅓ c. brown sugar
5 c. flour
Coarse salt

Dissolve the yeast in the warm water. In a large bowl, put 3 cups of the flour and the brown sugar. Add the warm water and stir until you have a soft dough, adding more flour if necessary. Turn onto lightly floured surface and knead for 5 minutes. Cover dough with plastic wrap and let rise for 10 minutes.

Form pretzels and place on greased cookie sheets to rise for about 10 minutes. Sprinkle with coarse salt. Bake at 475° about 8 minutes until golden brown.
(Dropping each pretzel into rapidly boiling water before baking will give it a shinier coating when baked.)

MARCH 10

Older children often enjoy learning about the different plagues that besieged Egypt before the exodus of the Hebrews. Exodus 7:14–11:10 lists these plagues. Read about these in your Bible and talk about them together. How many plagues are there? Which are the easiest to imagine? the hardest? If you had been the Pharaoh at that time, when would enough have been enough?

MARCH 21

Plan an outing soon to see wildflowers, visit an arboretum, or do some spring gardening at home.

MARCH 29

Sandwich hugs are great any time, but they certainly fit with today's devotion. In sandwich hugs, one person gets to be the filling in the middle and two others are the bread. Take turns being the middle of the sandwich.

APRIL 1

Read the other Gospel accounts of the Resurrection, comparing stories of how the women and disciples respond to the amazing news of Jesus' resurrection. See Matthew 28:1-10; Mark 16:1-8, 9-14; or Luke 24:1-12.

APRIL 4

Talk together about what happens at a funeral or memorial service. If your family has attended such a service, share your memories of what it was like.

APRIL 6

Look at current newspapers and magazines to find stories about individuals working for peace.

APRIL 12

Choose one of the ways to feed my sheep and find out how your family can act on it. Your pastor or a committee at church may have ideas of people and places that need your help.

APRIL 14

Make a sign to put with the seeds you planted so that everyone who sees those plants will read Seeds of Peace or Seeds of Kindness, etc.

Read the children's book *Miss Rumphius* (see Books and Resources for more details) and discuss how each family member can make the world a better place.

APRIL 18

Ask your pastor if there is someone in your church who has had an experience of healing and would be willing to tell your family about it. Invite that person to your home or meet after church to hear the story.

APRIL 21

Read more about Paul's life in the Book of Acts or find a library book about him.

APRIL 23

Work together to find all the words in this puzzle:

parable	new life
beginning	Jesus
everlasting life	Christ
unshrunk	patches
new wine	cloth
old wine	sew
wineskins	

Words can be horizontal, vertical, or diagonal either direction.

```
O E V E L A T I G M O F O J A Z G E
A D F W W I L S C A C O X T I V F V
C B E G H Q Q N O K C L O T H I O E
V I T E M R A L O V W D X Y L S R R
K U N X S T D K D U C W B W B H G L
I W C J H U K E O O L I E M N I J A
Y Z H B O B J J O X H N N T B Z T S
F O R R M N E W W I N E O E H I M T
Y Q I J G M S N I K G T I Y T P E I
O P S S F T U N N B C I T K A S T N
P A T C H E S E E L E M O N C N I G
A A E I O A K G S S O G E T A H N L
R N S H E I I J K D L W I V E N G I
A C L O W N B K I L E M M D O G G F
B L K S N O P U N S H R U N K U G E
L H I I G F A F S K F G J E S O P I
E O N R Q S U S O I Z O B W A L L H
L G M S I L H E G T D S T X E U N G
```

APRIL 29

There are many ways your family can show the love of Jesus even to those you may never meet. You can ask your pastor what opportunities your church offers or check the Social Service Organizations in your phone directory listing. Here are some possibilities:

- Give money to mission offerings—set aside money from the family budget to give to special offerings for mission work. You might forgo dessert or a treat once a week to raise the money.

- Adopt a child in another country—for a small amount of money, you can provide help to a needy child and also have a personal connection with him or her.
- Collect food or clothing for the needy—join an organized collection group or start your own project in your church or community.
- Work at a soup kitchen for the hungry—your family could volunteer once a month to help cook and serve food.

MAY 1

Give each family member two or three sheets of lined paper. Ask them to write MAY at the top of one of the sheets and to number the lines one to thirty-one, skipping a line between each number. Each day for a month, each person is to list one gift he or she receives by being awake to God's gifts. It may be something noticed in nature or something received from another or the gift of joy received from doing something for someone else. It may be simply seeing a kindness exchanged between others or something a pet does. At the end of the month family members may share their lists with one another during this family time together.

MAY 5

Find out if someone in your church who lives alone or in a nursing home has a birthday this month. As a family, do something special for that person for his or her birthday. You might make a card or pot a little plant or bake some cookies. Take your gift or card on the person's birthday and sit down for a while and visit.

MAY 21

During a quiet dinner, talk with one another about a place each of you has been that is special to you, a place where it is easy to feel God is present with you. Let each family member describe where that place is for her or him, what it is like, and why it is so special. You may want to make plans to go to these places soon.

MAY 25

Ask family members to draw pictures of three memories that stand out in their lives. Each memory picture can be drawn simply with stick figures—these are not intended to be works of art. Take turns telling about these memories. It is okay to share both happy and unhappy ones. Listening to one another, without being defensive or judgmental, is very important during this activity.

MAY 29

Gather some putty or clay and give each person a ball of it. Play with it, get the feel of it, and begin to shape it. What form emerges as you work with the material? Reshape it as you go. This is not a task to complete, but to enjoy.

As you play with the clay, you may want to ask the following, but do not expect answers:

- What kind of person do you want to become? (Adults are included here; we are never finished.)
- What kinds of things have shaped you?
- What have you done in shaping yourself?
- What do you want to do in reshaping yourself?

Conclude with the statement that we are always in the process of being shaped and also shaping ourselves.

Recommended Books for Adults

Many books are available to help parents as they attempt to nurture their children's faith journeys. The following is certainly not an exhaustive list, but it does give some of the titles that the authors of this book have found to be helpful. You may want to ask your pastor or other church staff members for additional recommendations.

Cloyd, Betty Shannon. *Children and Prayer: A Shared Pilgrimage*. Nashville, Tenn.: Upper Room Books, 1997.

Cloyd, Betty Shannon. *Parents and Grandparents as Spiritual Guides*. Nashville, Tenn.: Upper Room Books, 2000.

Coffey, Kathy. *Experiencing God with Your Children*. New York: The Crossroad Publishing Company, 1997.

Downing, Sue. *Hand in Hand: Growing Spiritually with Our Children*. Nashville, Tenn.: Discipleship Resources, 1998.

Edelman, Marian Wright. *Guide My Feet: Prayers and Meditations on Loving and Working for Children*. Boston: Beacon Press, 1995.

Gellman, Marc and Thomas Hartman. *Where Does God Live? Questions and Answers for Parents and Children*. New York / Liguori, Mo.: Triumph / Liguori Publications, 1991.

Halverson, Delia. *How Do Children Grow? Introducing Children to God, Jesus, the Bible, Prayer, Church*. St. Louis, Mo.: Chalice Press, 1999.

Heller, David. *Talking to Your Child about God*. New York: Berkley Publishing Group, 1994.

Hughs, Ina. *A Prayer for Children*. New York: William Morrow & Company, Inc., 1995.

Marrocco, Nancy. *Homemade Christians*. Winona, Minn.: Saint Mary's Press, 1995.

Morris, Margie. *Helping Children Feel at Home in Church*. Nashville, Tenn.: Discipleship Resources, 1997.

Murray, Dick. *Teaching the Bible to Elementary Children*. Nashville, Tenn.: Discipleship Resources, 1997.

Persky, Margaret McMillan. *Living in God's Time: A Parent's Guide to Nurturing Children throughout the Christian Year*. Nashville, Tenn.: Upper Room Books, 1999.

Pierce-Norton, MaryJane. *Children Worship!* Nashville, Tenn.: Discipleship Resources, 1997.

Pierce-Norton, MaryJane. *Teaching Young Children: A Guide for Teachers and Leaders*. Nashville, Tenn.: Discipleship Resources, 1997.

Thompson, Marjorie J. *Family the Forming Center: A Vision of the Role of Family in Spiritual Formation*. Nashville, Tenn.: Upper Room Books, 1996.

Recommended Books for Children

Check with your local library or bookstore to find any of these excellent children's books. Most are picture books and can be read in one sitting.

Barner, Bob. *To Everything*. San Francisco: Chronicle Books, 1998. Bright and exuberant artwork makes the words from Ecclesiastes 3 come alive.

Baylor, Byrd. *Amigo*. New York: Aladdin Books, 1989. A lonely boy makes friends with a prairie dog.

Bradford, Sarah. *Harriet Tubman: The Moses of Her People*. Magnolia, Mass.: Peter Smith, 1990. The story of Harriet Tubman was first published in 1886. Much of it is written in Harriet's own words. Considered a classic biography, it is especially appropriate for older children.

The Brothers Grimm. *The Falling Stars*. New York: North-South Books, 1985. This poignant story about sacrifice and compassion includes a little girl who gives away everything she has and is rewarded.

Brumbeau, Jeff. *The Quiltmaker's Gift*. Duluth, Minn.: Pfeifer-Hamilton Publications, 2000. How a generous quiltmaker teaches a king the meaning of giving.

Carle, Eric. *Walter the Baker*. New York: Simon & Schuster Children's Publishing, 1993. In an endearing tale of fiction, this book tells the story of how the first pretzel came to be. Eric Carle's trademark illustrations bring this simple story to life.

Cooney, Barbara. *Miss Rumphius*. New York: Penguin Putnam Books for Young Readers, 1994. The classic story of how one woman was able to make the world more beautiful, this book encourages children to find their own way to give of themselves.

Cherry, Lynne. *The Great Kapok Tree: A Tale of the Amazon Rain Forest*. New York: Gulliver Books, Harcourt Brace Jovanovich, 1990. Rain forest creatures convince a man not to damage their habitat further.

Dearborn, Sabrina, comp. *A Child's Book of Blessings*. New York: Barefoot Books, 1999. Blessings from a wide range of authors and backgrounds with lovely illustrations.

Dengler, Marianna. *The Worry Stone*. Flagstaff, Ariz.: Northland Publishing, 1996. This story within a story, taken from the Chumash Indians, shows how friendship can heal pain.

de Paola, Tomie. Francis: *The Poor Man of Assisi*. New York: Holiday House, 1990. The life story of Saint Francis.

de Paola, Tomie. *Patrick: Patron Saint of Ireland*. New York: Holiday House, 1992. Beautiful companion illustrations, also by Tomie de Paola, complement this telling of Patrick's life story. It ends with several brief legends from his life, including tales of snakes and shamrocks.

Fox, Mem. *Wilfred Gordon McDonald Partridge*. Brooklyn, New York: Kane/Miller Book Publishers, 1985. A young boy helps a woman in a nursing home find her memories.

Freedman, Florence B. *Brothers: A Hebrew Legend*. New York: Harper and Row, 1985. A celebration of "how good it is for brothers to live together in friendship."

Hamanaka, Sheila. *All the Colors of the Earth*. New York: Morrow Junior Books, 1994. This glowing celebration praises the diversity of children.

Hazell, Rebecca. *The Barefoot Book of Heroic Children*. New York: Barefoot Books, 2000. Twelve stories of passionate and courageous children like Anne Frank, Wilma Rudolph, and Alexander Graham Bell.

Hippely, Hillary Horder. *A Song for Lena*. New York: Simon and Schuster Books for Young Readers, 1996. Young Lena and Grandmother give strudel to a hungry man and are rewarded for many years by his music. This book illustrates love, kindness, and giving from the heart.

Hunt, Angela Elwell. *The Tale of Three Trees*. Colorado Springs, Colo.: Cook Communications Ministries, 2001. The story traces the destiny of three trees. When cut down, each appears at first to arrive at a rather meaningless purpose but finally is shown to play a significant part in the life of Jesus.

Monk, Isabell. *Hope*. Minneapolis, Minnesota: Carolrhoda Books, 1999. A young girl learns about her mixed-race heritage and is able to affirm, "Yes, I am generations of faith mixed with love. I am HOPE!" This book reflects a message of love and respect for all heritages.

Jaffe, Nina and Steve Zeitlin. *The Cow of No Color: Riddle Stories and Justice Tales from around the World*. New York: Henry Holt and Company, 1998. Short stories that teach and encourage the reader to puzzle out what is right and what is wrong.

Jasinek, Doris and Pamela Bell Ryan. *A Family Is a Circle of People Who Love You*. Minneapolis, Minnesota: Compcare Publishers, 1988. A good look at different types of families and how love binds all families together.

Libby, Larry R. *Someday Heaven*. Grand Rapids, Michigan: Zonderkidz, 2001. One author answers many of the questions children have about heaven: Where is heaven? How do I get there? Will I be an angel?

Lindbergh, Reeve. *The Circle of Days*. Cambridge, Massachusetts: Candlewick Press, 1997. Words from Saint Francis of Assisi accompanied by beautiful collage paintings.

Loebel, Arnold. *Frog and Toad Are Friends, Frog and Toad All Year, Frog and Toad Together*. New York: HarperTrophy, 1979, 1984, 1979. The adventures of two dear friends reveal how to understand and support each other.

Matthews, Caitlin. *The Blessing Seed: A Creation Myth for the New Millennium*. United Kingdom: Barefoot Books, 1998. This picture book focuses more on creation (original blessing) than the fall (original sin).

McBratney, Sam. *Guess How Much I Love You*. Cambridge, Massachusetts: Candlewick Press, 1999. A story about how much a father rabbit loves his son.

Momaday, N. Scott. *Circle of Wonder: A Native American Christmas Story*. Albuquerque: University of New Mexico Press, 1994. A Native American family has the honor of keeping the statue of the Christ child during the twelve days of Christmas.

O'Keefe, Susan Heyboer. *Good Night, God Bless*. New York: Henry Holt and Company, 1999. Brief bedtime prayers with imaginative images and illustrations.

Pittman, Helena Clare. *The Gift of the Willows*. Minneapolis, Minn.: Carolrhoda Books, 1988. A story about a Japanese potter and his family with the focus "Life is growing."

Polacco, Patricia. *Pink and Say*. New York: Philomel Books, 1994. Beautifully moving true story of a friendship between two young Union soldiers in the Civil War, one white, the other African-American.

Sasso, Sandy Eisenberg. *A Prayer for the Earth: The Story of Naamah, Noah's Wife*. Woodstock, Vt.: Jewish Lights Publishing, 1996. How Noah's wife used courage and creativity to save all the plants on earth until after the flood (a nice addition to the story of Noah and the ark).

Sasso, Sandy Eisenberg. *God in Between*. Woodstock, Vt.: Jewish Lights Publishing,

1998. This beautiful picture book illustrates finding God in community.

Sasso, Sandy Eisenberg. *God's Paintbrush*. Woodstock, Vt.: Jewish Lights Publishing, 1992. This book uses common illustrations and questions to depict God as a special friend.

Sasso, Sandy Eisenberg. *In God's Name*. Woodstock, Vt.: Jewish Lights Publishing, 1994. Illustrations enhance how many different ways people understand who God is.

Schell, Mildred, translated from Leo Tolstoy's story *The Shoemaker's Dream*. Valley Forge, Pa.: Judson Press, 1982. Jesus comes to visit an old shoemaker in the guise of "the least of these."

Spinelli, Eileen. *Somebody Loves You, Mr. Hatch*. New York: Bradbury Press, 1991. A lonesome man's life is transformed when he receives a "somebody loves you" note.

Swartz, Nancy Sohn. *In Our Image: God's First Creatures*. Woodstock, Vt.: Jewish Lights Publishing, 1998. God asks all creatures to help in creating humankind in this celebration of the interconnectedness of all beings.

Thomas, Jane Resh. *Saying Good-Bye to Grandma*. New York: Houghton Mifflin Company, 1990. A sensitive story about what happens when a young girl's grandmother dies, this book matter-of-factly shows many of the rituals of death.

Udry, Janice May. *A Tree Is Nice*. New York: Harper Trophy, 1987. A classic book about our interrelatedness with nature.

Varley, Susan. *Badger's Parting Gifts*. New York: William Morrow and Company, 1984. Friends feel the loss of Badger's death, but as they remember his many gifts to them, they recognize that he is still part of their lives.

Von Olfers, Sibylle. *The Story of the Root Children*. Edinburgh, Scotland: Floris Books, 1992. A Mother Earth figure awakens her root children after a long winter's underground sleep in order to prepare them for the arrival of spring. The tiny elfin children emerge from darkness into sunlight to enjoy the beauty and brightness of spring.

Walsh, Mary Caswell. *Saint Francis Celebrates Christmas*. Chicago: Loyola Press, 1998. A retelling of how Saint Francis developed the first nativity scene, baby and all, with the help of villagers in Greco, Italy, nearly 800 years ago.

Wild, Margaret. *Old Pig*. New York: Dial Books for Young Readers, 1996. As Old Pig gets older, she helps prepare Grandaughter for her death in a celebration of life.

Williams, Jay. *Everyone Knows What a Dragon Looks Like*. New York: Four Winds Press, 1996. This story about how appearances can be deceiving shows that God, like the dragon in the book, may be different than we expect.

Williams, Margery. *The Velveteen Rabbit*. New York: Knopf, 1983. An enduring classic, this story of how a toy becomes real is a reminder of how love transforms both the lover and the loved one.

Wood, Douglas. *Grandad's Prayers of the Earth*. Cambridge, Mass.: Candlewick Press, 1999. A celebration of the earth through the story of a young boy and his grandfather (who teaches the connection between prayer and the natural world).

Wood, Douglas. *Old Turtle*. Duluth, Minn.: Pfeifer-Hamilton Publishers, 1995. A moving fable that explores how each creature perceives God differently, but all are bound as one in God's care.

Meet the Authors

ANNE BROYLES went to elementary school in Tucson, Arizona, where she enjoyed riding her bike and building forts in the desert after school. Her pets included dogs, horned toads, turtles, and a desert tortoise. Thanks to an older brother, she also experienced life with a tarantula, bull snake, and, at one time, a family of black widow spiders raised in a jar! When she grew up, Anne became a United Methodist minister and writer. She is married and has two young adult children, Trinity and Justus. She is the author of nine books, including a children's picture book, *Shy Mama's Halloween*.

For this book, Anne wrote the daily devotions and optional activities for October and April.

SUE DOWNING grew up in St. Louis, Missouri, where she loved pretend play with her friends, paper dolls, playing the piano, reading, and art. Her family was always very active in church, and Sue grew up wanting to help in the church, just as she saw her mother do. As an adult, Sue has been in ministry with children and is presently a preschool teacher at her church's day school. Sue and her husband, Jim, live in Brentwood, Tennesse. They are the parents of a daughter, Julie, and a son, Scottie, who died as an infant. Sue has written Sunday school curriculum and three books.

For this book, Sue wrote the daily devotions and optional activities for September and February.

ELIZABETH LYND ESCAMILLA has always enjoyed working with children—through pediatric nursing, Girl Scouting, Sunday school teaching, and her own parenting. She has a variety of ways of seeking beauty close to home, including gardening, singing, and dollmaking. She and her husband Paul make their home in Dallas.

PAUL LYND ESCAMILLA has never outgrown the thrill of running. He also likes to swim, read, and play the guitar. He is pastor of Walnut Hills United Methodist Church and enjoys being a dad to his and Elizabeth's three children. He has written articles, Sunday school curriculum, and a book.

For this book, Elizabeth and Paul wrote the daily devotions and optional activities for November and March.

MARILYN BROWN ODEN grew up in Woodward, Oklahoma, where she liked to play running games at recess, write stories in her playhouse, and hang by her legs on her swinging trapeze. She also liked playing tug-of-war with her collie, Pal, playing softball and the clarinet, riding her bike, and learning to fly with her dad. She grew up to become a wife and mother, a writer and counselor, and the author of eight books.

For this book, Marilyn wrote the introduction and the daily devotions and optional activities for December, January, and May.